W9-BBW-228

# Additional praise for *Taming the Big Data Tidal Wave*

This book is targeted for the business managers who wish to leverage the opportunities that big data can bring to their business. It is written in an easy flowing manner that motivates and mentors the non-technical person about the complex issues surrounding big data. Bill Franks continually focuses on the key success factor . . . How can companies improve their business through analytics that probe this big data? If the tidal wave of big data is about to crash upon your business, then I would recommend this book.
—*Richard Hackathorn, President, Bolder Technology, Inc.*

Most big data initiatives have grown both organically and rapidly. Under such conditions, it is easy to miss the big picture. This book takes a step back to show how all the pieces fit together, addressing varying facets from technology to analysis to organization. Bill approaches big data with a wonderful sense of practicality—"just get started" and "deliver value as you go" are phrases that characterize the ethos of successful big data organizations.
—*Eric Colson, Vice President of Data Science and Engineering, Netflix*

Bill Franks is a straight-talking industry insider who has written an invaluable guide for those who would first understand and then master the opportunities of big data.
—*Thornton May, Futurist and Executive Director, The IT Leadership Academy*

# Taming the Big Data Tidal Wave

# Wiley & SAS Business Series

The Wiley & SAS Business Series presents books that help senior-level managers with their critical management decisions.

Titles in the Wiley & SAS Business Series include:

For more information on any of the above titles, please visit **www.wiley.com**.

# Taming the Big Data Tidal Wave

*Finding Opportunities in Huge Data Streams with Advanced Analytics*

**Bill Franks**

**WILEY**

John Wiley & Sons, Inc.

Copyright © 2012 by Bill Franks. All rights reserved.

Published by John Wiley & Sons, Inc., Hoboken, New Jersey.
Published simultaneously in Canada.

No part of this publication may be reproduced, stored in a retrieval system, or transmitted in any form or by any means, electronic, mechanical, photocopying, recording, scanning, or otherwise, except as permitted under Section 107 or 108 of the 1976 United States Copyright Act, without either the prior written permission of the Publisher, or authorization through payment of the appropriate per-copy fee to the Copyright Clearance Center, Inc., 222 Rosewood Drive, Danvers, MA 01923, (978) 750-8400, fax (978) 646-8600, or on the Web at www.copyright.com. Requests to the Publisher for permission should be addressed to the Permissions Department, John Wiley & Sons, Inc., 111 River Street, Hoboken, NJ 07030, (201) 748-6011, fax (201) 748-6008, or online at www.wiley.com/go/permissions.

Limit of Liability/Disclaimer of Warranty: While the publisher and author have used their best efforts in preparing this book, they make no representations or warranties with respect to the accuracy or completeness of the contents of this book and specifically disclaim any implied warranties of merchantability or fitness for a particular purpose. No warranty may be created or extended by sales representatives or written sales materials. The advice and strategies contained herein may not be suitable for your situation. You should consult with a professional where appropriate. Neither the publisher nor author shall be liable for any loss of profit or any other commercial damages, including but not limited to special, incidental, consequential, or other damages.

For general information on our other products and services or for technical support, please contact our Customer Care Department within the United States at (800) 762-2974, outside the United States at (317) 572-3993 or fax (317) 572-4002.

Wiley also publishes its books in a variety of electronic formats. Some content that appears in print may not be available in electronic books. For more information about Wiley products, visit our web site at www.wiley.com.

*Library of Congress Cataloging-in-Publication Data:*
Franks, Bill
  Taming the big data tidal wave: finding opportunities in huge data streams with advanced analytics / Bill Franks.
       pages cm. — (Wiley & SAS business series)
   Includes bibliographical references and index.
   ISBN 978-1-118-20878-6 (cloth); ISBN 978-1-118-22866-1 (ebk);
ISBN 978-1-118-24117-2 (ebk); ISBN 978-1-118-26588-8 (ebk)
   1. Data mining.   2. Database searching.   I. Title.
   QA76.9.D343.F73 2012
   006.3'12—dc23

2011048536

Printed in the United States of America.

10  9  8  7  6  5  4

*This book is dedicated to Stacie, Jesse, and Danielle,
who put up with all the nights and weekends it took to
get this book completed.*

# Contents

# Foreword

L ike it or not, a massive amount of data will be coming your way soon. Perhaps it has reached you already. Perhaps you've been wrestling with it for a while—trying to figure out how to store it for later access, address its mistakes and imperfections, or classify it into structured categories. Now you are ready to actually extract some value out of this huge dataset by analyzing it and learning something about your customers, your business, or some aspect of the environment for your organization. Or maybe you're not quite there, but you see light at the end of the data management tunnel.

In either case, you've come to the right place. As Bill Franks suggests, there may soon be not only a flood of data, but also a flood of books about big data. I'll predict (with no analytics) that this book will be different from the rest. First, it's an early entry in the category. But most importantly, it has a different content focus.

Most of these big-data books will be about the management of big data: how to wrestle it into a database or data warehouse, or how to structure and categorize unstructured data. If you find yourself reading a lot about Hadoop or MapReduce or various approaches to data warehousing, you've stumbled upon—or were perhaps seeking—a "big data management" (BDM) book.

This is, of course, important work. No matter how much data you have of whatever quality, it won't be much good unless you get it into an environment and format in which it can be accessed and analyzed.

But the topic of BDM alone won't get you very far. You also have to analyze and act on it for data of any size to be of value. Just as traditional database management tools didn't automatically analyze transaction data from traditional systems, Hadoop and MapReduce won't automatically interpret the meaning of data from web sites, gene mapping, image analysis, or other sources of big data. Even before the recent big data era, many organizations have gotten caught up in data management for years (and sometimes decades) without ever getting any real value from their data in the form of better analysis and decision-making.

This book, then, puts the focus squarely where it belongs, in my opinion. It's primarily about the effective analysis of big data, rather than the BDM topic, per se. It starts with data and goes all the way into such topics as how to frame decisions, how to build an analytics center of excellence, and how to build an analytical culture. You will find some mentions of BDM topics, as you should. But the bulk of the content here is about how to create, organize, staff, and execute on analytical initiatives that make use of data as the input.

In case you have missed it, analytics are a very hot topic in business today. My work has primarily been around how companies compete on analytics, and my books and articles in these areas have been among the most popular of any I've written. Conferences on analytics are popping up all over the place. Large consulting firms such as Accenture, Deloitte, and IBM have formed major practices in the area. And many companies, public sector organizations, and even nonprofits have made analytics a strategic priority. Now people are also very excited about big data, but the focus should still remain on how to get such data into a form in which it can be analyzed and thus influence decisions and actions.

Bill Franks is uniquely positioned to discuss the intersection of big data and analytics. His company, Teradata, compared to other data warehouse/data appliance vendors, has always had the greatest degree of focus within that industry segment on actually analyzing data and extracting business value from it. And although the company is best known for enterprise data warehouse tools, Teradata has also provided a set of analytical applications for many years.

Over the past several years Teradata has forged a close partnership with SAS, the leading analytics software vendor, to develop highly scalable tools for analytics on large databases. These tools, which often involve embedding analysis within the data warehouse environment itself, are for large-volume analytical applications such as real-time fraud detection and large-scale scoring of customer buying propensities. Bill Franks is the chief analytics officer for the partnership and therefore has had access to a large volume of ideas and expertise on production-scale analytics and "in-database processing." There is perhaps no better source on this topic.

So what else is particularly interesting and important between these covers? There are a variety of high points:

- Chapter 1 provides an overview of the big data concept, and explains that "size doesn't always matter" in this context. In fact, throughout the book, Franks points out that much of the volume of big data isn't useful anyway, and that it's important to focus on filtering out the dross data.

- The overview of big data sources in Chapter 3 is a creative, useful catalog, and unusually thorough. And the book's treatment of web data and web analytics in Chapter 2 is very useful for anyone or any organization wishing to understand online customer behavior. It goes well beyond the usual reporting-oriented focus of web analytics.

- Chapter 4, devoted to "The Evolution of Analytical Scalability," will provide you with a perspective on the technology platforms for big data and analytics that I am pretty sure you won't find anywhere else on this earth. It also puts recent technologies like MapReduce in perspective, and sensibly argues that most big data analytics efforts will require a combination of environments.

- This book has some up-to-the-minute content about how to create and manage analytical data environments that you also won't find anywhere else. If you want the best and latest thinking about "analytic sandboxes" and "enterprise analytic data sets" (that was a new topic for me, but I now know what they are and why they're important), you'll find it in Chapter 5. This chapter also has some important messages about the need for model and scoring management systems and processes.

- Chapter 6 has a very useful discussion of the types of analytical software tools that are available today, including the open source package R. It's very difficult to find commonsense advice about the strengths and weaknesses of different analytical environments, but it is present in this chapter. Finally, the discussion of ensemble and commodity analytical methods in this chapter is refreshingly easy to understand for nontechnical types like me.

- Part Three of the book leaves the technical realm for advice on how to manage the human and organizational sides of analytics. Again, the perspective is heavily endowed with good sense. I particularly liked, for example, the emphasis on the framing of decisions and problems in Chapter 7. Too many analysts jump into analysis without thinking about the larger questions of how the problem is being framed.

- Someone recently asked me if there was any description of analytical culture outside of my own writings. I said I didn't know of any, but that was before I read Part Four of Franks's book. It ties analytical culture to innovation culture in a way that I like and have never seen before.

Although the book doesn't shrink from technical topics, it treats them all with a straightforward, explanatory approach. This keeps the book accessible to a wide audience, including those with limited technical backgrounds. Franks's advice about data visualization tools summarizes the tone and perspective of the entire book: "Simple is best. Only get fancy or complex when there is a specific need."

If your organization is going to do analytical work—and it definitely should—you will need to address many of the issues raised in this book. Even if you're not a technical person, you will need to be familiar with some of the topics involved in building an enterprise analytical capability. And if you are a technical person, you will learn much about the human side of analytics. If you're browsing this foreword in a bookstore or through "search inside this book," go ahead and buy it. If you've already bought it, get busy and read!

THOMAS H. DAVENPORT
President's Distinguished Professor of IT and
Management, Babson College
Co-Founder and Research Director, International
Institute for Analytics

# Preface

You receive an e-mail. It contains an offer for a complete personal computer system. It seems like the retailer read your mind since you were exploring computers on their web site just a few hours prior. . . .

As you drive to the store to buy the computer bundle, you get an offer for a discounted coffee from the coffee shop you are getting ready to drive past. It says that since you're in the area, you can get 10% off if you stop by in the next 20 minutes. . . .

As you drink your coffee, you receive an apology from the manufacturer of a product that you complained about yesterday on your Facebook page, as well as on the company's web site. . . .

Finally, once you get back home, you receive notice of a special armor upgrade available for purchase in your favorite online video game. It is just what is needed to get past some spots you've been struggling with. . . .

Sound crazy? Are these things that can only happen in the distant future? No. All of these scenarios are possible today! Big data. Advanced analytics. Big data analytics. It seems you can't escape such terms today. Everywhere you turn people are discussing, writing about, and promoting big data and advanced analytics. Well, you can now add this book to the discussion.

What is real and what is hype? Such attention can lead one to the suspicion that perhaps the analysis of big data is something that is more hype than substance. While there has been a lot of hype over the past few years, the reality is that we are in a transformative era in terms of analytic capabilities and the leveraging of massive amounts of data. If you take the time to cut through the sometimes overzealous hype present in the media, you'll find something very real and very powerful underneath it. With big data, the hype is driven by genuine excitement and anticipation of the business and consumer benefits that analyzing it will yield over time.

Big data is the next wave of new data sources that will drive the next wave of analytic innovation in business, government, and academia. These innovations have the potential to radically change how organizations view their business. The analysis that big data enables will lead to decisions that are more informed and, in some cases, different from what they are today. It will yield insights that many can only dream about today. As you'll see, there are many consistencies with the requirements to tame big data and what has always been needed to tame new data sources. However, the additional scale of big data necessitates utilizing the newest tools, technologies, methods, and processes. The old way of approaching analysis just won't work. It is time to evolve the world of advanced analytics to the next level. That's what this book is about.

*Taming the Big Data Tidal Wave* isn't just the title of this book, but rather an activity that will determine which businesses win and which lose in the next decade. By preparing and taking the initiative, organizations can ride the big data tidal wave to success rather than being pummeled underneath the crushing surf. What do you need to know and how do you prepare in order to start taming big data and generating exciting new analytics from it? Sit back, get comfortable, and prepare to find out!

## INTENDED AUDIENCE

There have been myriad books on advanced analytics over the years. There have also been a number of books on big data more recently. This book attempts to come from a different angle than the others. The primary focus is educating the reader on what big data is all about and how it can be utilized through analytics, and providing guidance on how to approach the creation and evolution of a world-class advanced analytics ecosystem in today's big data environment. A wide range of readers will find this book to be of value and interest. Whether you are an analytics professional, a businessperson who uses the results that analysts produce, or just someone with an interest in big data and advanced analytics, this book has something for you.

The book will not provide deeply detailed technical reviews of the topics covered. Rather, the book aims to be just technical enough to provide a high-level understanding of the concepts discussed. The goal is to enable readers to understand and begin to apply the concepts while also helping identify where more research is desired. This book is more of a handbook than a textbook, and it is accessible to non-technical readers. At the same time, those who already have a deeper understanding of the topics will be able to read between the lines to see the more technical implications of the discussions.

## OVERVIEW OF THE CONTENTS

This book is comprised of four parts, each of which covers one aspect of taming the big data tidal wave. Part One focuses on what big data is, why it is important, and how it can be applied. Part Two focuses on the tools, technologies, and methods required to analyze and act on big data successfully. Part Three focuses on the people, teams, and analysis principles that are required to be effective. Part Four brings everything together and focuses on how to enable innovative analytics through an analytic innovation center and a change in culture. Below is a brief outline with more detail on what each part and chapter are about.

## PART ONE: THE RISE OF BIG DATA

Part One is focused on what big data is, why it is important, and the benefits of analyzing it. It covers a total of 10 big data sources and how those sources can be applied to help organizations improve their business. If readers are unclear when picking up the book about what big data is or how broadly big data applies, Part One will provide clarity.

**Chapter 1: What Is Big Data and Why Does It Matter?** This chapter begins with some background on big data and what it is all about. It then covers a number of considerations related to how organizations can make use of big data. Readers will need to understand what is in this chapter as much as anything else in the book if they are to help their organizations tame the big data tidal wave successfully.

**Chapter 2: Web Data: The Original Big Data.** Probably the most widely used and best-known source of big data today is the detailed data collected from web sites. The logs generated by users navigating the web hold a treasure trove of information just waiting to be analyzed. Organizations across a number of industries have integrated detailed, customer-level data sourced from their web sites into their enterprise analytics environments. This chapter explores how that data is enhancing and changing a variety of business decisions.

**Chapter 3: A Cross-Section of Big Data Sources and the Value They Hold.** In this chapter, we look at nine more sources of big data at a high level. The purpose is to introduce what each data source is and then review some of the applications and implications that each data source has for businesses. One trend that becomes clear is how the same underlying technologies can lead to multiple big data sources in different industries. In addition, different industries can leverage some of the same sources of big data. Big data is not a one-trick pony with narrow application.

## PART TWO: TAMING BIG DATA: THE TECHNOLOGIES, PROCESSES, AND METHODS

Part Two focuses on the technologies, processes, and methods required to tame big data. Major advances have increased the scalability of all three of those areas over the years. Organizations can't continue to rely on outdated approaches and expect to stay competitive in the world of big data. This part of the book is by far the most technical, but should still be accessible to almost all readers. After reading these chapters, readers will be familiar with a number of concepts that they will come across as they enter the world of analyzing big data.

**Chapter 4: The Evolution of Analytic Scalability.** The growth of data has always been at a pace that strains the most scalable options available at any point in time. The traditional ways of performing advanced analytics were already reaching their limits before big data. Now, traditional approaches just won't do. This chapter discusses the convergence of the analytic and data environments, massively parallel processing (MPP) architectures, the cloud, grid computing, and

MapReduce. Each of these paradigms enables greater scalability and will play a role in the analysis of big data.

**Chapter 5: The Evolution of Analytic Processes.** With a vastly increased level of scalability comes the need to update analytic processes to take advantage of it. This chapter starts by outlining the use of analytical sandboxes to provide analytic professionals with a scalable environment to build advanced analytics processes. Then, it covers how enterprise analytic data sets can help infuse more consistency and less risk in the creation of analytic data while increasing analyst productivity. The chapter ends with a discussion of how embedded scoring processes allow results from advanced analytics processes to be deployed and widely consumed by users and applications.

**Chapter 6: The Evolution of Analytic Tools and Methods.** This chapter covers several ways in which the advanced analytic tool space has evolved and how such advances will continue to change the way analytic professionals do their jobs and handle big data. Topics include the evolution of visual point and click interfaces, analytic point solutions, open source tools, and data visualization tools. The chapter also covers how analytic professionals have changed their approaches to building models to better leverage the advances available to them. Topics include ensemble modeling, commodity models, and text analysis.

## PART THREE: TAMING BIG DATA: THE PEOPLE AND APPROACHES

Part Three is focused on the people that drive analytic results, the teams they belong to, and the approaches they use to ensure that they provide great analysis. The most important factor in any analytics endeavor, including the analysis of big data, is having the right people in the driver's seat who are following the right analysis principles. After reading Part Three, readers will better understand what sets great analysis, great analytic professionals, and great analytics teams apart from the rest.

**Chapter 7: What Makes a Great Analysis?** Computing statistics, writing a report, and applying a modeling algorithm are each only one step of many required for generating a great analysis. This chapter starts by clarifying a few definitions, and then discusses a variety of themes that relate to creating great analysis. With big data adding even more complexity to the mix than organizations are used to dealing with, it's more crucial than ever to keep the principles discussed in this chapter in mind.

**Chapter 8: What Makes a Great Analytic Professional?** Skill in math, statistics, and programming are necessary, but not sufficient, traits of a great analytic professional. Great analytic professionals also have traits that are often not the first things that come to most people's minds. These traits include commitment, creativity, business savvy, presentation skills, and intuition. This chapter explores why each of these traits are so important in defining a great analytic professional and why they can't be overlooked.

**Chapter 9: What Makes a Great Analytics Team?** How should an organization structure and maintain advanced analytics teams for optimal impact? Where do the teams fit in the organization? How should they operate? Who should be creating advanced analytics? This chapter talks about some common challenges and principles that must be considered to build a great analytics team.

## PART FOUR: BRINGING IT TOGETHER: THE ANALYTICS CULTURE

Part Four focuses on some well-known underlying principles that must be applied for an organization to successfully innovate with advanced analytics and big data. While these principles apply broadly to other disciplines as well, the focus will be on providing a perspective on how the principles relate to advanced analytics within today's enterprise environments. The concepts covered will be familiar to readers, but perhaps not the way that the concepts are applied to the world of advanced analytics and big data.

**Chapter 10: Enabling Analytic Innovation.** This chapter starts by reviewing some of the basic principles behind successful innovation. Then, it applies them to the world of big data and advanced analytics through the concept of an analytic innovation center. The goal is to provide readers with some tangible ideas of how to better enable analytic innovation and the taming of big data within their organizations.

**Chapter 11: Creating a Culture of Innovation and Discovery.** This chapter wraps things up with some perspectives on how to create a culture of innovation and discovery. It is meant to be fun and light-hearted, and to provide food for thought in terms of what it takes to create a culture that is able to produce innovative analytics. The principles covered are commonly discussed and well-known. However, it is worth reviewing them and then considering how an organization can apply the well-established principles to big data and advanced analytics.

# Acknowledgments

Many people deserve credit for assisting me in getting this book written. Thanks to my colleagues at Teradata, SAS, and the International Institute for Analytics, who encouraged me to write this, as well as to the authors I know who helped me to understand what I was getting into.

I also owe a big thanks to the people who volunteered to review and provide input on the book as I developed it. Reading hundreds of pages of rough drafts isn't exactly a party! Thanks for the great input that helped me tune the flow and message.

A last thanks goes to all of the analytic professionals, business professionals, and IT professionals who I have worked with over the years. You have all helped me learn and apply the concepts in this book. Without getting a chance to see these concepts in action in real situations, it wouldn't have been possible to write about them.

BILL FRANKS

# PART
# ONE

---

# The Rise of
# Big Data

# CHAPTER 1

# What Is Big Data and Why Does It Matter?

**P**erhaps nothing will have as large an impact on advanced analytics in the coming years as the ongoing explosion of new and powerful data sources. When analyzing customers, for example, the days of relying exclusively on demographics and sales history are past. Virtually every industry has at least one completely new data source coming online soon, if it isn't here already. Some of the data sources apply widely across industries; others are primarily relevant to a very small number of industries or niches. Many of these data sources fall under a new term that is receiving a lot of buzz: big data.

Big data is sprouting up everywhere and using it appropriately will drive competitive advantage. Ignoring big data will put an organization at risk and cause it to fall behind the competition. To stay competitive, it is imperative that organizations aggressively pursue capturing and analyzing these new data sources to gain the insights that they offer. Analytic professionals have a lot of work to do! It won't be easy to incorporate big data alongside all the other data that has been used for analysis for years.

This chapter begins with some background on big data and what it is all about. Then it will cover a number of considerations in terms of how an organization can make use of big data. Readers will need

3

to understand what is in this chapter as much as or more than anything else in the book if they are to tame the big data tidal wave successfully.

## WHAT IS BIG DATA?

There is not a consensus in the marketplace as to how to define big data, but there are a couple of consistent themes. Two sources have done a good job of capturing the essence of what most would agree big data is all about. The first definition is from Gartner's Merv Adrian in a Q1, 2011 *Teradata Magazine* article. He said, "Big data exceeds the reach of commonly used hardware environments and software tools to capture, manage, and process it within a tolerable elapsed time for its user population."[1] Another good definition is from a paper by the McKinsey Global Institute in May 2011: "Big data refers to data sets whose size is beyond the ability of typical database software tools to capture, store, manage and analyze."[2]

These definitions imply that what qualifies as big data will change over time as technology advances. What was big data historically or what is big data today won't be big data tomorrow. This aspect of the definition of big data is one that some people find unsettling. The preceding definitions also imply that what constitutes big data can vary by industry, or even organization, if the tools and technologies in place vary greatly in capability. We will talk more about this later in the chapter in the section titled "Today's Big Data Is Not Tomorrow's Big Data."

A couple of interesting facts in the McKinsey paper help bring into focus how much data is out there today:

- $600 today can buy a disk drive that will store all of the world's music.
- There are 30 billion pieces of information shared on Facebook each month.
- Fifteen of 17 industry sectors in the United States have more data per company on average than the U.S. Library of Congress.[3]

## THE "BIG" IN BIG DATA ISN'T JUST ABOUT VOLUME

While big data certainly involves having a lot of data, big data doesn't refer to data volume alone. Big data also has increased velocity (i.e., the rate at which data is transmitted and received), complexity, and variety compared to data sources of the past.

Big data isn't just about the size of the data in terms of how much data there is. According to the Gartner Group, the "big" in big data also refers to several other characteristics of a big data source.[4] These aspects include not just increased volume but increased velocity and increased variety. These factors, of course, lead to extra complexity as well. What this means is that you aren't just getting a lot of data when you work with big data. It's also coming at you fast, it's coming at you in complex formats, and it's coming at you from a variety of sources.

It is easy to see why the wealth of big data coming toward us can be likened to a tidal wave and why taming it will be such a challenge! The analytics techniques, processes, and systems within organizations will be strained up to, or even beyond, their limits. It will be necessary to develop additional analysis techniques and processes utilizing updated technologies and methods in order to analyze and act upon big data effectively. We will talk about all these topics before the book is done with the goal of demonstrating why the effort to tame big data is more than worth it.

## IS THE "BIG" PART OR THE "DATA" PART MORE IMPORTANT?

It is already time to take a brief quiz! Stop for a minute and consider the following question before you read on: What is the most important part of the term *big data*? Is it (1) the "big" part, (2) the "data" part, (3) both, or (4) neither? Take a minute to think about it and once you've locked in your answer, proceed to the next paragraph. In the meantime, imagine the "contestants are thinking" music from a game show playing in the background.

Okay, now that you've locked in your answer let's find out if you got the right answer. The answer to the question is choice (4). Neither the "big" part nor the "data" part is the most important part of big data. Not by a long shot. What organizations do with big data is what is most important. The analysis your organization does against big data combined with the actions that are taken to improve your business are what matters.

Having a big source of data does not in and of itself add any value whatsoever. Maybe your data *is* bigger than mine. Who cares? In fact, having any set of data, however big or small it may be, doesn't add any value by itself. Data that is captured but not used for anything is of no more value than some of the old junk stored in an attic or basement. Data is irrelevant without being put into context and put to use. As with any source of data big or small, the power of big data is in what is done with that data. How is it analyzed? What actions are taken based on the findings? How is the data used to make changes to a business?

Reading a lot of the hype around big data, many people are led to believe that just because big data has high volume, velocity, and variety, it is somehow better or more important than other data. This is not true. As we will discuss later in the chapter in the section titled *Most Big Data Doesn't Matter*, many big data sources have a far higher percentage of useless or low-value content than virtually any historical data source. By the time you trim down a big data source to what you actually need, it may not even be so big any more. But that doesn't really matter, because whether it stays big or whether it ends up being small when you're done processing it, the size isn't important. It's what you do with it.

 ## IT ISN'T HOW BIG IT IS. IT'S HOW YOU USE IT!

We're talking about big data of course! Neither the fact that big data is big nor the fact that it is data adds any inherent value. The value is in how you analyze and act upon the data to improve your business.

The first critical point to remember as we start into the book is that big data is both big and it's data. However, that's not what's going to make it exciting for you and your organization. The exciting part comes from all the new and powerful analytics that will be possible as the data is utilized. We're going to talk about a number of those new analytics as we proceed.

## HOW IS BIG DATA DIFFERENT?

There are some important ways that big data is different from traditional data sources. Not every big data source will have every feature that follows, but most big data sources will have several of them.

First, big data is often automatically generated by a machine. Instead of a person being involved in creating new data, it's generated purely by machines in an automated way. If you think about traditional data sources, there was always a person involved. Consider retail or bank transactions, telephone call detail records, product shipments, or invoice payments. All of those involve a person doing something in order for a data record to be generated. Somebody had to deposit money, or make a purchase, or make a phone call, or send a shipment, or make a payment. In each case, there is a person who is taking action as part of the process of new data being created. This is not so for big data in many cases. A lot of sources of big data are generated without any human interaction at all. A sensor embedded in an engine, for example, spits out data about its surroundings even if nobody touches it or asks it to.

Second, big data is typically an entirely new source of data. It is not simply an extended collection of existing data. For example, with the use of the Internet, customers can now execute a transaction with a bank or retailer online. But the transactions they execute are not fundamentally different transactions from what they would have done traditionally. They've simply executed the transactions through a different channel. An organization may capture web transactions, but they are really just more of the same old transactions that have been captured for years. However, actually capturing browsing behaviors as customers execute a transaction creates fundamentally new data which we'll discuss in detail in Chapter 2.

Sometimes "more of the same" can be taken to such an extreme that the data becomes something new. For example, your power meter has probably been read manually each month for years. An argument can be made that automatic readings every 15 minutes by a Smart Meter is more of the same. It can also be argued that it is so much more of the same and that it enables such a different, more in-depth level of analytics that such data is really a new data source. We'll discuss this data in Chapter 3.

Third, many big data sources are not designed to be friendly. In fact, some of the sources aren't designed at all! Take text streams from a social media site. There is no way to ask users to follow certain standards of grammar, or sentence ordering, or vocabulary. You are going to get what you get when people make a posting. It can be difficult to work with such data at best and very, very ugly at worst. We'll discuss text data in Chapters 3 and 6. Most traditional data sources were designed up-front to be friendly. Systems used to capture transactions, for example, provide data in a clean, preformatted template that makes the data easy to load and use. This was driven in part by the historical need to be highly efficient with space. There was no room for excess fluff.

## BIG DATA CAN BE MESSY AND UGLY

Traditional data sources were very tightly defined up-front. Every bit of data had a high level of value or it would not be included. With the cost of storage space becoming almost negligible, big data sources are not always tightly defined up-front and typically capture everything that may be of use. This can lead to having to wade through messy, junk-filled data when doing an analysis.

Last, large swaths of big data streams may not have much value. In fact, much of the data may even be close to worthless. Within a web log, there is information that is very powerful. There is also a lot of information that doesn't have much value at all. It is necessary to weed through and pull out the valuable and relevant pieces. Traditional data sources were defined up-front to be 100 percent relevant. This is because of the scalability limitations that were present. It was far too expensive to have anything included in a data feed that wasn't critical. Not only were data records predefined, but every piece of data in them was high-value. Storage space is no longer a primary constraint. This has led to the default with big data being to capture everything possible and worry later about what matters. This ensures nothing will be missed, but also can make the process of analyzing big data more painful.

## HOW IS BIG DATA MORE OF THE SAME?

As with any new topic getting a lot of attention, there are all sorts of claims about how big data is going to fundamentally change everything about how analysis is done and how it is used. If you take the time to think about it, however, it really isn't the case. It is an example where the hype is going beyond the reality.

The fact that big data is big and poses scalability issues isn't new. Most new data sources were considered big and difficult when they first came into use. Big data is just the next wave of new, bigger data that pushes current limits. Analysts were able to tame past data sources, given the constraints at the time, and big data will be tamed as well. After all, analysts have been at the forefront of exploring new data sources for a long time. That's going to continue.

Who first started to analyze call detail records within telecom companies? Analysts did. I was doing churn analysis against mainframe tapes at my first job. At the time, the data was mind-boggling big. Who first started digging into retail point-of-sale data to figure out what nuggets it held? Analysts did. Originally, the thought of analyzing data about tens to hundreds of thousands of products across thousands of stores was considered a huge problem. Today, not so much.

The analytical professionals who first dipped their toe into such sources were dealing with what at the time were unthinkably large amounts of data. They had to figure out how to analyze it and make use of it within the constraints in place at the time. Many people doubted it was possible, and some even questioned the value of such data. That sounds a lot like big data today, doesn't it?

Big data really isn't going to change what analytic professionals are trying to do or why they are doing it. Even as some begin to define themselves as data scientists, rather than analysts, the goals and objectives are the same. Certainly the problems addressed will evolve with big data, just as they have always evolved. But at the end of the day, analysts and data scientists will simply be exploring new and unthinkably large data sets to uncover valuable trends and patterns as they have always done. For the purposes of this book, we'll include both traditional analysts and data scientists under the umbrella term "analytic professionals." We'll also cover these professionals in much more detail in Chapters 7, 8, and 9. The key takeaway here is that the challenge of big data isn't as new as it first sounds.

 ## YOU HAVE NOTHING TO FEAR

In many ways, big data doesn't pose any problems that your organization hasn't faced before. Taming new, large data sources that push the current limits of scalability is an ongoing theme in the world of analytics. Big data is simply the next generation of such data. Analytical professionals are well-versed in dealing with these situations. If your organization has tamed other data sources, it can tame big data, too.

Big data will change some of the tactics analytic professionals use as they do their work. New tools, methods, and technologies will be added alongside traditional analytic tools to help deal more effectively with the flood of big data. Complex filtering algorithms will be developed to siphon off the meaningful pieces from a raw stream of big data. Modeling and forecasting processes will be updated to include big data inputs on top of currently exiting inputs. We'll discuss these topics more in Chapters 4, 5, and 6.

The preceding tactical changes don't fundamentally alter the goals or purpose of analysis, or the analysis process itself. Big data will certainly drive new and innovative analytics, and it will force analytic professionals to continue to get creative within their scalability constraints. Big data will also only get bigger over time. However, incorporating big data really isn't that much different from what analysts have always done. They are ready to meet the challenge.

### RISKS OF BIG DATA

Big data does come with risks. One risk is that an organization will be so overwhelmed with big data that it won't make any progress. The key here, as we will discuss in Chapter 8, is to get the right people involved so that doesn't happen. You need the right people attacking big data and attempting to solve the right kinds of problems. With the right people addressing the right problems, organizations can avoid spinning their wheels and failing to make progress.

Another risk is that costs escalate too fast as too much big data is captured before an organization knows what to do with it. As with anything, avoiding this is a matter of making sure that progress moves at a pace that allows the organization to keep up. It isn't necessary to go for it all at once and capture 100 percent of every new data source starting tomorrow. What is necessary is to start capturing samples of the new data sources to learn about them. Using those initial samples, experimental analysis can be performed to determine what is truly important within each source and how each can be used. Building from that base, an organization will be ready to effectively tackle a data source on a large scale.

Perhaps the biggest risk with many sources of big data is privacy. If everyone in the world was good and honest, then we wouldn't have to worry much about privacy. But everyone is not good and honest. In fact, in addition to individuals, there are also companies that are not good and honest. There are even entire governments that are not good and honest. Big data has the potential to be problematic here. Privacy will need to be addressed with respect to big data, or it may never meet its potential. Without proper restraints, big data has the potential to unleash such a groundswell of protest that some sources of it may be shut down completely.

Consider the attention received by recent security breaches that led to credit card numbers and classified government documents being stolen and posted online. It isn't a stretch to say that if data is being stored, somebody will try and steal it. Once the bad guys get their hands on data they will do bad things with it. There have also been high-profile cases of major organizations getting into trouble for having ambiguous or poorly defined privacy policies. This has led to data being used in ways that consumers didn't understand or support, causing a backlash. Both self-regulation and legal regulation of the uses of big data will need to evolve as the use of big data explodes.

Self-regulation is critical. After all, it shows that an industry cares. Industries should regulate themselves and develop rules that everyone can live with. Self-imposed rules are usually better and less restrictive than those created when a government entity steps in because an industry didn't do a good job of policing itself.

## PRIVACY WILL BE A HUGE ISSUE WITH BIG DATA

Given the sensitive nature of many sources of big data, privacy concerns will be a major focal point. Once data exists, dishonest people will try to use it in ways you wouldn't approve of without your consent. Policies and protocols for the handling, storage, and application of big data are going to need to catch up with the analysis capabilities that already exist. Be sure to think through your organization's approach to privacy up front and make your position totally clear and transparent.

People are already concerned about how their web browsing history is tracked. There are also concerns about the tracking of people's locations and actions through cell phone applications and GPS systems. Nefarious uses of big data are possible, and if it is possible someone will try it. Therefore, steps need to be taken to stop that from happening. Organizations will need to clearly explain how they will keep data secure and how they will use it if the general population is going to accept having their data captured and analyzed.

## WHY YOU NEED TO TAME BIG DATA

Many organizations have done little, if anything, with big data yet. Luckily, your organization is not too far behind in 2012 if you have ignored big data so far, unless you are in an industry, such as ecommerce, where analyzing big data is already standard. That will change soon, however, as momentum is picking up rapidly. So far, most organizations have missed only the chance to be on the leading edge. That is actually just fine with many organizations. Today, they have a chance to get ahead of the pack. Within a few years, any organization that isn't analyzing big data will be late to the game and will be stuck playing catch up for years to come. The time to start taming big data is now.

It isn't often that a company can leverage totally new data sources and drive value for its business while the competition isn't doing the same thing. That is the huge opportunity in big data today. You have a chance to get ahead of much of your competition and beat them to the punch. We will continue to see examples in the coming years of businesses transforming themselves with the analysis of big data. Case studies will tell the story about how the competition was left in the dust and caught totally off guard. It is already possible to find compelling results being discussed in articles, at conferences, and elsewhere today. Some of these case studies are from companies in industries considered dull, old, and stodgy. It isn't just the sexy, new industries like ecommerce that are involved. We'll look at a variety of examples of how big data can be used in Chapters 2 and 3.

 ## THE TIME IS NOW!

Your organization needs to start taming big data now. As of today, you've only missed the chance to be on the bleeding edge if you've ignored big data. Today, you can still get ahead of the pack. In a few years, you'll be left behind if you are still sitting on the sidelines. If your organization is already committed to capturing data and using analysis to make decisions, then going after big data isn't a stretch. It is simply an extension of what you are already doing today.

The fact is that the decision to start taming big data shouldn't be a big stretch. Most organizations have already committed to collecting and analyzing data as a core part of their strategy. Data warehousing, reporting, and analysis are ubiquitous. Once an organization has bought into the idea that data has value, then taming and analyzing big data is just an extension of that commitment. Don't let a naysayer tell you it isn't worth exploring big data, or that it isn't proven, or that it's too risky. Those same excuses would have prevented any of the progress made in the past few decades with data and analysis. Focus those who are uncertain or nervous about big data on the fact that big data is simply an extension of what the organization is already doing. There is nothing earth-shatteringly new and different about it and nothing to fear.

## THE STRUCTURE OF BIG DATA

As you read about big data, you will come across a lot of discussion on the concept of data being structured, unstructured, semi-structured, or even multi-structured. Big data is often described as unstructured and traditional data as structured. The lines aren't as clean as such labels suggest, however. Let's explore these three types of data structure from a layman's perspective. Highly technical details are out of scope for this book.

Most traditional data sources are fully in the structured realm. This means traditional data sources come in a clear, predefined format that is specified in detail. There is no variation from the defined formats on a day-to-day or update-to-update basis. For a stock trade, the first field received might be a date in a MM/DD/YYYY format. Next might be an account number in a 12-digit numeric format. Next might be a stock symbol that is a three- to five-digit character field. And so on. Every piece of information included is known ahead of time, comes in a specified format, and occurs in a specified order. This makes it easy to work with.

Unstructured data sources are those that you have little or no control over. You are going to get what you get. Text data, video data, and audio data all fall into this classification. A picture has a format of individual pixels set up in rows, but how those pixels fit together to create the picture seen by an observer is going to vary substantially in each case. There are sources of big data that are truly unstructured such as those preceding. However, most data is at least semi-structured.

Semi-structured data has a logical flow and format to it that can be understood, but the format is not user-friendly. Sometimes semi-structured data is referred to as multi-structured data. There can be a lot of noise or unnecessary data intermixed with the nuggets of high value in such a feed. Reading semi-structured data to analyze it isn't as simple as specifying a fixed file format. To read semi-structured data, it is necessary to employ complex rules that dynamically determine how to proceed after reading each piece of information.

Web logs are a perfect example of semi-structured data. Web logs are pretty ugly when you look at them; however, each piece of information does, in fact, serve a purpose of some sort. Whether any given piece of a web log serves your purposes is another question. See Figure 1.1 for an example of a raw web log.

## WHAT STRUCTURE DOES YOUR BIG DATA HAVE?

Many sources of big data are actually semi-structured or multi-structured, not unstructured. Such data does have a logical flow to it that can be understood so that information can be extracted from it for analysis. It just isn't as easy to deal with as traditional structured data sources. Taming semi-structured data is largely a matter of putting in the extra time and effort to figure out the best way to process it.

There is logic to the information in the web log even if it isn't entirely clear at first glance. There are fields, there are delimiters, and there are values just like in a structured source. However, they do not follow each other consistently or in a set way. The log text generated by a click on a web site right now can be longer or shorter than the log text generated by a click from a different page one minute from now. In the end, however, it's important to understand that semi-structured data does have an underlying logic. It is possible to develop relationships between various pieces of it. It simply takes more effort than structured data.

### Raw Web Log Data

```
96.255.99.50 - - [01/Jun/2010:05:28:07 +0000] "GET /origin-
log.enquisite.com/d.js?id=a1a3af-
ly6l645&referrer=http://www.google.com/search?hl=en&q=budget+planner&aq=5&aqi=g
10&aql=&oq=budget+&gs_rfai=&location=https://money.strands.com/content/simple-
and-free-monthly-budget-planner&ua=Mozilla/4.0 (compatible; MSIE 7.0; Windows NT 6.0;
SLCC1; .NET CLR 2.0.50727; .NET CLR 3.0.30618; .NET CLR 3.5.30729;
InfoPath.2)&pc=pgys63w0xgn102in8ms37wka8quxe74e&sc=cr1kto0wmxqik1wlr9p9weh
6yxy8q8sa&r=0.07550191624904945 HTTP/1.1" 200 380 "-" "Mozilla/4.0 (compatible;
MSIE 7.0; Windows NT 6.0; SLCC1; .NET CLR 2.0.50727; .NET CLR 3.0.30618; .NET CLR
3.5.30729; InfoPath.2)" "ac=bd76aad174480000679a044cfda00e005b130000"
```

**Figure 1.1** Example of a Raw Web Log

Analytic professionals will be more intimidated by truly unstructured data than by semi-structured data. They may have to wrestle with semi-structured data to bend it to their will, but they can do it. Analysts can get semi-structured data into a form that is well structured and can incorporate it into their analytical processes. Truly unstructured data can be much harder to tame and will remain a challenge for organizations even as they tame semi-structured data.

## EXPLORING BIG DATA

Getting started with big data isn't difficult. Simply collect some big data and let your organization's analytics team start exploring what it offers. It isn't necessary for an organization to design a production-quality, ongoing data feed to start. It just needs to get the analytics team's hands and tools on some of the data so that exploratory analysis can begin. This is what analysts and data scientists do.

There is an old rule of thumb that 70 to 80 percent of the time developing an analysis is spent gathering and preparing data and only 20 to 30 percent is spent analyzing it. Expect that those guidelines will be low when initially working with big data. Analytic professionals will initially probably spend at least 95 percent, if not close to 100 percent, of their time just figuring out a big data source before they can even think about doing in-depth analysis with it.

It is important to understand that that's okay. Figuring out what a data source is all about is an important part of the analysis process. It may not be glamorous or exciting, but iteratively loading data, examining what it looks like, and adjusting the load processes in order to better target the data that is needed are immensely important. Without completing those steps, it won't be possible to proceed to the analysis phase.

The process of identifying the pieces of big data that contain value and determining how best to extract those pieces accurately is critical. Expect this to take time and do not get frustrated if it takes longer than anticipated. As the process of figuring out the new data sources progresses, analytic professionals and their business sponsors should look for ways to deliver small, quick wins. Showing the organization something of value, no matter how small, will keep people interested in the process and help them see that there is progress being made. A cross-functional team can't get started and a year later claim they are still figuring out how to do something with big data. It is necessary to come up with some ideas, even if they are small, and make something happen quickly.

 ## DELIVER VALUE AS YOU GO

It will take a lot of effort to figure out how to apply a source of big data to your business. An organization's analytic professionals and their business sponsors must be sure to look for ways to deliver small, quick wins as they go. It will demonstrate to the organization that progress is being made and will build support for further efforts. Such wins can also generate a solid return on investment.

A great example comes from a European retailer. The company wanted to start leveraging detailed web log data. As they built complex, long-term processes to capture the data, they first put in place a few simple processes. They started by identifying what products each customer browsed. The browsing information was used for a basic follow-up e-mail campaign that sent each customer a message if they left the site after viewing products, but did not end up purchasing them. This simple exercise generated a huge amount of revenue for the organization.

Along with a handful of other similarly basic first steps, the company paid for the entire long-term effort of capturing and loading the web data. More important, they hadn't even gotten fancy or dealt with the entire data stream yet. Imagine the returns they are going to see as they proceed to more deeply analyze the data in the future. Due to the quick and early wins, everyone in the organization is excited to continue because they have seen how powerful even the first, basic uses of the data were. Plus, the further efforts are already paid for!

## MOST BIG DATA DOESN'T MATTER

The fact is that most big data just doesn't matter. That sure sounds harsh, doesn't it? But it's not meant to be. As we have already discussed, a big data stream is going to be large in terms of volume, velocity, variety, and complexity. Much of the content of a big data stream won't matter for any given purpose, and some of it won't matter much at all. Taming the big data tidal wave isn't about getting all the water from the wave nicely controlled in a swimming pool. It's more like sipping water from a hose: You slurp out just what you need and let the rest run by.

Within a big data feed there will be some information that has long-term strategic value, some that will be useful only for immediate and tactical use, and some data that won't be used for anything. A key part of taming big data is to determine which pieces fall into which category.

A great example of this is related to the radio frequency identification (RFID) tags we discuss in Chapter 3 that are being placed today on pallets of products when they are shipped. For expensive items, tags are even being placed on individual items. Eventually, tagging is going to move to individual items as the rule rather than the exception. Today, that is cost prohibitive in most cases, so the tags are often placed on each pallet. The tags make it easier to track where the pallets are, when they are loaded and unloaded, and where they are stored.

Imagine a warehouse with tens of thousands of pallets. Each pallet has an RFID tag. RFID readers query the warehouse every 10 seconds saying, basically, "Who is out there?" Each of the pallets responds back: "I am." Let's discuss how in this case big data starts to be narrowed down very quickly.

A pallet first arrives today and first chimes in: "This is pallet 123456789. I'm here." Every 10 seconds over the next three weeks while that pallet is in the warehouse, it is going to reply again and again: "I'm here. I'm here. I'm here." Upon completion of each of the 10 second polls taken, it's very well worth the effort to parse through all the replies and identify any pallets that have had a change in status. This way, it can be validated that any changes were expected, and action can be taken if a pallet changed status unexpectedly.

Once a pallet actually leaves the warehouse, it is no longer responding. After validating that the pallet was expected to leave when it did, all of the intermediate "I'm here" records really don't matter. Over time, all that really matters are the date and time when the pallet entered the warehouse and the date and time when it left. If those times are three weeks apart, it only makes sense to keep the two time stamps associated with the entry and exit of the pallet. All of the responses at 10 second intervals in between, saying "I'm here. I'm here. I'm here," have no long-term value whatsoever, but it was necessary to collect them. It was necessary to analyze each at the moment it was generated. But the responses outside the first and last have no long-term value. They can be safely thrown away once the pallet is gone.

 **GET READY TO THROW DATA AWAY**

One key to taming big data will be to identify what pieces matter. There will be pieces that have long-term strategic use, pieces that have short-term tactical use, and pieces that don't matter at all. It will seem odd to let a lot of data slip past, but that is par for the course with big data. Throwing data away will take some getting used to.

If raw big data feeds can be kept available for a period of time, this will provide the capability to go back and extract additional data missed when it was first processed. One good example of this is the way that web activity tracking is done today. Most web sites use what is known as a tag-based methodology. With a tag-based methodology, it is necessary to identify up front what text, images, or links it is desired to track users' interactions with. The tags, which are not seen by the user, will report back that a user has done something. Since only tagged items are reported, most browsing information is ignored from the start. The problem is if a request to have a new promotional image tagged is inadvertently missed, there will be no ability to go back and analyze interactions with that image. It has to be tagged before a user browses. It is possible to add a tag later, but only activity from that point forward will be captured.

There are newer methodologies that will parse through raw web logs and enable the identification of anything that occurred without having predefined it. These methods are log-based since they leverage a raw web log directly. The value of this is that if you realize later that you forgot to capture interactions with the promotion image, you can go and parse through the data again and pull it out. In this case, nothing is thrown away up front, but what to keep will need to be determined at the time of analysis. That is an important capability and is why keeping some historical big data, as long as it is cost-effective to do so, makes sense. How much historical data can be kept will depend on the size of a data feed and how much storage is reasonably available. It is a good idea to leave as much flexibility as possible within those constraints by keeping as much history as available storage will economically allow.

## FILTERING BIG DATA EFFECTIVELY

The biggest challenge with big data may not be the analytics you do with it, but the extract, transform, and load (ETL) processes you have to build to get it ready for analysis. ETL is the process of taking a raw feed of data, reading it, and producing a usable set of output. The data is extracted (E) from whatever source it is starting from. The data is next transformed (T) through various aggregations, functions, and combinations to get it into a usable state. Last, the data is loaded (L) into whatever environment will be leveraged to analyze the data. That is the process of ETL.

Let's go back to the analogy we discussed earlier: sipping water out of a hose. When you're drinking water out of a hose, you don't really care which parts of the stream of water get in your mouth. With big data, you care very much about which parts of the data stream get captured. It will be necessary to explore and understand the entire data stream first. Only then can you filter down to the pieces that you need. This is why the up-front effort to tame big data can take so long.

 **SIPPING FROM THE HOSE**

Working with big data is a lot like taking a drink from a hose. Most of the data will run past, just like most of the water does. The goal is to sip the right amount of data out of the data stream as it flows past, not to try and drink it all. By focusing on the important pieces of the data, it makes big data easier to handle and keeps efforts focused on what is important.

Analytic processes may require filters on the front end to remove portions of a big data stream when it first arrives. There will be other filters along the way as the data is processed. For example, when working with a web log, a rule might be to filter out up front any information on browser versions or operating systems. Such data is rarely needed except for operational reasons. Later in the process, the data may be filtered to specific pages or user actions that need to be examined for the business issues to be addressed.

The complexity of the rules and the magnitude of the data being removed or kept at each stage will vary by data source and by business problem. The load processes and filters that are put on top of big data are absolutely critical. Without getting those correct, it will be very difficult to succeed. Traditional structured data doesn't require as much effort in these areas since it is specified, understood, and standardized in advance. With big data, it is necessary to specify, understand, and standardize it as part of the analysis process in many cases.

## MIXING BIG DATA WITH TRADITIONAL DATA

Perhaps the most exciting thing about big data isn't what it will do for a business by itself. It's what it will do for a business when combined with an organization's other data.

Browsing history, for example, is very powerful. Knowing how valuable a customer is and what they have bought in the past across all channels makes web data even more powerful by putting it in a larger context. We'll explore this in detail in Chapter 2.

Smart-grid data is very powerful for a utility company. Knowing the historical billing patterns of customers, their dwelling type, and other factors makes data from a smart meter even more powerful by putting it in a larger context. We'll look at this in Chapter 3.

The text from customer service online chats and e-mails is powerful. Knowing the detailed product specifications of the products being discussed, the sales data related to those products, and historical product defect information makes that text data even more powerful by putting it in a larger context. We'll explore this topic from different perspectives in Chapters 3 and 6.

A large part of the reason why Enterprise Data Warehouses (EDWs) have become such a widespread corporate tool isn't to centralize a bunch of data marts to save hardware and software costs. An EDW adds value by allowing different data sources to intermix and enhance one another. With an EDW, it is possible to analyze customer and employee data together since they are in one location. They are no longer completely separate. For example, do certain employees increase customer value through their interactions more than others? Such questions are much easier to answer if the data is all in one place. As big data is added in, it just continues to evolve the number and magnitude of problems that can be addressed as ever more types of data can be combined together to add new perspectives and contexts.

 **MIX IT UP!**

The biggest value in big data can be driven by combining big data with other corporate data. By putting what is found in big data in a larger context, the quantity and quality of insights will increase exponentially. This is why big data needs to be folded into an overall data strategy as opposed to having a stand-alone big data strategy.

This is why it is critically important that organizations don't develop a big data strategy that is distinct from their traditional data strategy. That will fail. Big data and traditional data are both pieces of the overall strategy. To succeed, organizations need to develop a cohesive strategy where big data isn't a distinct, standalone concept. Rather, big data must be simply another facet of an enterprise data strategy. From the start, it is necessary to think through and plan not just how to capture and analyze big data by itself, but also how to use it in combination with other corporate data and as a component of a more holistic approach to corporate data.

## THE NEED FOR STANDARDS

Will big data continue to be a wild west of crazy formats, unconstrained streams, and lack of definition? Probably not. Over time, standards will be developed. Many semi-structured data sources will become more structured over time, and individual organizations will fine-tune their big data feeds to be friendlier for analysis. But more important, there will be a move toward industry standards. While text data like e-mail or social media commentary can't be controlled very much on the input end, it *is* possible to standardize the approaches to interpreting such data and using it for analytics. This is already starting to happen.

For example, what words are "good" and what words are "bad"? What contexts exist where the default rules don't apply? Which e-mails are worth exhaustive parsing and analysis, and which can be processed minimally? Standards for the production and generation of big data will develop, as will the standards for the processing and analysis of big data. Both the input and output sides will be addressed. As a result, life will get easier for those tasked with taming it. It will take time and many of the standards that develop will be more of a set of commonly accepted best practices among practitioners than formally stated rules or policies from an official standards organization. Nevertheless, standardization will increase.

 ## STANDARDIZE TO THE EXTENT POSSIBLE

While text data like e-mail can't be controlled very much on the input end, it is possible to standardize the approaches to interpreting such data and using it for analytics. You won't be able to standardize everything about big data, but you can standardize enough to make life much easier. Focus on standardizing the use of big data as much as on standardizing the input feed itself.

Organizations that are quick to embrace big data will have the ability to define and influence the developing standards and therefore be sure that their specific needs are met. Some industries are even getting ahead of the curve. There has been a lot of work to define the parameters of smart-grid data within the utility industry even before the ability to collect the data is in place. By starting out with formal definitions and guidelines, smart-grid data will be much more manageable than if every utility had just started creating data in their own way without thinking it through ahead of time with their peers.

## TODAY'S BIG DATA IS NOT TOMORROW'S BIG DATA

As discussed at the start of the chapter, the accepted definitions of big data are somewhat "squishy." There is no specific, universal definition in terms of what qualifies as big data. Rather, big data is defined in relative terms tied to available technology and resources. As a result, what counts as big data to one company or industry may not count as big data to another. A large e-commerce company is going to have a much "bigger" definition of big data than a small manufacturer will.

More important, what qualifies as big data will necessarily change over time as the tools and techniques to handle it evolve alongside raw storage size and processing power. Household demographic files with hundreds of fields and millions of customers were huge and tough to manage a decade or two ago. Now such data fits on a thumb drive and can be analyzed by a low-end laptop. As what qualifies as high volume, high velocity, high variety, and high complexity evolves, so will big data.

 **"BIG" WILL CHANGE**

What's big data today won't be considered big data tomorrow any more than what was considered big a decade ago is considered big today. Big data will continue to evolve. What is impossible or unthinkable today in terms of data volume, velocity, variety, and complexity won't be so years down the road. That's how it has always been, and it will continue as such in the era of big data.

Transactional data in the retail, telecommunications, and banking industries were very big and hard to handle even a decade ago. In fact, such data wasn't widely available for analytics and reporting in many organizations in the late 1990s. Today, such data is considered a necessary and fundamental asset. Virtually every company of any size has access to it.

Similarly, what we are intimidated by today won't be so scary a few years down the road. Clickstream data from the web may be a standard, easily handled data source in 10 years. Actively processing every e-mail, customer service chat, and social media comment may become a standard practice for most organizations. The tracking of hundreds of metrics per second from an engine may not make anyone break a sweat.

As we tame the current generation of big data streams, other even bigger data sources are going to come along and take their place. What will they be? Nobody has all the answers today. However, following are a few ideas on how current data sources can be upgraded to another magnitude of "big" pretty quickly:

- Imagine web browsing data that expands to include millisecond-level eyeball and mouse movement so that every tiny detail of a user's navigation is captured, instead of just what was clicked on. This is another order of big.

- Imagine video game telemetry data being upgraded to go beyond every button pressed or movement made. Imagine it also containing the eye and body movement of the player along with the location and status of every single object within the scene being played instead of just the objects that are interacted with. That gets massive fast.

- Imagine RFID information being available for every single individual item in every single store, distribution facility, and manufacturing plant globally. Imagine those chips evolving to capture dozens of metrics per second, such as temperatures, humidity, speed, acceleration, pressure, and more. The volume of such data is unthinkable today.

- Imagine capturing and translating to text every conversation anyone has with a customer service or sales line. Add to that all the associated e-mails, online chats, and comments from places such as social media sites or product review sites. Now, go parse, combine, and analyze all of that text. Is your head exploding yet?

The point is that big data is here to stay. Though what we find intimidating today won't be what we find intimidating a few years from now, some new data source will be intimidating. Organizations will need to continue to adjust their methods and their goals to make use of the data as it evolves. Your organization can't adjust and update its methods for handling big data until it has some methods in place, however. So you need to get started!

## WRAP-UP

The most important lessons to take away from this chapter are:

- Big data is often defined as data that exceeds the capability of commonly used hardware environments and software tools to capture, manage, and process it within a tolerable elapsed time for its user population.

- Big data is big not just in terms of volume, but also in terms of variety, velocity, and complexity.

- The power of big data is in the analysis you do and the actions you take. It is in neither the "big" part nor the "data" part.

- Big data is often automatically generated by a machine of some sort and is usually not in a user-friendly format. The default is to capture everything and worry about what matters later.

- Big data is just the next wave of new, bigger data that pushes today's limits. From an analytics perspective it isn't any different from past data sources that were large and difficult to handle when they first became available.

- Big data will change some of the tactics and tools that analytic professionals utilize, but it won't fundamentally change why analytics are done or how the value of analytics is assessed.

- Many big data sources are semi-structured. There is logic to a semi-structured data feed, but it may not be pretty. Big data can also be unstructured. In some cases, it is even structured like traditional data sources.

- The biggest risks of big data are the privacy implications that some of the data sources involve. Both self-regulation and legal regulation will be needed as the use of big data evolves.

- Taming the big data tidal wave isn't about controlling all of the data. It is like sipping from a hose. Just skim off the important pieces.

- The most exciting thing about big data is what it will do for a business when combined with other data.

- Big data and traditional data are both pieces of an overall data and analytics strategy. Don't develop a big data strategy that is distinct from your traditional data strategy.

■ Big data will continue to evolve. What we think is big and intimidating today won't raise an eyebrow in a decade, but another new data source will!

## NOTES

1. Merv Adrian, "Big Data," *Teradata Magazine*, 1:11, www. teradatamagazine.com/v11n01/Features/Big-Data/.
2. McKinsey Global Institute, *Big Data: The Next Frontier for Innovation, Competition, and Productivity*, May 2011.
3. Ibid.
4. *CEO Advisory: "Big Data" Equals Big Opportunity*, Gartner, March 31, 2011.

# CHAPTER 2

# Web Data: The Original Big Data

Wouldn't it be great to understand customer intent instead of just customer action? Wouldn't it be great to understand each customer's thought processes as they determine if they'll make a purchase or not? It had been virtually impossible to get insights into such topics in the past. Today, such topics can be addressed with the use of detailed web data. That's what this chapter is all about.

There is no better way to understand what big data is all about than to actually learn about some specific examples of big data and how it can be used to drive business value. Perhaps no big data source is as widely used today as web data. We'll dedicate this entire chapter to web data so that we can dive deeply into the topic and discuss applications of web data in detail.[1] In Chapter 3, we'll then have shorter discussions of nine other important big data sources that represent a cross-section of what is available and how such data can be used.

Organizations across a number of industries have integrated detailed, customer-level behavioral data sourced from a web site into their enterprise analytics environments. Most organizations, however, still end web integration with the inclusion of online transactions. Traditional web analytics vendors provide operational reporting on click-through rates, traffic sources, and metrics based only on web data. However, detailed web behavior data was not historically leveraged outside of web reporting.

Leading companies have shown that detailed web data can provide previously untapped corporate value. This chapter will outline what those leaders are doing, why they are doing it, and why every organization should consider such analytics today. The examples are quite compelling and promise to be eye-opening to those who have not yet given much thought to integrating detailed clickstream data with other data as opposed to keeping it isolated by itself.

The core theme of this chapter isn't simply the taming of web data by itself. Instead of aggregated web metrics from a distinct data silo, organizations should focus on the integration of web data with all the other relevant information about their customers. Utilizing such information in a scalable analytics environment enables moving beyond purchasing insights about customers and into individual intentions, purchase decision processes, and preferences. By tapping into the rich insight provided by this new data source, huge strides forward can occur within an organization.

How does an organization capture, analyze, and utilize this rich information to drive insight? First, we'll discuss what data needs to be acquired and why. Then, we'll explore some examples of what that data can reveal. Finally, we'll discuss specific examples of how analytics processes can be transformed through the integration of web data. Web data is one big data source that has already been tamed by many organizations. Add yours to the list!

## WEB DATA OVERVIEW

Organizations have talked about a 360-degree view of their customers for years. At any point in time, one organization or the other claims that it has achieved a true 360-degree view. In reality, it is impossible to have a true 360-degree view as that implies you literally know everything there is to know about your customers. When a 360-degree view is discussed, what is really meant is that the organization has as full a view of its customers as possible considering the technology and data available at that point in time. However, the finish line is always moving. Just when you think you have finally arrived, the finish line moves farther out again.

A few decades ago, companies were at the top of their game if they had the names and addresses of their customers and they were able to append demographic information to those names through the then-new third-party data enhancement services. Eventually, cutting-edge companies started to have basic recency, frequency, and monetary value (RFM) metrics attached to customers. Such metrics look at when a customer last purchased (recency), how often they have purchased (frequency), and how much they spent (monetary value). These RFM summaries might be tallied for the past year and possibly over a customer's lifetime. In the past 10 to 15 years, virtually all businesses started to collect and analyze the detailed transaction histories of their customers. This led to an explosion of analytical power and a much deeper understanding of customer behavior.

 ## GET YOUR 360-DEGREE VIEW UP-TO-DATE

Many organizations haven't yet moved beyond yesterday's standard transactional view of customers. The integration of new data sources, such as web data, is now possible and is driving huge value for early adopters. Is your organization's view of its customers up-to-date?

Many organizations are still frozen at the transactional history stage. Today, while this transactional view is still important, many companies incorrectly assume that it remains the closest view possible to a 360-degree view of their customers. Today, organizations need to be collecting newly evolving big data sources related to their customers from a variety of extended and newly emerging touch points such as web browsers, mobile applications, kiosks, social media sites, and more.

Just as transactional data enabled a revolution in the power and depth of analysis, so too do these new data sources enable taking analytics to a new level. With today's data storage and processing capabilities, it is absolutely possible to achieve success, and many forward-thinking companies have already proven it by applying the data to a variety of problems, some of which we'll discuss shortly.

## What Are You Missing?

Have you ever stopped to think about what happens if only the trans-actions generated by a web site are captured? Perhaps for a web site, 95 percent of browsing sessions do not result in a basket being created. Of that 5 percent, only about half, or 2.5 percent, actually begin the check out process. And, of that 2.5 percent only two-thirds, or 1.7 percent, actually complete a purchase. These figures are not unrealistic in many cases.

What this means is that information is missing on more than 98 percent of web sessions if only transactions are tracked. But more important, an even higher percentage of available data is missing. For every purchase transaction, there might be dozens or hundreds of specific actions taken on the site to get to that sale. That information needs to be collected and analyzed alongside the final sales data.

It is important to note that this is not just the same old web ana-lytics story from years past. Traditional web analytics focus on aggre-gated behavior, summarized in an environment where only web data was included. The goal needs to be moving beyond reporting of summary statistics, even if they can be viewed in some detail, to actually combining customer level web behavior data with other cross-channel customer data. This is moving far beyond click-through reports and page view summaries.

Just as RFM is only a small piece of what transaction data can yield, so, too, are traditional web analytics only a portion of what web data can yield. Web data is a game-changing, amazing new frontier that can revolutionize organizations' customer insights and the impacts those insights have on their businesses.

## Imagine the Possibilities

Imagine knowing everything customers do as they go through the process of doing business with your organization. Not just what they buy, but what they are thinking about buying along with what key decision criteria they use. Such knowledge enables a new level of understanding about your customers and a new level of interaction with your customers. It allows you to meet their needs more quickly and keep them satisfied.

- Imagine you are a retailer. Imagine walking through the aisles with customers and recording every place they go, every item they look at, every item they pick up, every item they put in the cart and then take back out. Imagine knowing whether they read nutritional information, if they look at laundry instructions, if they read the promotional brochure on the shelf, or if they look at other information made available to them in the store.

- Imagine you are a bank. Imagine being able to identify every credit card option customers considered. Imagine being able to understand if it was a reward program, interest rates, or annual fees that drove their choice. Imagine knowing what they say about each product after they own it.

- Imagine you are an airline. Imagine being able to identify every flight customers viewed before choosing their final itinerary. Imagine knowing if they cared more about price or convenience. Imagine knowing all the destinations they consider and when they first consider them.

- Imagine you are a telecom company. Imagine being able to identify every phone model, rate plan, data plan, and accessory that customers considered before making a final decision. Imagine knowing that the way they came back to your site was by typing into a search engine "renew contract" or "contract cancellation."

It certainly sounds exciting to have the information outlined in this list. You can also have it right now by making a commitment to collect it and make it available for analytics. There are organizations in each of these industries that are already doing this.

## A Fundamentally New Source of Information

The beauty of exploring customers' detailed web behavior is that it moves beyond just knowing what they buy. You can now gain insights into how they made their decisions. Instead of seeing just the results, you have visibility into the entire buying process. This big data source isn't a simple extension of existing data sources. Many organizations were excited over the integration of web transactions with their traditional transactions. But, at base, a web transaction is simply another transaction record with a new "transaction type" or "transaction location" flag. In the case of detailed web behavior, there is no existing analog to most of the data that can be collected. It is a fundamentally new source of information.

 ## A RARE OPPORTUNITY

It isn't often that an organization has the opportunity to collect a completely new and distinct set of data. Detailed web data is one of the rare opportunities to do this. There simply isn't an existing data source that provides much of what web data provides outside of expensive surveys or research studies that only provide data on a small subset of customers.

One of the most exciting aspects of web data is that it provides factual information on customer preferences, future intentions, and motivations that are virtually impossible to get from other sources outside of a direct conversation or survey. Why do customers choose one offering over another? Perhaps organizations think they know. However, they will likely find that there are many customers making choices in ways that were not anticipated.

Once customers' intentions, preferences, and motivations are known, there are completely new ways of communicating with them, driving further business, and increasing their loyalty. The glorious part of this story happens when you marry web data with all that has been learned from the prior 360-degree view. Now that view can be extended with all the rich new web behavior data available.

### What Data Should Be Collected?

Any action that a customer takes while interacting with an organization should be captured if it is possible to capture it. That means detailed event history from any customer touch point. Common touch points today include web sites, kiosks, mobile apps, and social media. A wide range of customer events can be captured, including the examples in Table 2.1.

**Table 2.1** Behaviors That Can Be Captured

| Purchases | Requesting help |
|---|---|
| Product views | Forwarding a link |
| Shopping basket additions | Posting a comment |
| Watching a video | Registering for a webinar |
| Accessing a download | Executing a search |
| Reading / writing a review | And many more! |

While this chapter will focus on web data, the same principles apply for the other sources listed in the first paragraph. While the examples that follow will be web site–centric, keep in mind that the same concepts apply across the board to all touch points from which data can be collected.

 **IT ISN'T JUST ABOUT WEB DATA**

There are a variety of touch points for which the concepts discussed in this chapter apply. These include things such as kiosks and mobile applications. Don't limit your thinking just to web data.

## What about Privacy?

Privacy is a big issue today and may become an even bigger issue as time passes. Serious consideration needs to be given to what data is captured and how it is used. You need to respect not just formal legal restrictions, but also what your customers will view as appropriate. The last thing an organization wants to do is to create programs that customers view as being "creepy" or intrusive. Privacy is an issue worthy of a deep discussion within your organization. It is outside the scope of this book to cover all of the issues surrounding privacy. However, we will examine one option to address privacy concerns while still gaining value from the analysis of web data.

Even if an organization wants to be conservative with its actions, there are options for realizing tremendous value from web data. If there is no desire to interact with customers individually or tie the data back to identifiable customer data, web data is still valuable. An arbitrary identification number that is not personally identifiable can be matched to each unique customer based on a logon, cookie, or similar piece of information. This creates what might be called a "faceless" customer record. While all of the data associated with one of these identifiers is from one person, the people doing the analysis have no ability to tie the ID back to the actual customer. Analysis can still be done to look for patterns across customers, however. These patterns are powerful and can be found without ever worrying specifically which given individual did what.

 **CONSIDER FACELESS CUSTOMER ANALYSIS**

Much of the value in customer analysis is in the aggregate patterns that can be identified. You only need to identify an individual by name or address if you want to do direct marketing. A lot of high-value analysis can be done by simply looking at faceless customer data. In this approach, analysts only know each customer by an arbitrary, non-traceable number. Don't miss out on the benefits of such analysis.

It is the patterns across faceless customers that matter, not the behavior of any specific customer. The individuals in this example are only important as an input to the pattern analysis. Nobody needs to identify who each individual actually is in order to derive value. With today's database technologies, it is possible to enable analytic professionals to do analysis without having any ability to identify the individuals involved. This can remove many privacy concerns. Of course, many organizations are in fact identifying and targeting specific customers as a result of such analytics. They have presumably put in place privacy policies, including opt-out options, and are careful to follow them.

## WHAT WEB DATA REVEALS

Now that we've covered what web data is, let's dive into it in more detail. There are a number of specific areas where web data can help organizations understand their customers better than is possible without web data. Without taming this source of big data, such insights will be very difficult, if not impossible, to come by. We'll establish some broad areas of the kind of insights you can gain from web data in this section of the chapter before moving on to detailed use cases and applications in the final section.

## Shopping Behaviors

A good starting point to understanding shopping behavior is identifying how customers come to a site to begin shopping. What search engine do they use? What specific search terms are entered? Do they use a bookmark they created previously? Analytic professionals can take this information and look for patterns in terms of which search terms, search engines, and referring sites are associated with higher sales rates. Note that analysts will be able to look into higher sales rates not just within a given web session, but also for the same customer over time. This can be combined with a view of sales on the web site along with a cross-channel view of the customer's purchase behavior over time. That is where the value resides.

Once customers are on a site, start to examine all the products they explore. Identify who simply looked at a product landing page and left, and who drilled down further. Who viewed extra photos? Who read product reviews? Who looked at detailed product specifications? Who looked at shipping information? Who took advantage of any other information that is available on the site? For example, identify which products were chosen for a "Compare" view. Last, it is easy to identify which products were added to a wish list or basket, as well as if they were later removed.

 **READ YOUR CUSTOMERS' MINDS**

Web data is unique in that it allows you to gain insights into what customers are thinking of buying next and how their decision processes work. This provides the capability to be proactive and nudge a customer down a purchase path they have yet to complete. Provide the right offer, and they'll almost think you're reading their mind as they make a purchase.

One very interesting capability enabled by web data is to identify product bundles that are of interest to a customer *before* they make a purchase. Move beyond trying to up-sell a customer with a follow-up offer after a purchase. Instead, examine what they are browsing and make them an offer to buy a complete bundle in the first place.

For example, consider a customer who views computers, backup disks, printers, and monitors. It is likely the customer is considering a complete PC system upgrade. Offer a package right away that contains the specific mix of items the customer has browsed. Do not wait until after customers purchase the computer and then offer generic bundles of accessories. A customized bundle offer before customers buy is more powerful than a generic one after they have already purchased.

## Customer Purchase Paths and Preferences

Using web data, it is possible to identify the ways customers arrive at their buying decisions by watching how they navigate a site. It is also possible to gain insight into their preferences. Consider for a moment an airline. An airline can tell a number of things about preferences based on the ticket that is booked. For example, how far in advance was the ticket booked? What fare class was booked? Did the trip span a weekend or not? This is all useful, but an airline can get even more from web data.

An airline can identify customers who value convenience. Such customers typically start searches with specific times and direct flights only. They will only deviate from the most convenient direct flight if there is a huge price difference for a minimal change in convenience. Perhaps a customer can save $700 by flying into New York's JFK airport instead of LaGuardia. He can land at JFK within 30 minutes of the LaGuardia flight and the extra cab fare is only about $20. In that case, a convenience-oriented customer might decide it is worth $700 in savings to deal with the extra hassle of JFK. But, if the difference is only $200 and the time of arrival is two hours later, a convenience-oriented customer will stick with the most convenient option.

Airlines can also identify customers who value price first and foremost and are willing to consider many flight options to get the best price. Such customers will only deviate from the cheapest option if there is a moderate price difference for a huge gain in convenience. For example, perhaps a customer can leave at 10:00 a.m. for $220 versus leaving at 6:00 a.m. for $200. The four hours of extra sleep are worth $20 to a price-oriented customer, and she pays the $20 premium for the later flight.

Based on search patterns, airlines can also tell how tied to deals or specific destinations a given customer is. Does she research all of the special deals available and then choose one of those for her trip? Or does she only look at a certain destination and pay what is required to get there? For example, a college student may be open to any number of spring break destinations and will take the one with the best deal. On the other hand, a customer who visits family on a regular basis will only be interested in flying to where the family is.

Simply knowing that customers regularly browse weekend deals for certain destinations can be a good indicator of what's important to them. Some customers are open to visiting family any time they see a deal to the right city. If they see a deal, they book it. Once that pattern is identified, an airline can anticipate customers' needs better.

The preceding are examples where a combination of historical insight into purchase history is invaluable when married with current browsing and research patterns. Of course, it will take time and effort to change analytical processes to account for such patterns. But, once the aspects of a site that appeal to customers on an individual basis are known, they can be targeted with messages that meet their needs much more effectively.

## Research Behaviors

Understanding how customers utilize the research content on a site can lead to tremendous insights into how to interact with each individual customer, as well as how different aspects of the site do or do not add value in driving sales. As the options customers explore on their way to a purchase are examined, it is possible to infer what is important to them.

For example, consider an online store focused on selling movies. If some customers routinely look at the standard, widescreen, extended, and HD versions of a video before making a final decision, that says they are open to various format options even if they often end up buying one format most of the time. Once customers' patterns are known, it is possible to alter what they see when they visit a site in order to make it easier for them to find their favorite options quickly. A customer who views a lot of formats might be shown all the formats every time. However, why make a customer sort through all DVD formats if it is known that she neither browses nor buys anything but a single format?

Another way to use web data to understand customers' research patterns is to identify which of the pieces of information offered on a site are valued by the customer base overall and the best customers specifically. How often do customers look at a previews, additional photos, or technical specs before making a purchase? Note that when tracking across sessions and combining with other customer data, it is possible to know if people researched one day and then bought later on another day. A final purchase event will often be a highly targeted web session that simply executes the purchase. The historical browsing history is needed to put the whole picture together. Perhaps a little-used web site feature the organization was considering removing is a big favorite among a critical segment of customers. In that case, the feature might be kept.

 **THE POWER OF RESEARCH**

It is no longer necessary to execute expensive, small-scale surveys to gain insights into how customers research and study products before making a purchase. Web data can provide detailed insights into what is important to each customer individually, as well as customers in aggregate. Plus, it eliminates the risk of having a customer tell you he'll do one thing on a survey when he will really do another. You'll see the truth.

An organization may see an unusual number of customers dropping a specific product after looking at the detailed specifications page, but not in cases where customers don't view the specs. After looking into what is on the page, it may be uncovered that the product description is not clear or that one of the specs is not accurate. With an updated description, sales will increase.

The reading of reviews is a tremendous indicator of what is important to people. Which customers value reviews? Which do not? Which products are routinely losing customers after reviews are read? Reviews have the power to make or break a sale. Once you know which customers usually buy after reading reviews, if you see many of them deciding not to purchase a specific product after reading its reviews, you should look into it. Perhaps some negative reviews are posted. If so, you can identify if they are valid, what points they raise, and how you will address those points.

In the end, identifying which site features are important to each customer and how each customer leverages the site for research can help better tailor a site to the individual. For customers who always drill to detailed product specifications, perhaps those specifications come up as soon as a product is viewed. For those who always want to see photos, perhaps photos are featured in full size instead of as thumbnails. The point is to make research easier for your customers so they will come to you instead of the competition when they are ready to research and buy.

## Feedback Behaviors

Some of the best information customers can provide is detailed feedback on products and services. Simply the fact that customers are willing to take the time to do so indicates that they are engaged with a brand. By using text mining to understand the tone, intent, and topic of a customer's feedback, a better picture of what is important to that individual begins to form.

Do certain customers post reviews of what they buy on a regular basis? If those reviews are often positive and are read by other customers, then perhaps it is smart to give such customers special incentives to keep the good words coming. Similarly, by parsing the questions and comments submitted via online help chats with customers, it is possible to get a feel not just for what customers in general are asking about, but what each specific customer is asking about. If analysis shows that certain features are always important for a specific customer, then point the customer in the direction of other items with similar attributes.

Is a customer a fan on Facebook? Does he or she follow you on Twitter? By looking at the comments and questions customers pose through such interfaces, much can be learned about their likes and dislikes. Additionally, when very active customers who are always saying things about a company on social media sites are identified, an organization may want to cultivate them as an influential brand ambassador. Give such customers the extra attention they deserve given the influence they have over your brand. Note that customers' influence will not always be strongly correlated with their individual value. A mid-sized customer who usually warrants a standard treatment can be very vocal. It may be smart to upgrade them beyond what their dollar value implies due to the influence they wield.

## WEB DATA IN ACTION

What an organization knows about its customers is never the complete picture. It is always necessary to make assumptions based on the information available. If there is only a partial view, the full view can often be extrapolated accurately enough to get the job done. But, it is also possible that the information missing paints a totally different picture than expected. In the cases where the missing information differs from the assumptions, it is possible to make suboptimal, if not totally wrong, decisions.

Therefore, organizations should strive to collect and analyze as much data as possible. We've discussed a number of different types of web data and some broad uses of them. Now, let's move on to some specific examples of how organizations can apply web data to enhance existing analytics, enable new analytics, and improve their business.

## The Next Best Offer

A very common marketing analysis is to predict what the next best offer is for each customer. Of all the available options, which single offer should next be suggested to a customer to maximize the chances of success? Having web behavior data can totally change the decision as to what a customer's next best offer is and make those decisions much more robust.

Let's assume you work at a bank and that you know the following information about a customer named Mr. Smith:

- He has four accounts: checking, savings, credit card, and a car loan.
- He makes five deposits and 25 withdrawals per month.
- He never visits a branch in person.
- He has a total of $50,000 in assets deposited.
- He owes a total of $15,000 between his credit card and car loan.

What is the best offer to place in an e-mail to Mr. Smith later today? Based on Mr. Smith's profile, it would be reasonable to argue for any number of things such as a lower credit card interest rate or an offer of a CD for his sizable cash holdings. One thing that would not come up high on most people's lists is offering a mortgage because we have nothing that says it is remotely relevant. However, once Mr. Smith's web behavior is examined, a couple of key facts jump right off the page at us:

- He browsed mortgage rates five times in past month.
- He viewed information about homeowners' insurance.
- He viewed information about flood insurance.
- He explored home loan options (i.e., fixed versus variable, 15- versus 30-year) twice in the past month.

It's pretty easy to decide what to discuss next with Mr. Smith now, isn't it?

 **GET AHEAD OF THE CURVE**

With web browsing behavior, it is possible to gain insights that totally change the direction that might otherwise have been taken. Decisions can be based on what a customer has been browsing recently, which in many cases will be products or product lines that the customer hasn't purchased before. Once the web data to alerts you to the unseen opportunity, you can take action to pull the customer into the new product line.

It can be difficult for any business to determine if its customer base is still engaged. The web provides direct clues as to what is of interest to customers and if they are still engaged. Consider the case of a catalog retailer that also has many store locations. The cataloger collects the following for each customer, among other data:

- Last products browsed
- Last products reviewed
- Historical purchases
- Marketing campaign and response history

The data is compiled and analyzed to determine which products each customer appears most interested in. Adjustments are made to the content of catalogs sent, as well as the length of the catalogs, and the offers within each catalog. The effort leads to major changes in the promotional efforts versus the cataloger's traditional approach, providing the following results:

- A decrease in total mailings
- A reduction in total catalog promotions pages
- A materially significant increase in total revenues

Web data can help completely overhaul activities for the better.

## Attrition Modeling

In the telecommunications industry, companies have invested massive amounts of time and effort to create, enhance, and perfect "churn" models. Churn models flag those customers most at risk of cancelling their accounts so that action can be taken proactively to prevent them from doing so. Churn is a major issue for the industry and there are huge amounts of money at stake. The models have a major impact on the bottom line.

Management of customer churn has been, and remains, critical to understanding patterns of customer usage and profitability. Imagine how this has been invigorated today with the use of web data put into the right context. Mrs. Smith, as a customer of telecom Provider 101, goes to Google and types "How do I cancel my Provider 101 contract?"

She then follows a link back to Provider 101's cancellation policies page. Imagine how much stronger, more time-sensitive, and usable this customer data is for a churn model and for taking meaningful action compared to other data.

It is hard to think of an indicator of cancellation that is stronger than knowing that Mrs. Smith researched cancelling aside from her actually taking the final step of making the cancellation request. Perhaps analysts would have seen her usage dropping, perhaps not. It would take weeks to months to identify such a change in usage pattern anyway. By capturing Mrs. Smith's actions on the web, Provider 101 is able to move more quickly to avert losing Mrs. Smith.

Missing the opportunity to identify customers who are exploring cancellation options in the early stages means trying to win them back when their mind is already made up and another carrier may have already won their business. It will be too late in most cases and the customer will be lost for good.

## Response Modeling

Many models are created to help predict the choice a customer will make when presented with a request for action. Models typically try to predict which customers will make a purchase, or accept an offer, or click on an e-mail link. For such models, a technique called logistic regression is often used. These models are usually referred to as response models or propensity models. Our attrition model example a moment ago is in the same class of model. The main difference is that in an attrition model, the goal is predicting a negative behavior (churn) rather than a positive behavior (purchase or response).

When using a response or propensity model, all customers are scored and ranked by likelihood of taking action. Then, appropriate segments are created based on those ranks in order to reach out to the customers. In theory, every customer has a unique score. In practice, since only a small number of variables define most models, many customers end up with identical or nearly identical scores. This is particularly true among customers who are not very frequent or high-spending. In such cases, many customers can end up in big groups with very similar, very low scores.

Web data can help greatly increase differentiation among customers. This is especially true among low-value or infrequent customers where customers can have a large uplift in score based on the web data. Let's look at an example where four customers are scored by a response model with a handful of variables. Each customer in the example has the exact same score due to having the same value for each of the model's variables. The scores are hypothetical, so don't worry about how the scores were computed. The four customers' profiles are each as follows:

- Last purchase was within 90 days
- Six purchases in the past year
- Spent $200 to $300 in total
- Homeowner with estimated household income of $100,000 to $150,000
- Member of the loyalty program
- Has purchased the featured product category in the past year

In this case, all customers get the exact same score and look identical in terms of likelihood to respond. Let's assume they all score a 0.62. Any marketing program based on this model will treat each of these four customers the exact same way. After all, based on the preceding information there is nothing differentiating them, and they are exactly the same!

Now, using web data, let's see how drastically the view changes. Look how the web data provides powerful new information:

- Customer 1 has never browsed your site so his score drops to 0.54.
- Customer 2 viewed the product category featured in the offer within the past month so her score rises to 0.67.
- Customer 3 viewed the specific product featured in the offer within the past month so his score rises to 0.78.
- Customer 4 browsed the specific product featured three times last week, added it to a basket once, abandoned the basket, then viewed the product again later. Her score rises to 0.86.

The web behavior allows us to identify customers with a current interest, if not intention, to purchase. It is possible to score customers better and end up with solid differentiation among them, where originally there was no differentiation. Now, repeat the example of these four customers across millions of customers across multiple channels and dramatic changes can be driven!

When asked about the value of incorporating web data, a director of marketing from a multichannel American specialty retailer replied, "It's like printing money!" The good news is that it is very easy to build a model both with and without web data to prove exactly how results improve for any given situation. There is virtually no risk to testing the impact in your organization's environment.

## Customer Segmentation

Web data also enables a variety of completely new analytics. One of those is to segment customers based solely upon their typical browsing patterns. Such segmentation will provide a completely different view of customers than traditional demographic or sales-based segmentation schemas. In addition, such segmentation can yield unique insights and actions.

Consider a segment called the Dreamers that has been derived purely from browsing behavior. Dreamers repeatedly put an item in their basket, but then abandon it. Dreamers often add and abandon the same item many times. This may be especially true for a high-value item like a TV or computer. It isn't difficult to clearly identify the segment of people that does this repeatedly. So, what can be done once they are found?

One option is to look at what the customers are abandoning. Perhaps a customer is looking at a high-end TV that is quite expensive. You've seen in the past that this customer often aims too high and after a time will buy a less-expensive product than the one that was abandoned repeatedly. Sending an e-mail pointing out less-expensive options that have many of the same features may be a way to get them to pull the trigger and buy a TV sooner.

**NEW ANALYTICS ARISE FROM WEB DATA**

There are a variety of data sources used for customer segmentation. Sales, demographics, and survey responses are a few. It is now possible to segment customers on their browsing behavior as well. This provides insight into customers' shopping styles and thought processes, and is a terrific additional dimension to add to your mix of segmentation criteria.

Another option is operational in nature. Abandoned basket statistics can be adjusted to account for the Dreamer segment. Abandoned baskets are often viewed as a failure by organizations. However, through the examination of browsing history, it can be clearly identified that 10 abandons were due to one customer who is known to repeatedly abandon a lot of products on a regular basis. As a result, the abandoned basket count can be reduced and all the customer's abandons for that product can be counted as a single abandonment. This will yield a cleaner view of abandonment. By the time statistics are adjusted for all such customers, the average abandonment rate might look quite a bit better from where it started. Not only will the new figures look better, but they will be a more accurate reflection of reality.

## Assessing Advertising Results

Better assessing paid search and online advertising results is another high-impact analysis enabled with customer level web behavior data. Traditional web analytics provide high-level summaries such as total clicks, number of searches, cost per click or impression, keywords leading to the most clicks, and page position statistics. However, these metrics are at an aggregate level and are rolled up only from the individual browsing session level. The context is also traditionally limited solely to the web channel.

This means that all statistics are based only on what happened during the single session generated from the search or ad click. Once a customer leaves the web site and his web session ends, the scope of the analysis is complete. There is no attempt to account for past or future visits in the statistics. By incorporating customers' browsing data and extending the view to other channels as well, it is possible to assess search and advertising results at a much deeper level.

- Were the site visits each ad or search term generated associated with the most valuable or least valuable customers?
- How many sales did the initial session lead to in the days or weeks that followed the customer's first click?
- Are certain referring web sites drawing visitors that return for more visits and make more total purchases than visitors referred from other sites?
- By doing a cross-channel analysis that accounts for activity in other channels, are a lot of sales closed in a second channel after an interest is generated on the web via an ad or search?

Let's consider an example from a financial institution. Credit card applications are everywhere. They are in the mail, they are in magazines, and they are available all over the web. The bank in our example understands that "eyeballs and clicks" are truly only a portion of the picture. What happens after the initial click is the telling information about the value of an advertising placement.

The bank does extensive analytics to dive deeper and not just look at clicks from the initial session. Customers were examined across time and sessions to also assess application completion, customer service inquiries, card issuance, card activation, and initial credit spending. This view of advertising beyond the click provides a more complete view of advertising success and leads to smarter allocation of advertising budgets.

 ## WHY LIMIT YOURSELF TO THE IMMEDIATE?

Identifying the outcome of the single web session started with an advertisement, e-mail click, or search misses the mark. Many customers will come back later to finish what they started, perhaps even in a different channel. Traditional web analytics do not account for future behavior after an initial session, nor do they account for historical behavior that happened prior to the session. Upgrade your capabilities to allow you to do both.

Through detailed, customer-level web data, it is possible to get down to understanding which ads, keywords, or referring sites generate the "best" clicks based on a much larger picture than simply aggregated results from initial web sessions. With the additional insight provided by the extended cross-channel, cross-time view, it is possible to see a picture that has previously been unavailable. Organizations that understand the deeper context will have an opportunity to take advantage of new strategies that those using traditional levels of analysis will not be able to identify. That is a distinct competitive advantage.

## WRAP-UP

The most important lessons to take away from this chapter are:

- The integration of detailed, customer-level web behavior data has the ability to transform what organizations understand about their customers.

- Just as transactional data enabled a revolution in the power and depth of analysis when it became available, so, too, will web data enable taking analytics to a new level.

- There are other customer touch points that can be tracked in a similar fashion as a web site such as kiosks and mobile phone applications. The same principles apply to those.

- Any data that can be captured should be. This includes page views, searches, downloads, and any other activity on a web site.

- Privacy is a major concern with web data and caution should be used when defining policies on how such data will be used. Those policies must also be rigorously followed and enforced.

- Tremendous value can be generated from analysis of faceless customers who are identified only by an arbitrary identification number. This way, neither analysts, nor anyone else, can identify who each customer actually is. Only the patterns matter.

- Web data lets you understand detailed customer shopping behaviors, purchase paths, research behaviors, and feedback behaviors. It is almost as if you can read your customers' minds.

- Web data enables stronger results in areas such as next best offer, attrition modeling, response modeling, customer segmentation, paid search, and online advertising analysis.

- The opportunity to be an early adopter and get ahead of the competition is almost closed. Get started taming this big data source now!

## NOTE

1. The content for this chapter is based on a conference talk created with my colleague Rebecca Bucnis. We also generated a white paper on the topic called *Taking Your Analytics Up a Notch by Integrating Clickstream Data* for SAS Global Forum 2011.

# CHAPTER 3

# A Cross-Section of Big Data Sources and the Value They Hold

**W**ouldn't it be neat to receive an offer on your mobile phone for a discounted meal at a restaurant as you are driving past its parking lot? How happy would you be if a pit boss at a casino gave you the $20 that a dealer forgot to pay you? Imagine being able to quickly find people who match to your playing style in an online video game because the game can tell you who they are. Would you like to lower your car insurance rates? All of these are possible through big data.

In Chapter 2 we discussed web data. If web data isn't the original big data, it is probably the most widely used and recognized source of big data. But there are many other sources of big data as well, and they all have their own valuable uses. Some are fairly well-known and some are relatively obscure. In this chapter, we're going to take a look at nine more sources of big data and some ways to use them. Each will be covered at a high level. The purpose is to provide an introduction to what each data source is about and then review some of the applications and implications that each data source has for businesses.

Chapters 2 and 3 are not a top-10 list, because the claim is not that these are the most important sources of big data. The order in which the sources are discussed doesn't imply any ranking either. The point is to provide a representative cross-section of big data sources so that the reader will understand the breadth and types of big data available, as well as the breadth of analysis that the data enables. Every reader should see at least a few to take a personal interest in.

One trend that becomes clear is how the same underlying technologies can lead to multiple big data sources in different industries. Also, different industries can leverage some of the same sources of big data. Big data is truly not a one-trick pony with narrow application. Its impacts will be far-reaching.

The big data sources we'll cover include:

- Auto insurance: The value of telematics data.
- Multiple industries: The value of text data.
- Multiple industries: The value of time and location data.
- Retail and manufacturing: The value of radio frequency identification (RFID) data.
- Utilities: The value of smart-grid data.
- Gaming: The value of casino chip tracking data.
- Industrial engines and equipment: The value of sensor data.
- Video games: The value of telemetry data.
- Telecommunications and other industries: The value of social network data.

## AUTO INSURANCE: THE VALUE OF TELEMATICS DATA

Telematics has started to receive serious attention in the auto insurance industry. Telematics involves putting a sensor, or black box, into a car to capture information about what's happening with the car. This black box can measure any number of things depending on how it is configured. It can monitor speed, mileage driven, or if there has been any heavy braking. Telematics data helps insurance companies better understand customer risk levels and set insurance rates. If privacy concerns are ignored and it is taken to the extreme, a telematics device could keep track of everywhere a car went, when it was there, how fast it was going, and what features of the car were in use.

Telematics has the potential to lower rates for most drivers and increase profits for insurers. How can it both lower rates and increase profits? The answer is that insurers have to price insurance based on a risk estimate. Using traditional risk estimates, based on data such as age and demographics along with personal accident history, provides only a high-level profile. Especially for drivers with a clean driving record, there isn't much to differentiate them from the other people in a neighborhood.

Insurance companies have to plan for the worst. So they'll figure out what band they think people fall into on the scale of risk and then to be safe will assume their risk is at the higher end of that band. The more detail that an auto insurance company can get on people's specific habits and how risky they actually are, the narrower the risk bands will be and the less assuming the worst case within a band will increase their rate. That's how rates can lower and margins can go up at the same time. Insurers will have a much better feel for individual risk and they'll have less variability in the projected payouts that will have to be paid.

There are insurance companies pursuing telematics-based insurance in many countries throughout the globe, and the number is growing. Early programs focus on collecting minimal information from cars. They don't track everywhere a car has been, for example. What the early programs do track is how far a car is driven, what time of day it is driven, if speeding occurs, and if there is a lot of heavy braking. It is fairly basic information with limited privacy concerns, which is intentional. By avoiding the collection of highly sensitive information, a wider level of adoption will occur. The same principles are also being applied to commercial fleets. It is easier to set rates for a company's fleet of trucks if the insurer knows more specifically how the trucks are utilized.

Telematics data is taking hold initially as a tool to help consumers and companies get better, more effective auto and fleet insurance. Over time, telematics devices may end up being present in a large number of vehicles and uses for telematics data outside of insurance will emerge. There are already onboard computers managing systems within an automobile, but a telematics device can take it to an entirely new level. There are some very interesting uses for telematics data. Let's take a look at a few.

## Using Telematics Data

There are some mind-blowing analytics possible if telematics truly takes off. Just imagine that a critical mass of millions or tens of millions of cars end up with telematics devices within your country. Let's also imagine that a third-party research firm arranges with consumers to collect very detailed telematics data from their cars in an anonymous fashion. As opposed to the limited data collected for insurance purposes, the data in this case has minute-by-minute or second-by-second updates on speed, location, direction, and other useful information.

This data feed will provide information on thousands of cars in any given traffic jam on any given day. Researchers will know how fast each car was moving along the way. They will know where traffic started, where it ended, and how long it lasted. This is an amazingly detailed view of the reality of traffic flow. Imagine the impact on the study of traffic jams and the planning of road systems!

 **LOOK BEYOND THE INTENDED USE**

The wealth of possibilities for telematics data is a terrific example of putting big data to use in a way that wasn't initially foreseen. Often, the most powerful uses for a given data source will be something entirely different from why it was created. Be sure to consider alternative uses for every big data stream encountered.

Once researchers have access to thousands of cars in every rush hour, every day, in every city, they will have the ability to diagnose traffic causes and effects in immense detail. They'll be able to pinpoint the answers to questions such as:

- How does a tire in the road impact traffic?
- What happens if a left lane gets blocked?
- When a traffic light gets out of sync, what are the effects?
- Which traffic intersections are poorly timed, even if they're acting the way they were intended to act?
- How fast does a backup in one lane spread to other lanes?

It's almost impossible to effectively study such questions today, outside of very focused and expensive testing. It is possible to physically send people out to monitor a given stretch of road and record information. Or, to put down sensors to count cars that go by. Or, to install a video camera. But those options are very limited in practice due to costs.

It's a traffic engineer's dream to have the telematics information outlined here. If telematics devices do become common, any location populated enough to have traffic can be studied. The changes that are made to roads and traffic management systems, as well as the plans for how roads are built in the first place, will provide huge benefits to all of us. Telematics got its start as a mechanism to assist in insurance pricing. But it may well revolutionize how we manage our highway systems and improve our lives by reducing the stress and frustration we experience when sitting in traffic.

## MULTIPLE INDUSTRIES: THE VALUE OF TEXT DATA

Text is one of the biggest and most common sources of big data. Just imagine how much text is out there. There are e-mails, text messages, tweets, social media postings, instant messages, real-time chats, and audio recordings that have been translated into text. Text data is one of the least structured and largest sources of big data in existence today. Luckily, a lot of work has been done already to tame text data and utilize it to make better business decisions.

Text analytics typically starts by parsing text and assigning meaning to the various words, phrases, and components that comprise it. This can be done by simple frequency counts or more sophisticated methods. There's an entire discipline called natural language processing that comes into play heavily in such analytics. We won't get into that here. Text mining tools are available as part of major analytical tool suites, and there are also standalone text mining packages available. Some of these text analysis tools focus on a rules-based approach where users have to tune the software to identify the patterns that they're interested in. Others use machine learning and other algorithms that will help to find patterns within the data automatically. Each approach has advantages and disadvantages, but that discussion is out of scope for our purposes. We'll focus here on how to use the results, not produce them.

Once the parsing and classification phases are done, the results of those processes can be analyzed. The output of a text mining exercise is often an input to other analytic processes. For example, once the sentiment of a customer's e-mail is identified, it is possible to generate a variable that tags the customer's sentiment as negative or positive. That tag is now a piece of structured data that can be fed into an analytics process. Creating structured data out of unstructured text is often called information extraction.

For another example, assume that we've identified which specific products a customer commented about in his or her communications with our company. We can then generate a set of variables that identify the products discussed by the customer. Those variables are again metrics that are structured and can be used for analysis purposes. These examples illustrate how it is possible to capture pieces of unstructured data and create relevant and structured data from it.

 ## CREATE STRUCTURE WHERE NONE EXISTS

Text analysis is a terrific example of taking purely unstructured data, processing it, and creating structured data that can be used by traditional analytics and reporting processes. One major part of taming big data is getting creative in the ways that unstructured and semi-structured data is made usable in this way.

Interpreting text data is actually quite difficult. The words we say change meaning based on which words we emphasize and also the context in which we state them. When looking at pure text, you won't know where the emphasis was placed, and you often won't know the full context. This means that you'll have to make some assumptions. We'll discuss this issue more in Chapter 6.

Text analysis is both an art and a science and it will always contain a level of uncertainty. When doing text analysis, there will be issues with misclassification as well as issues with ambiguity. That's okay. If a pattern can be found within a set of text that enables a better decision to be made, then it should be used. The goal of text analysis is improvement of the decisions being made, not perfection. Text data can easily cross the bar of improving decisions and providing better information than was present without it. This is true even given the noise and ambiguity that it contains.

## Using Text Data

One popular use of text analysis today is what's known as sentiment analysis. Sentiment analysis looks at the general direction of opinion across a large number of people to provide information on what the market is saying, thinking, and feeling about an organization. It often uses data from social media sites. Examples include:

- What's the "buzz" around a company or product?
- Which corporate initiatives are people talking about?
- Are people saying good or bad things about an organization and the products and services it offers?

As discussed earlier, one tough part of text analysis is that words can be good or bad depending on the context. It will be necessary to take that into account, but across a lot of individuals the direction of sentiment should become clear. Getting a read on the trends of what people are saying across social media outlets or within customer service interactions can be immensely valuable in planning what to do next.

If an organization captures sentiment information at an individual customer level, it will provide a view into customers' intent and attitudes. Similar to how it is possible to use web data to infer intent, knowing whether a customer's general sentiment about a product is positive or negative is valuable information. This is particularly true if the customer hasn't yet purchased that product. Sentiment analysis will provide information on how easy it is going to be to convince that customer to purchase that product.

Another use for text data is pattern recognition. By sorting through complaints, repair notes, and other comments made by customers, an organization will be more quickly able to identify and fix problems before they become bigger issues. As a product is first released and complaints start to come in, text analysis can identify the specific areas where customers are having problems. It may even be possible to identify a brewing issue in advance of a wave of customer service calls coming in. This will enable a much faster, more proactive reaction. The corporate response will be better both in terms of putting in place a fix to address the problem in future products, and also in what can be done to reach out to customers and mitigate the issues that they're experiencing today.

Fraud detection is also a major application for text data. Within health insurance or disability insurance claims, for example, it's possible to use text analysis to parse out the comments and justifications that have been submitted. Then, patterns can be identified that are associated with fraud so that claims can be flagged as high or low risk. Claims with higher risk patterns can be checked much more carefully. On the flip side, it's possible to do some claims automation. If there are patterns, terms, and phrases that are associated with clean, valid claims, those claims can be identified as low-risk and can be expedited through the system while resources are focused on the claims that have a higher risk.

Legal endeavors also benefit from text analysis. In a legal case, it is routine that e-mail or other messaging histories are subpoenaed. The messages are then examined in bulk to identify statements that may contain information tied to the case at hand. For example, which e-mails have potential insider information in them? Which people made fraudulent statements as they interacted with others? What is the specific nature of threats that were made?

Applying such analytics in a legal setting is often called eDiscovery. All of the preceding analytics can lead to successful prosecutions. Without text analysis, it would be almost impossible to manually scan all the documents required. Even if an effort was made to manually scan them, there would be a good chance of missing key information due to the monotonous nature of the task.

Text data has the potential to impact every industry. It will be one of the most widely used forms of big data. Learning how to capture, parse, and analyze text is critical for organizations. Text is one big data source that must be tamed.

## MULTIPLE INDUSTRIES: THE VALUE OF TIME AND LOCATION DATA

With the advent of global positioning systems (GPS), personal GPS devices, and cellular phones, time and location information is a growing source of data. A wide variety of services and applications from foursquare, to Google Places, to Facebook Places are centered on registering where a person is at a given point in time. Cell phone applications can record your location and movement on your behalf. Cell phones can even provide a fairly accurate location using cell tower signals if a phone is not formally GPS-enabled.

There are some very novel ways that consumer applications use this information, which leads to individuals allowing it to be captured. For example, there are applications that allow you to track the exact routes you travel when you exercise, how long the routes are, and how long it takes you to complete the routes. The fact is, if you carry a cell phone, you can keep a record of everywhere you've been. You can also open up that data to others if you choose. As more individuals open up their time and location data more publicly, very interesting possibilities start to emerge.

Many organizations are starting to realize the power of knowing "when" their customers are "where" and are attempting to get permission to collect such information from their customers. Of course, this should always be done on an opt-in basis, and very clear privacy policies should be developed and adhered to rigorously. Today, organizations are coming up with compelling value propositions to convince customers to release time and location information to them.

Time and location data isn't just about consumers, however. The owner of a fleet of trucks is going to want to know where each is at any point in time. A pizza restaurant will want to know where each delivery person is at any given moment. Pet owners want to be able to locate pets if they get out of the house. A large banquet facility wants to know how efficiently servers are moving around and covering patrons in all areas of the facility.

As an organization collects time and location data on individual people and assets, it starts to get into the realm of big data quickly. This is especially true if frequent updates to that information are made. It's one thing to know where every truck ends up at the start and end of every day. It's another thing to know where every truck is every second of every day. Time and location data is going to continue to grow in adoption, application, and impact.

## Using Time and Location Data

Time and location data is one of the most privacy-sensitive types of big data. There are serious questions that deal not just with privacy, but even with ethical and moral issues. Should chips be placed in children's arms so that they can be tracked down if they go missing? What about elderly people with dementia who are known to walk away from their house or care facility? Certainly the potential for the misuse of time and location data is high. But the upside when it is used appropriately is also high. Let's look at some examples.

Soon, people may be able to register with local police and fire agencies and provide information on where they typically travel. This way, if there's an event like a major accident, flood, fire, or closed road, people can receive an alert from the fire or police department telling them that one of the spots along their typical route has trouble and that they may want to go a different way. This could mitigate traffic disruption as people proactively avoid a problem area and save a lot of time individually by preventing them from getting stuck. Eventually, agencies may even be able to receive real time information on your location if you allow it.

One application of this data that's only beginning to be leveraged is the development of time- and location-sensitive offers. This is going to be huge in the future of marketing. It's no longer just about what offer to develop for a customer today or this week, but it's about what offer is best for that customer based on when they will be where. Today, this is typically achieved by having customers check in and report where they are so they can receive an offer. Eventually, organizations may track the whereabouts of customers continually and react as necessary.

For example, perhaps a customer communicates that he's going to be commuting home from the office at 5:30 and he's going to drive by Exit 5 sometime between 5:45 and 6:00. He's looking for dinner and wants to know what you have to offer if he stops by your store or restaurant. You need to provide him something that matches his need at that point in time in that place. Giving him an offer tomorrow morning via e-mail will be too late. You want to give him an offer that's good at only the location he'll pass and only in the brief time around when he'll pass it.

**PROVIDE OFFERS FOR THE "HERE" AND "NOW"**

An emerging trend in marketing is the generation of offers for customers that are only good for a specific time period and a specific location. Such offers can be far more powerful and targeted than offers for a broad range of time and locations. Early adopters of these approaches have seen eye-opening results.

Of course, the complexity of managing offers goes up a few notches because now it isn't just about keeping track of what offers each person is eligible for this week. Instead, it is necessary to worry about where each person is at any point in time and what offers they are eligible for as a result. Time- and location-based offers do add complexity and will be more difficult to manage. Over time, however, the success rate of such offers should greatly surpass traditional personalized offers if they are done well. History has repeatedly shown that the more targeted and specific an offer, the better the response will be.

Another application of time and location data deals with enhancing social network analysis. In addition to a wireless carrier being able to identify relationships based on voice or text interactions, time and location data allows identification of what people were at the same place at the same time. For example, who attended a given concert or movie? Who went to a specific sporting event? Who was dining at a specific restaurant at the same time?

By identifying who ends up in similar locations at similar times repeatedly, it is possible to identify people who may not know each other or be part of the same social network today, but who have a lot of common interests. Imagine a dating service with this information to help you find your match! It could be worth encouraging people to get to know each other or giving them offers for products that are relevant to the type of people and communities that they appear to be associated with.

Time and location data not only helps understand customers' historical patterns, but also allows accurately predicting where customers will be in the future. This is especially true for customers who stick to a regular schedule. If you know where a given person is and where they're heading, you can predict where they might be in 10 minutes or an hour based on that information. By looking at where customers were going historically when on the same route, you can make an even more educated prediction as to where they are going now. At minimum, you can greatly narrow down the list of possibilities. This enables better targeting.

Watch for an explosion in the use of time and location data in the coming years. Opt-in processes and incentives for consumers will begin to mature. For now, be very cautious and ensure your customers explicitly agree to let you use information in these ways before you do it. This will enable messaging to become even more targeted and personal than it is today. The idea of getting offers that aren't targeted to the here and now may well be considered old-fashioned in the not-too-distant future.

## RETAIL AND MANUFACTURING: THE VALUE OF RADIO FREQUENCY IDENTIFICATION DATA

A radio frequency identification tag, or RFID tag, is a small tag placed on objects like shipping pallets or product packages. It is important to note that an RFID tag contains a unique serial number, as opposed to a generic product identifier like a UPC code. In other words, it doesn't just identify that a pallet contains some Model 123 computers. It identifies the pallet as being a specific, unique set of Model 123 computers.

When an RFID reader sends out a signal, the RFID tag responds by sending information back. It's possible to have many tags respond to one query if they're all within range of the reader. This makes accounting for a lot of items easy. Even when items are stacked on top of one another or behind a wall, as long as the signals can penetrate, it will be possible to get a response. RFID tags remove the need to manually log or inventory each item and allow a census to be taken much more rapidly.

Most RFID tags used outside of very high value applications are known as passive. This means that the tags do not have an embedded battery. The radio waves from a reader create a magnetic field that is used to provide just enough power to allow a tag to send out the information embedded within it. While RFID technology has been around for a long time, costs were prohibitive for most applications. Today a passive tag costs just a few cents and prices continue to drop.

As prices continue to drop, the feasible uses will continue to expand. There are some technical issues with today's RFID technology. One example is that liquids can block signals. As time progresses, these issues should be solved with updates to the technologies used.

There are uses of RFID today that most people will have come in contact with. One use is the automated toll tags that allow drivers to pass through a toll booth on a highway without stopping. The way it works is that the card provided by the toll authority has an RFID tag in it. There are also readers placed on the road. As a car drives through, the tag will transmit back the car's data so that the fact that you went through the toll can be registered.

Another major use of RFID data is asset tracking. For example, an organization might tag every single PC, desk, or television that it owns. Such tags enable robust inventory tracking. They also enable alerts if items are moved outside of approved areas. For example, readers might be placed by exits. If a corporate asset moves through the door without having been granted prior approval, an alarm can be sounded and security can be alerted. This is similar to how the item tags at retail stores sound an alarm if they haven't been deactivated.

One of the biggest uses for RFID today is item and pallet tracking in the manufacturing and retail spaces. Each pallet a manufacturer sends a retailer, for example, may have a tag. It makes it easy to take stock of what's in a given distribution center or store. Eventually, it is possible that every individual product in a store that is above a trivial price point will end up being tagged with an RFID chip, or an updated technology that serves the same purpose. Now that we've covered what RFID data is, let's look at some examples of how RFID data can improve businesses today.

## Using Radio Frequency Identification Data

One application where RFID can add value is in identifying situations where an item has no units on the shelf in a retail environment. If a reader is constantly polling the shelves to identify how many of each item remains, it can provide an alert when restocking is needed. RFID enables much better tracking of shelf availability because there's a key difference between being out of stock and having shelf availability. It's entirely possible that the shelf in a store has no product on it, yet simultaneously there are five cases in the storage room in the back.

In such a scenario, any traditional out-of-stock analysis is going to show that there is plenty of stock remaining and nothing to worry about. When sales start to drop, people are going to wonder why. If products have an RFID tag, it is possible to identify that there are five units in the back, yet no product on the shelf. As a result, the problem can be fixed by moving product from the back room to the shelf. There are some challenges in terms of cost and technology in this example today, but work is being done to overcome them.

RFID can also be a big help for tracking the impact of promotional displays. Often, during a promotion, product may be displayed in multiple locations throughout a store. From traditional point-of-sale data, all that will be known is that an item on promotion sold. It isn't possible to know which display it came from. Through RFID tags, it is possible to identify which products were pulled from which displays. That makes it possible to assess how different locations in the store impact performance.

As RFID is combined with other data, it gets even more powerful. If a company has been collecting temperature data within a distribution center, product spoilage can be traced for items that were present during a specific power outage or other extreme event. Perhaps the temperature of a section of a warehouse got up to 90 degrees for 90 minutes during a power outage. With RFID it is possible to know exactly which pallets were in that part of distribution center at exactly that point in time and appropriate action can be taken. The warehouse data can then be matched to shipment data. A targeted recall can be issued if the products were likely to be damaged or retailers can be alerted to double-check their product as it arrives.

 ## IT'S THE COMBINATION THAT COUNTS

With RFID data, like many other big data sources, the power isn't just in what RFID data can tell you uniquely by itself. It is in what it can tell you when combined with other data. It can't be stressed enough that a big data strategy must aim to incorporate big data into the same processes as other data. Big data can't be a stand-alone effort.

There are operational applications as well. Some distribution centers may tend to be too rough with merchandise and cause a high level of breakage. Perhaps this is true only for specific work teams or even specific workers. A human resources (HR) system will report who was working at any point in time. By combining that data with RFID data that shows when product was moved, it is possible to identify employees who have an unusually high rate of breakage, shrinkage, and theft. The combination of data allows stronger, better quality action.

A very interesting future application of RFID is tracking store shopping in a similar fashion as web shopping. If RFID readers are placed in shopping carts, it is possible to know exactly what customers put into their carts and exactly what order that they added those items. Even if individual items aren't tagged, the cart's path can still be identified. Many of the advantages of web data discussed in Chapter 2 are possible in a store environment through such a use of RFID. These last two examples are again cases where privacy is an issue that must be considered. Perhaps customers won't want their shopping in the store tracked to them. In that case, "anonymous" shopping trips can be tracked where the person who generated the data is not identified.

One last application of RFID relates to how fraud can be reduced as criminals attempt to return stolen items. If an item has an RFID tag, the retailer can identify through the tag's unique identifier that an item being returned was part of a stolen batch of product and take appropriate action. In fact, it may come to the point where an RFID tag identifier is included as part of a receipt and required by the returns process. A retailer will know which specific RFID tag was on the item you purchased, not just that you purchased an item generically. When you come to the returns desk, you need to be returning that specific item with that specific tag. You can't pick up another of the same item from the shelf and fraudulently return it with your receipt. Using RFID in this manner will make it much harder to perpetrate fraud.

RFID has the potential to have huge implications within the manufacturing and retail industries in the years to come. It has had a slower adoption rate than many hoped. But as tag prices continue to drop and the quality of the tags and readers continues to improve, it will make financial sense to pursue wider adoption.

## UTILITIES: THE VALUE OF SMART-GRID DATA

Smart grids are the next generation of electrical power infrastructure. A smart grid is much more advanced and robust than the traditional transmission lines all around us. A smart grid has highly sophisticated monitoring, communications, and generation systems that enable more consistent service and better recovery from outages or other problems. Various sensors and monitors keep tabs on many aspects of the power grid itself and the electricity flowing through it.

One aspect of a smart grid is what's known as a smart meter. A smart meter is an electric meter that replaces traditional meters. On the surface, a smart meter won't look much different than the meters we've always had; but a smart meter is much more functional than a traditional meter. Instead of a human meter reader having to physically visit a property and manually record consumption every few weeks or months, a smart meter automatically collects data on a regular basis, typically every 15 minutes to every hour. As a result, it's possible to have a much more robust view of power usage both for every household or business individually, as well as across a neighborhood or even the entire grid.

While we'll focus on smart meters here, the sensors placed throughout a smart grid deserve a mention. The data that utilities capture from unseen sensors placed throughout the smart grid dwarfs smart meter data in size. Synchrophasors that take 60 readings per second across the power system, and home area networks recording each appliance cycling on or off are just two examples. The average person won't have any idea that most of these other sensors exist, but they will be crucial for the utilities. Such sensors will capture a full range of data on the flow of power and the state of equipment throughout the power grid. The data generated will be very, very big.

Smart-grid technology is already in place in some parts of Europe and the Americas. Virtually every power grid in the world will be replaced with smart-grid technology over time. The amount of data on electricity usage that utility companies will have available to them as a result of smart grids is going to grow exponentially. How might such data be used? Let's take a look.

## Using Smart-Grid Data

From a power management perspective, the data from smart meters will help people to better understand demand levels from customers all the way up the chain. But the data can also benefit consumers. An individual homeowner, for example, will be able to explicitly test how much power various appliances use by simply turning them on while holding other things constant and then monitoring the detailed power usage statistics that flow from their smart meter.

Utilities around the world are already aggressively moving to pricing models that vary by time of day or demand, and the smart grid will only accelerate that. One of the primary goals of the utility firms is to utilize new pricing programs to influence customer behavior and reduce the demand during peak times. It is the peaks that require additional generation to be built, which drives significant costs and environmental impacts. If the cost of power can be flexibly applied by time of day and measured by the meter, customers can be incented to change their behavior. Lower peaks and more even demand equate to fewer new infrastructure requirements and lower costs.

The power company, of course, will be able to identify all sorts of additional trends through the data provided by smart meters. Which locations are drawing power on off-peak cycles? What customers have a similar daily or weekly cycle of power needs? A utility can segment customers based on usage patterns and develop products and programs that target specific segments. The data will also enable identification of specific locations that appear to have very unusual patterns. That might point to problems needing correction.

In effect, power companies will have the ability to do all of the customer analytics other industries have been able to do for years. Imagine a phone company knowing your month-end total bill, but none of your calls. Consider a retailer knowing only your total sales, but none of your purchase details. Think about a financial institution knowing only your month-end balances, but none of the movements of money and funds throughout the month. In many ways, power companies have been dealing with data that is equally poor for understanding their customers. They had a simple month-end total usage, and even that month-end figure was often an estimated, not an actual, usage amount.

 ## BIG DATA CAN TRANSFORM AN INDUSTRY

In some cases, big data will literally transform an industry and allow it to take the use of analytics to a whole new level. Smart-grid data in the utility industry is an example. No longer limited by monthly meter readings, information on usage will be available at intervals measured in seconds or minutes. Add to that the sophisticated sensors throughout the grid, and it is a whole different world from a data perspective. The analysis of this data will lead to innovation in rate plans, power management, and more.

With smart meter data, a whole variety of new analytics will be enabled that will benefit all. Consumers will have customized rate plans based on their individual usage patterns, similar to how telematics enables individualized rates for auto insurance. A customer who's using power during peak periods is going to be charged more than non-peak users. It will encourage us all to shift our usage patterns once we are able to see the incentives to do so. Perhaps we'll run the dishwasher late in the afternoon instead of right after lunch, for example.

Utilities will have much better forecasts of demand, as they are able to identify where demand is coming from in more detail. They'll know what types of customers are demanding power at what points in time. The utility can look for ways to drive different behaviors to even out demand and lower the frequency of unusual spikes in demand. All of this will limit the need for expensive new generation facilities.

Each household or business will gain the power through smart meter data to better track and proactively manage its energy usage. This will not only save energy and make the world more green, but it's going to help everyone save money. After all, if you are able to identify where you're spending more than you intended, you will adjust as needed. With only a monthly bill, it is impossible to identify such opportunities. Smart-meter data makes it simple.

## GAMING: THE VALUE OF CASINO CHIP TRACKING DATA

Earlier, we discussed RFID technology as it is applied to the retail and manufacturing industries. However, RFID technology has a wide range of uses, many of which also lead to big data. One other use for RFID tags is to place them within the chips at a casino. Each chip, particularly high-value chips, can have its own embedded tag so that it can be uniquely identified via the tag's serial number.

Within a casino environment, slot machine play has been tracked for many years. Once you slide your frequent player card or credit card in the machine, every time you pull the handle or push a button it is tracked. Of course, so are the amounts of your wagers and any payouts that you receive. Robust analysis of slot patterns has been possible for years. Casinos did not have the capacity to capture such details from table games. By embedding tags within gaming chips, they're now evolving to have it.

Traditionally, a casino primarily tracked chips via robust security camera networks and people on the ground tasked with ensuring that chips are moving around appropriately. A pit boss watched frequent players and estimated their average bets and lengths of play in order to award frequent-player benefits. While pit bosses are very good at this and also leverage the help of other staff, it is still possible to end up giving too much or too little credit for play. This happens if a player is watched when he happens to bet more or less than usual. In fact, some players even try to game the system by increasing their bets when they think they are being watched.

 ## THE SAME TECHNOLOGY CAN DRIVE MULTIPLE BIG DATA STREAMS

Retailers and manufacturers leverage RFID technology. So do casinos. How they use RFID is totally different in many ways, and has similarities in others. The interesting part is that a single technology can be used by different industries to create their own distinct sources of big data.

Just as the example of casino chip tracking is a unique, but additional, application of RFID, there will be others. This example illustrates that some of the same underlying technologies will enable different big data streams that are similar in nature but completely different in scope and application. What's exciting is how one fundamental technology can have different and completely distinct uses that generate multiple forms of big data in multiple industries.

## Using Casino Chip Tracking Data

One obvious benefit of casino chip tags is the ability to precisely track each player's wagers. This ensures a player gets full credit in a frequent-player program, but no more or less. This benefits players and the casino. For the casino, resources will be allocated more precisely to the correct players. Over-rewarding the wrong players and under-rewarding the right players both lead to suboptimal allocation of limited marketing resources. Players, of course, always want their credits to be accurate.

Wager data collected across players will allow casinos to better segment players and understand betting patterns. Who typically bets $5 at a time, yet every once in a while jumps up to a $100 bet? Who bets $10 every time? Players can be segmented based on these patterns. The betting patterns can also point to those who are card counting in blackjack as there are certain patterns of wagers that will become clear when a player is using card counting techniques.

With chip tracking, it is also a lot harder to purposely defraud a casino or even for a dealer to make a mistake. Since bets and payouts can be tracked to the chip, it's easy to go back and compare video of the results of a blackjack hand and the payouts that were made. Even if arms or heads obscure what chips were put down or picked up, the RFID readings will provide the details. It will allow casinos to identify errors or fraud that took place. One example is when a player puts down extra chips after the fact when the dealer is looking the other way.

Analysis over time can identify dealers or players involved in an unusual number of mistakes. This will lead to either addressing fraudulent activity or providing additional training for a dealer who just happens to make a lot of innocent mistakes. Errors will also be lowered in the counting of chips in the casino cage. Counting large stacks of chips of different denomination is monotonous, and people can make mistakes. RFID allows faster, more accurate tallying.

Taking the preceding example further, the tracking of individual chips is a terrific deterrent for thieves. If a stack of chips is stolen, the RFID identifiers for those chips can be flagged as stolen. When someone comes in to cash the chips, or even sits at a table with the chips, the system can realize it and alert security. If thieves remove or alter the chips so that they can't be read, that will be a flag. The casino will know exactly what chip IDs exist and will expect each chip to report a valid ID. When a chip doesn't report an ID, or when the ID reported isn't valid, they can take action.

As with any business, the more a casino can stop fraud and ensure that appropriate payouts are being made, the less risk it has. This will lead to the ability to provide both better service and better odds to players since there will be fewer expenses to cover. It can be a win for both casinos and their players.

## INDUSTRIAL ENGINES AND EQUIPMENT: THE VALUE OF SENSOR DATA

There are a lot of complex machines and engines in the world. These include aircraft, trains, military vehicles, construction equipment, drilling equipment, and others. Keeping such equipment running smoothly is absolutely critical given how much it costs. In recent years, embedded sensors have begun to be utilized in everything from air-craft engines to tanks in order to monitor the second-by-second or millisecond-by-millisecond status of the equipment.

Monitoring may be done in immense detail, particularly during testing and development. For example, as a new engine is developed, it's worth capturing as much detailed data as possible to identify if it's working as expected. It's quite expensive to replace a flawed compo-nent once an engine is released, so it is necessary to analyze perfor-mance carefully up front. Monitoring is also an ongoing endeavor. Perhaps not every detail is captured for every millisecond on an ongoing basis, but a large amount of detail is captured in order to assess equipment lifecycles and identify recurring issues.

Consider an engine. A sensor can capture everything from tem-perature, to revolutions per minute, to fuel intake rate, to oil pressure level. This data can be captured as frequently as desired. All of this data gets massive quickly as the frequency of readings, number of metrics being read, and number of items being monitored in such a fashion increases. Why should we care? Let's look at a few examples.

## Using Sensor Data

Engines are very complex. They contain many moving parts, must operate at high temperatures, and experience a wide range of operating conditions. Because of their cost they are expected to last many years. Stable and predictable performance is crucial, and lives often quite literally depend on it. For example, taking an aircraft out of service for maintenance will cost an airline or a country's air force a lot of money, but it must be done if a safety issue is identified. It's imperative to minimize the time that aircraft and aircraft engines, as well as other equipment, are out of service.

Strategies for minimizing down time include holding spare parts or engines that can be quickly swapped for the asset requiring maintenance, creating diagnostics to quickly identify the parts that must be replaced, and investing in more reliable versions of problem parts. All three of these strategies depend on data for effective implementation. Data is used to create diagnostic algorithms and as input to the algorithms to diagnose a specific problem. Engineering organizations can use sensor data to pinpoint the underlying causes of failure and design new safeguards for longer, more dependable operation. These considerations apply whether the engine is in an aircraft, watercraft, or ground-based equipment.

By capturing and analyzing detailed data on engine operations, it's possible to pinpoint specific patterns that lead to imminent failures. Patterns over time that lead to lower engine life and/or more frequent repair can also be identified. The number of permutations of the various readings, especially over time, makes analysis of this data a challenge. Not only does the process involve big data, but the analysis that must be developed is complex and difficult. Some examples of the types of questions that can be studied:

- Does a sudden drop in pressure indicate imminent failure with near certainty?

- Does a steady decrease in temperature over a period of a few hours point to other problems?
- What do unusual vibration levels imply?
- Does heavy engine revving upon start-up seriously degrade certain components and increase the frequency of maintenance required?
- Does a slightly low fuel pressure over a period of months lead to damage to some of the engine's components?

 ## LACK OF STRUCTURE WITHIN STRUCTURED DATA

Sensor data offers a difficult challenge. While the data collected is structured and its individual data elements are well understood, the relationships and patterns between the elements over time may not be understood at all. Time delays and unmeasured external factors can add to the problem's difficulty. The process of identifying the long-term interactions of various readings is extremely difficult given all the information to consider. Having structured data doesn't guarantee a highly structured and standardized approach to analyzing it.

When major problems arise, it's immensely helpful to go back and examine what was taking place in the moments up until the problem manifested itself. In this case, sensors act similarly to how well-known airplane black boxes help diagnose the cause of an accident. The data from the sensors in an engine also provide data that can be leveraged for diagnostic and research purposes. The sensors being discussed here are conceptually a more sophisticated form of the telematics devices discussed in the auto insurance example. The use of data from sensors that are continually surveying their surroundings is a recurrent theme in the world of big data. While we have focused on engines here, there are countless other ways that sensors are also being used today, and the same principles discussed here apply to those uses.

If the sensor data capture process is repeated across a lot of engines and a long period of time, it leads to a wealth of data to analyze. Analyze it well, and it is possible to find glitches in equipment that can be proactively fixed. Weak points can also be identified. Then, procedures can be developed to mitigate the problems that result from those findings. The benefits aren't just added safety but also lowered cost. As sensor data enables safer engines and equipment that remain in service a higher percentage of the time, it will enable both smoother operations and lower costs. That is a win all around.

## VIDEO GAMES: THE VALUE OF TELEMETRY DATA

Telemetry is the term used in the video game industry to describe the capture of in-game activities. It has conceptual similarities to the web log data discussed in Chapter 2. This is because telemetry data captures the actions players take while navigating a game. Telemetry is most often captured for online games as opposed to game consoles.

In a hockey game, telemetry data will capture things such as where a player was when a shot on goal was taken, what type of shot it was, what speed the shot had, and if the shot was successful. In a war game, telemetry data will capture what weapon was fired, from where it was fired, what direction it was fired, and what damage the weapon did to various objects. Theoretically, any level of detail about the scene and actions can be captured.

This takes a video game producer well beyond simply knowing how many customers bought a game and perhaps how many hours games are played. Telemetry data makes it possible for game producers to know intimate details about how customers actually play and interact with the games they've created. The amount of data captured can be huge, and the video game industry is just starting to analyze this data in earnest. There are many areas where telemetry can have an impact. It will be easy to see the parallel between telemetry data and web data in terms of its advantages and uses. Let's take a look at a few.

### Using Telemetry Data

Many games make money through subscriptions, so maintaining renewal rates is absolutely critical. By mining players' playing patterns, insights can be obtained into what types of game behavior are associated with renewals and which are not. For example, perhaps playing tournaments in a sports game while leveraging certain additional features leads to a large increase in renewal rates. The game manufacturer can then incent players to give tournaments a try while using those features if they haven't already done so.

 **TELEMETRY DATA WILL ONLY GET BIGGER**

Currently, telemetry data largely captures controller or keyboard actions. As interactive games evolve that track player motions as opposed to depending on controllers, the amount of data will increase immensely. Knowing a player pressed a given button at a point in time is a lot less data than knowing where in space each of his many body parts was at the time and in what direction and with what speed each body part was moving.

Newer games often offer in-game purchases for a small fee. These are known as microtransactions. A special weapon might be available for 10 cents, for example. By analyzing game play, it's possible to identify specific areas in the game where such a microtransaction will have a high success rate. Perhaps there's a certain point in the game where a special weapon comes in very handy because many players struggle. A quick reminder on the screen that the weapon is available will lead to many players accepting that offer and making the purchase.

Customer satisfaction is as big an issue in the video game industry as in any other industry. What is unique is that video games have a very, very fine line to walk. A game has to offer a challenge to its players, but it can't be so challenging that it becomes frustrating and causes people to give up. If a game is either too easy or too hard, players will tire of it and move on.

By analyzing game play, it is possible to identify specific parts of a game that are easily passed by almost every player and specific parts that even top players have a very hard time completing. Such areas might be tweaked by adding or removing enemies, for example, to even out the difficulty level. Stabilizing the difficulty level across a game will provide a more consistent, more satisfying experience for the players. This will lead to higher renewal rates and additional purchases.

Through telemetry data, players can also be segmented by the style of play they utilize. Such information can be used to both design new games and cross-sell other existing products. One player segment may go as fast as possible to beat a level without concern for anything but completing the level. Another segment may try to collect all the bonus items available before completing a level. Yet another segment might aim to explore every nook and cranny of a level as they work to the end. Based on those traits, a player can be educated about other games that benefit from his or her preferred method of play.

The level of knowledge about players that telemetry data can provide has the potential to totally change the video game industry. While the industry is just starting to use telemetry data, look for rapid advances in this area to occur in the near future. Also look for major changes to how games are made and marketed as a result of what the analysis of telemetry data unveils.

## TELECOMMUNICATIONS AND OTHER INDUSTRIES: THE VALUE OF SOCIAL NETWORK DATA

Social network data qualifies as a big data source even though in many ways it's more of an analysis methodology against traditional data. The reason is that the process of executing social network analysis requires taking already-large data sets and using them in a way that effectively increases their size by orders of magnitude.

One could argue that the complete set of cell phone calls or text message records captured by a cellular carrier is big data in and of itself. Such data is routinely used for a variety of purposes. Social network analysis, however, is going to take it up a notch by looking into several degrees of association instead of just one. That's why social network analysis can turn traditional data sources into big data.

For a modern phone company, it is no longer sufficient to look at all calls and analyze them as individual entities. With social network analysis, it is necessary to look at who the calls were between and then extend that view deeper. You not only need to know who I called, but who the people I called in turn called, and who those people in turn called, and so on. To get a more complete picture of a social network it is possible to go as many layers deep as analysis systems can handle. The need to navigate from customer to customer and call to call for several layers makes the volume of data become multiplied. It also increases the difficulty of analyzing it, particularly when it comes to traditional tools.

The same concepts apply to social networking sites. When analyzing any given member of a social network, it isn't that hard to identify how many connections the member has, how often she posts messages, how often she visits the site, and other standard metrics. However, knowing how wide a network a given member has when including friends, friends of friends, and friends of friends of friends, requires much more processing.

One thousand members or subscribers aren't hard to keep track of. But, they can have up to one million direct connections between them and up to one billion connections when "friends of friends" are considered. That is why social networking analysis is a big data problem. The analysis of such connections has a number of applications being pursued today.

## Using Social Network Data

Social network data, and the analysis of it, has some high-impact applications. One important application is changing the way organizations value customers. Instead of solely looking at a customer's individual value, it is now possible to explore the value of his or her overall network. The example we're about to discuss could apply to a wide range of other industries where relationships between people or groups are known, but we'll focus on wireless phones since that is where the methods have been most widely adopted.

Assume a wireless carrier has a relatively low-value customer as a subscriber. The customer has only a basic call plan and doesn't generate any ancillary revenue. In fact, the customer is barely profitable, if the customer generates profit at all. A carrier would traditionally value this customer based on his or her individual account. Historically speaking, when such a customer calls to complain and threaten to leave, the company may have let the customer go. The customer just isn't worth the cost of saving.

With social network analysis it is possible identify that the few people our customer does call on that cheap calling plan are very heavy users who have very wide networks of friends. In other words, the connections that customer has are very valuable to the organization. Studies have shown that once one member of a calling circle leaves, others are more likely to leave and follow the first. As more members of the circle leave, it can catch like a contagion and soon circle members are dropping fast. This is obviously a bad thing.

 ## LOOK BEYOND INDIVIDUAL VALUE

A very compelling benefit of social network data is the ability to identify the total revenue that a customer influences rather than just the direct revenue that he or she provides. This can lead to drastically different decisions about how to invest in that customer. A highly influential customer needs to be coddled well beyond what his or her direct value indicates if maximizing a network's total profitability takes priority over maximizing each account's individual profitability.

Using social network analysis, it is possible to understand the total value that the customer in our example influences for the organization rather than only the revenue directly generated. This allows a completely different decision regarding how to handle that customer. The wireless carrier may overinvest in the customer to make sure that they protect the network the customer is a part of. A business case can be made to provide incentives that dwarf the customer's individual value if doing so will protect the wider circle of customers that he or she is a part of.

This is a terrific example of how the analysis of big data can help provide new contexts in which decisions that would have never happened in the past now make perfect sense. Without big data, the customer would have been allowed to cancel and the wireless carrier would not have seen the avalanche of losses that soon came as the customer's friends followed. The goal shifts from maximizing individual account profitability to maximizing the profitability of the customer's network.

Identification of highly connected customers can also pinpoint where to focus efforts to influence brand image. Highly connected customers can be provided free trials and their feedback can be solicited. Attempts can be made to get them active on corporate social networking sites through incentives to provide commentary and opinion. Some organizations actively recruit influential customers and shower them with perks, advance trials, and other goodies. In return, those influential customers continue to wield their influence, and it should be even more positive in tone given the special treatment they are receiving.

Within social networking sites like LinkedIn or Facebook, social network analysis can yield insights into what advertisements might appeal to given users. This is done by considering not just interests customers have personally stated. Equally important, it is based on knowing what it is that their circle of friends or colleagues has an interest in. Members will never declare all of their interests on a social networking site, and every detail about them will never be known. However, if a good portion of a customer's friends have an interest in biking, for example, it can be inferred that the customer does as well, even though the customer never stated that directly.

Law enforcement and antiterrorism efforts can leverage social network analysis. Is it possible to identify people who are linked, even if indirectly, to known trouble groups or persons? Analysis of this type is often referred to as link analysis. It could be an individual, a group, or even a club or restaurant that is known to attract a bad element. If a person is found to be hanging out with a lot of these elements in a lot of these places, he or she might be targeted for a deeper look. While this is another analysis that raises privacy concerns, it is being used in real life situations today.

Online video gaming is another area where such analysis can be valuable. Who plays with whom? How does that pattern change across games? Social network analysis can augment the telemetry data we discussed earlier. It is possible to identify a player's preferred partners on a game-by-game basis. We earlier discussed how players can be segmented based on individual playing style. Do players of similar styles team up when playing together? Or do players seek a mix of styles? Knowing such information can be valuable to know if a game producer wants to suggest groups for players to team up with (for example, providing suggestions as to which group, out of the many options available in a list, a player might prefer to join in with when he or she logs in to play).

There have also been interesting studies on how organizations are connected. It starts by looking at the connections established through e-mail, phone calls, and text messages within an organization. Are departments interacting as expected? Are some employees going outside typical channels to make things happen? Who has a wide internal influence and would be a good person to take part in a study on how to better improve communications within the organization? This type of analysis can help organizations better understand how their people communicate.

Social network analysis will continue to grow in prevalence and impact. One of the neat features it has is that it is always going to make a data source much bigger than it began due to the exponentially expanding nature of the analysis process. Perhaps the neatest feature is how it can provide insights into a customer's total influence and value, which can completely change how that customer is viewed by an organization.

## WRAP-UP

The most important lessons to take away from this chapter are:

- While there are a wide range of big data sources across industries, common themes do exist. The same underlying technologies, such as RFID, can be utilized in multiple industries for different purposes.

- There are privacy implications with many big data sources, and privacy needs to be a serious consideration at all times.

- Telematics data is evolving to enable better pricing of auto insurance policies. However, the data collected also has the potential to revolutionize traffic management and planning.

- Text data is one of the biggest and most widely applicable types of big data. The focus is typically to extract key facts from the text and then use those facts as inputs to other analytic processes.

- Time and location data is a growing influence. Organizations will have to become much more sophisticated in order to target offers to customers at a given time and place.

- RFID data enables new analytics for retailers and manufacturers in areas from stock levels, to fraud, to employee performance.

- Smart grids will not only give utilities the ability to much better manage their power grids, but consumers will be enabled to better control their consumption.

- Tracking casino chips with RFID tags can help casinos more accurately track player activity, while also reducing payout errors and fraud.

- Sensor data provides powerful information on the performance of engines and machinery. It enables diagnosis of problems more easily and faster development of mitigation procedures.

- Telemetry data will enable video game producers to better target micro-transactions, make game flow improvements, and segment players by playing style.

- Social network data can lead to new ways of valuing customers. In the telecommunications industry, social network analysis has shifted focus from account profitability to network profitability.

# PART
## TWO

---

# Taming Big Data: The Technologies, Processes, and Methods

CHAPTER **4**

# The Evolution of Analytic Scalability

It goes without saying that the world of big data requires new levels of scalability. As the amount of data organizations process continues to increase, the same old methods for handling data just won't work anymore. Organizations that don't update their technologies to provide a higher level of scalability will quite simply choke on big data. Luckily, there are multiple technologies available that address different aspects of the process of taming big data and making use of it in analytic processes. Some of these advances are quite new, and organizations need to keep up with the times.

In this chapter, we'll discuss important technologies that make progress in the quest to tame the big data tidal wave possible. We'll discuss the convergence of the analytic and data environments, massively parallel processing (MPP) architectures, the cloud, grid computing, and MapReduce.

Before we start, remember that the intent of this book is not to get too technical. This chapter, along with Chapters 5 and 6, will be the most technical chapters, but the topics are covered at a conceptual level so that it is possible to understand the concepts even if you aren't technical. In keeping with this goal, it was necessary to take some liberties with over-simplification at times. If more detail is of interest, there are other books that can go as far into the technical weeds as desired!

## A HISTORY OF SCALABILITY

Until well into the 1900s, doing analytics was very, very difficult. To do a deep analysis, such as a predictive model, it required manually computing all of the statistics. For example, to perform a linear regression required manually computing a matrix and inverting the matrix by hand. All of the computations required on top of that matrix to get the parameter estimates were also done by hand. Everything was done by hand, or possibly with the assistance of fairly rudimentary mechanical calculating machines. While it was awfully hard to get data a century or more ago, it was even harder to make use of it. Scalability of any sort was virtually nonexistent.

Slide rules eventually eased the situation, and then calculators came along in the 1970s and helped make it easier to utilize more data. But the volume manageable with a calculator is still trivially small. Computers, which entered the mainstream in the 1980s, are what began to enable people to finally move away from manual computations for good. While computers existed before the 1980s, they were only available to a very select few, and they were difficult and expensive to work with.

As the decades have passed, data has moved far beyond the scale that people can handle manually. The amount of data has grown at least as fast as the computing power of the machines that process it. It may not be necessary to personally break a sweat and get a headache computing things by hand, but it is still very easy to cause computer and storage systems to start steaming as they struggle to process the data fed to them.

Technology has continued to advance at a pace that has made the volume of data that is "intimidating" grow larger every year. The thought of processing a terabyte of data a decade ago was reserved for only the biggest companies and wealthiest governments. In the year 2000, an organization that had a database holding a terabyte of data was at the forefront. Today you can buy a terabyte disk drive for your computer for under $100! In 2012, even many small companies have systems holding a terabyte or more of data. The companies at the forefront now measure their database size in petabytes. That's a thousand-fold difference in barely a decade!

Moreover, as new big data sources become available the boundaries are being pushed further. Many sources of big data can generate terabytes to petabytes of data in days or weeks, if not hours. Once again the limits of what can be handled are being tested today. However, over time, the big data tidal wave will be tamed just like all the intimidating data streams of the past have been tamed.

Today's first graders will probably have a multi-petabyte computer by the time they're in college and they'll work on systems that have exabytes, if not zettabytes, of storage. They'll also be expecting answers delivered in seconds or minutes, not hours or days. Table 4.1 lists today's commonly known data size terms as well as the next extensions along the scale of data. The first people to test the limits of data have realized big rewards in the past and that pattern will continue.

**Table 4.1** Measures of Data Size

| 1024 of these . . . | . . . equals 1 of these | Comment[1] |
| --- | --- | --- |
| Kilobyte | Megabyte | A standard music CD holds 600 megabytes. |
| Megabyte | Gigabyte | One gigabyte will hold data equivalent to about 30 feet of books on a shelf. |
| Gigabyte | Terabyte | Ten terabytes can hold the entire U.S. Library of Congress. |
| Terabyte | Petabyte | A petabyte can hold 20 million 4-door filing cabinets of text. |
| Petabyte | Exabyte | Five exabytes is equal to all of the words ever spoken by mankind. |
| Exabyte | Zettabyte | It would take approximately 11 billion years to download a zettabyte file from the Internet using high-power broadband. |
| Zettabyte | Yottabyte | The entire Internet makes up about a Yottabyte of data. |

## THE CONVERGENCE OF THE ANALYTIC AND DATA ENVIRONMENTS

It used to be that analytic professionals had to pull all their data together into a separate analytics environment to do analysis. There really wasn't a choice. None of the data that was required was together in one place, and the tools that did analysis didn't have a way to run where the data sat. The only option was to pull the data together in a separate analytics environment and then start performing analysis. Much of the work analytic professionals do falls into the realm of advanced analytics, which encompasses data mining, predictive modeling, and other advanced techniques. We'll discuss this in detail in Chapter 7.

There is an interesting parallel between what analysts did in the early days and what data warehousing is all about. Many are surprised at the similarities once they think about them. Analysts have been working with "data sets" for years. There's not much difference between a data set as analysts define it and a "table" in a database. Both a data set and a table contain rows and columns. Often, a single row represents an entity like a customer. The columns represent information about the customers such as name, spending level, or status.

Analysts have done "merges" of their data sets for years. Guess what? That is the exact same thing as a "join" of tables in a database. In both a merge and a join, two or more data sets or tables are combined together. They are typically merged/joined so that specific rows of one data set or table are combined with specific rows of another. In our customer example, one data set/table might contain customer demographics while another contains spending information. When data sets/tables are merged/joined by customer, the result will be that both demographics and spending information for each customer will be together.

Analysts do what is called "data preparation." In this process, they pull data from various sources and merge it all together to create the variables required for an analysis. In the data warehousing world this process is called "extract, transform, and load (ETL)." Basically, analysts were building custom data marts and mini–data warehouses before the terms data mart or data warehouse were invented! They were just doing it on a project-by-project basis for their own use instead of doing it in a standardized fashion intended for use by others.

Twenty years ago, most analysts were doing analysis on mainframes. All the data was on big round tapes. I still remember having to call the mainframe center when I was under a deadline to beg the guy on the phone to up the priority on my jobs so my tapes would get loaded faster. Over time, a major shift occurred, which was the move toward relational database management systems.

The relational database management system (RDBMS) started to not only become popular, but to become more scalable and more widely adopted. Today an RDBMS is the standard for managing data, and it's difficult to find a mainframe that's in heavy use for the purposes of analysis. As a result, most data used in analysis is now obtained from a relational database. A growing exception to the ubiquity of relational databases is unstructured data processed via a MapReduce paradigm, which we'll cover later in the chapter in the section titled "MapReduce."

 **THE POWER OF CENTRALIZATION**

The trend toward centralized enterprise data warehouses has had huge impacts on the way advanced analytics are done. With so much data in one place, there is no need to do the usual moving and combining of data just for an analysis process. The data is right there waiting to be analyzed! This opens up a whole new world of scalability and possibility.

Initially, databases were built for each specific purpose or team, and relational databases were spread all over an organization. Such single-purpose databases are often called "data marts." While many organizations still leverage data marts heavily, leading organizations now see value in combining the various database systems into one big system called an Enterprise Data Warehouse (EDW).

With an EDW, the goal is to get all corporate data that has importance together in one central database that has a single version of the truth. This allows all the different data to cross-pollinate so it is possible to run reports and mix data related to vastly differently topics or subject areas. No longer is marketing data totally separate from financial data.

Here is where it starts to get interesting. Once all the data is together, there are no longer disparate sources that need to be pulled together just for an analysis. More analysis can be done where the data sits. Figures 4.1 and 4.2 illustrate the difference between the old way of doing things and the new way of doing things.

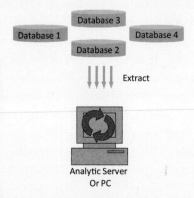

In traditional architectures, the heavy processing occurs in the analytic environment. This may even be a PC!

**Figure 4.1** Traditional Analytic Architecture

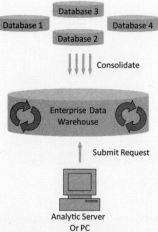

In an in-database environment, the processing stays in the database where the data has been consolidated. The user's machine just submits the request; it doesn't do heavy lifting.

**Figure 4.2** Modern In-Database Architecture

In an enterprise data warehousing environment, most of the data sources have already been brought into one place. If some small pieces of data are missing from the EDW, it doesn't really make sense to pull out the 90 to 95 percent of the data that's in the EDW and match it offline with the other 5 to 10 percent. It makes a lot more sense to get the other 5 to 10 percent into the EDW and analyze all of the data there. In other words, move the analysis to the data instead of moving the data to the analysis. This is the concept of in-database analytics.

 ## MODERNIZE YOUR ARCHITECTURE

Why spend a lot of time, effort, and money to move the data to the analysis when it is possible to take the analysis to the data? That is the simple premise behind in-database analytics, and it has huge implications for scalability. Taming big data without using in-database analytics will be much harder than it needs to be.

Teradata Corporation was the first to pursue in-database analytics in the 1990s, but now every database vendor is on board with the concept. Enterprise data warehouses, as well as data marts, are scalable and flexible enough today to support in-database processing. This is especially true for the massively parallel processing systems we'll discuss next. The key concept here, as mentioned, is to move the analysis to the data, not to move the data to the analysis. Let the database system do what it does best, which is crunch through lots of data.

University students today don't know much about mainframes and can't imagine running analysis off of tape drives. Soon, students won't understand why an advanced analytics environment and a data environment were ever separate. They won't differentiate between a storage environment and a data analysis environment. Those environments will be one and the same to them. As it should be!

## MASSIVELY PARALLEL PROCESSING SYSTEMS

Massively parallel processing (MPP) database systems have been around for decades. While individual vendor architectures may vary, MPP is the most mature, proven, and widely deployed mechanism for storing and analyzing large amounts of data. So what is an MPP database, and why is it special?

An MPP database spreads data out into independent pieces managed by independent storage and central processing unit (CPU) resources. Conceptually, it is like having pieces of data loaded onto multiple network connected personal computers around a house. It removes the constraints of having one central server with only a single set CPU and disk to manage it. The data in an MPP system gets split across a variety of disks managed by a variety of CPUs spread across a number of servers. See Figure 4.3 for an illustration.

Why is this architecture so powerful? Think about driving down a six-lane highway. If those six lanes go down to one lane for even a very short stretch of road, the traffic will be hideous. If six lanes are open all the way from your starting point to your destination, the ride will be much smoother. Traffic can still build up at peak times, but it lasts for a shorter period of time and is nowhere near as bad. In non-MPP database architectures, there are at least a few points during processing where the number of lanes is reduced to one, if not for the entire drive. With light traffic volume, a single lane is fine; not with heavy volume. That is what makes the MPP architecture so compelling for analyzing large amounts of data: It allows all lanes to stay open for the entire process.

Let's look at an example in the database world. A traditional database will query a one-terabyte table one row at time. If an MPP system with 10 processing units is used, however, the data is broken into 10 independent 100-gigabyte chunks. This means it will execute 10 simultaneous 100-gigabyte queries. If more processing power and

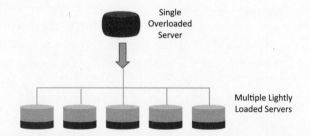

Single
Overloaded
Server

Multiple Lightly
Loaded Servers

Instead of a single overloaded database, an MPP database breaks the data
into independent chunks with independent disk and CPU.

**Figure 4.3** Massively Parallel Processing System Data Storage

more speed are required, just bolt on additional capacity in the form of additional processing units.

 **SHARE THE WORK!**

A massively parallel processing (MPP) database spreads data out across multiple sets of CPU and disk space. Think logically about dozens or hundreds of personal computers each holding a small piece of a large set of data. This allows much faster query execution, since many independent smaller queries are running simultaneously instead of just one big query.

If the system is upgraded to have 20 processing units in our example, there will be 20 independent chunks of 50 gigabytes running simultaneously instead of 10 chunks of 100 gigabytes. There will therefore be an equivalent increase in performance. It gets a little more complicated in cases where data must be moved from one processing unit to another processing unit as part of the requirements of the query, but MPP systems are built to handle that in a very, very fast way as well. See Figure 4.4 for an illustration.

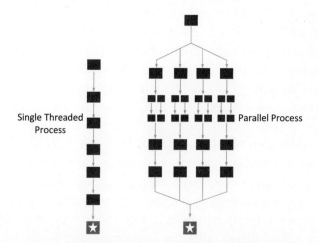

Single Threaded Process

Parallel Process

Instead of a single threaded process to work through the data, an MPP system breaks the job into pieces and allows the different sets of CPU and disk to run the process concurrently.

**Figure 4.4** Traditional Query versus an MPP Query

MPP systems build in redundancy so that data is stored in more than one location to make recovery easy in cases where there's equipment failure. They also have resource management tools to manage the CPU and disk space, query optimizers to make sure queries are being optimally executed, and other items that make it easier and more efficient for users to leverage the systems. Getting into any greater depth on these topics is out of the scope of this book.

## Using MPP Systems for Data Preparation and Scoring

The reason MPP can be a huge benefit to advanced analytics is because most of the processing pain in advanced analytics comes during the data preparation stages. Data preparation is made up of joins, aggregations, derivations, and transformations. This is the process of combining various data sources to pull together all the information needed for an analysis. Aggregations involve combining information from multiple records into one. One example is computing total and average sales for a customer across multiple transactions. Derivations and transformations involve actions such as computing ratios like sales per transaction and applying functions like a log or square root to variables in order to create additional variables.

The logic required for most data preparation tasks is actually relatively simple. It is exactly the kind of thing that a relational database and its native language, called structured query language (SQL), are meant to do. Today's SQL can handle most, if not all, data preparation tasks required for the majority of analysis. The use of SQL is where in-database processing started on MPP systems. Analysts simply pushed tasks into the database by writing SQL instead of writing in an analytics language that requires pulling the data off the database.

Even 10 years ago SQL had some limitations when it came to some of the complex computations required to support advanced analytics. These days it is far more robust. In fact, the old rule that a query will have no knowledge of other rows when working with a given row is no longer valid. There are SQL functions called "windowed aggregates," for example, that enable a query to account for data elsewhere when processing a given row. With such functions, it is possible for a query to know if a transaction is the customer's first or last, for example, and act differently when processing the data. Such functionality allows SQL to handle a lot of additional complex processing that advanced analytics tools provide for the data preparation process.

Before SQL was upgraded with more robust functionality, it led to the continued need to pull data off in order to do necessary analytical processing. Luckily, that's not true anymore, as SQL has greatly evolved. Most of the operations involved in data preparation can now be done via SQL right in the database. A lot of analytic professionals still code in SQL instead of an analytic tool today, but there are now more integrated options as well, which we'll discuss later in this section.

 ## DON'T UNDERESTIMATE SQL

SQL has evolved so much the past few years that it can handle virtually any common data preparation task. Between the use of SQL and the use of analytics tools that push processing into the database for users, analytic professionals can greatly increase the scale of their processes. Scale is required more than ever when working with big data.

As the concept of in-database processing has evolved, analytical tool vendors have started to enable their applications to push processing directly into the database system. Code is written in the native language of such tools, but the software now recognizes when an MPP database engine is being accessed, and the software will pass through instructions to the database and let the database handle the heavy lifting instead of performing a large extract.

The evolution of analytical tools pushing processing into the database on users' behalf means analytic professionals now have a choice to work in the environment that they are most comfortable with and still get the benefits of scalability. As analytic applications continue to push more of their features into MPP databases, it's only going to increase the influence of the in-database concept.

In-database processing is also very common for scoring. A model is often built on a sample, but scoring requires running against all of the data. For example, a propensity model can be built on a sample of customers, but every single customer will need to be scored when it is time to use the model to pick the highest scorers for a marketing campaign. In those cases the old methods of pulling all of the data out of the database can be impractical, if not completely impossible, due to the time it takes an extract-based approach to handle all that data.

Let's look at a more detailed example. Consider a retailer that has built a propensity model to identify which customers are most likely to respond to a promotion. Such a model is often built on a representative sample of a few hundred thousand customers. Those who have responded in the past are compared statistically to those who have not. The model creates a scoring algorithm that will compute the likelihood of response for each customer.

In building the model, pulling data off the database isn't so bad since it is a one-time action and involves only a sample. When it is time to use the model, the scoring algorithm must be applied to all of the tens of millions of customers the retailer has in order to accurately identify who is most and least likely to respond. This scoring process will be run on a regular basis. Since all the customers are included in the scoring process, extracting the data can kill performance. In-database processing avoids this.

There are at least four primary ways for data preparation and scoring to be pushed into a database today: (1) SQL push down, (2) user-defined functions (UDFs), (3) embedded processes, and (4) predictive modeling markup language (PMML) scoring. Let's look at each.

### SQL Push Down

SQL is the native language of an MPP system and it's efficient for a wide range of requirements. As discussed, this is particularly true for typical aggregations, joins, and transformations. Many core data preparation tasks can be either translated into SQL by the user, or an analytic tool can generate SQL on the user's behalf and "push it down" to the database. SQL is also easy to generate for many common analytical algorithms that have fairly simple scoring logic. Linear regression, logistic regression, and decision trees are examples that fall into this category. Analytic tools will often translate the logic from a model into SQL for the user. Or, sometimes, users will code an SQL script themselves once the model is complete. In either case, the data preparation or scoring processes end up being executed purely with SQL.

## User-Defined Functions

User-defined functions (UDFs) are a relatively new feature of relational databases. The capabilities of a UDF go beyond those of SQL. What UDFs do is extend SQL functionality by allowing a user to define logic that can be executed in the same manner as a native SQL function.

A request for total sales by customer might be written like this:

"Select Customer, Sum(Sales) . . ."

With a UDF, a request for an attrition score by customer might be written like this:

"Select Customer, Attrition_Score . . ."

In the latter example, "Attrition_Score" is a user-defined function that's been deployed on the database system. The UDF will apply whatever logic is required to the data, and this logic can be more complex than is possible in pure SQL.

User-defined functions are coded in languages like C++ or Java. As a result, some procedural language capabilities can be embedded within them. This extends core SQL, which does not have such capability directly. The downside of UDFs is that a lot of analytic professionals don't know how to program in the languages required. That's where analytic tools that automatically generate the functions are a very good thing. Such tools take care of generating appropriate user-defined functions for the analyst and loading it into the database so it is ready to use.

## Embedded Processes

A very new option for pushing processing into a database is the concept of an embedded process. An embedded process is an even higher level of integration than the user-defined functions just described. A user-defined function involves compiling code into new database functions that can be called from an SQL query just like any other function. To a user, the analytic function will behave just like the original analytic tool code and will efficiently run in parallel on the database, but it is no longer in the form of the analytic tool code. In effect, the analytical tool has had to translate what it needs into the language of the database.

An embedded process, however, is a version of an analytic tool's engine actually running on the database itself. An embedded process is therefore capable of running programs directly inside the database. Embedded processes leverage actual analytic tool code that has been published to the database engine. When a piece of code needs to be run and take advantage of the system's parallelism, it is passed to the analytic tool processes running on each of the database's processing units. There is no translation required. This method requires the least amount of change to underlying code but is also a much harder solution for tools to implement. Tool and database vendors are just starting to leverage embedded processes more widely. In the coming years, this is likely to become the method of choice.

## Predictive Modeling Markup Language

Predictive modeling markup language (PMML) is a way to pass model results from one tool to another. Conceptually it contains the minimum information needed to produce an accurate piece of scoring code. The type of information included in a PMML feed includes a model type, the variable names and formats, and the parameter values.[2] PMML lets analysts use any PMML-compliant tool desired to build a model. If a tool is PMML-compliant and the goal is to deploy a model on another PMML-compliant tool for scoring, simply pass the PMML from the first tool to the second tool, and the second tool will automatically generate a scoring process.

One drawback of PMML isn't immediately apparent. The exact same variables in the exact same format must be available in the system where the PMML is being deployed as were available in the system where the model and PMML were generated. For example, assume a model developed used an input variable called "SumOfSales" that holds the total sales by customer in a numeric format. "SumOfSales" must also be available as a numeric variable on the system where the PMML will be deployed. This requires recreating it on that system.

Initially, analytic professionals often thought that PMML meant they didn't have to worry about working in-database during development of models because they could build a model on their tool of choice and then simply deploy it with PMML into their relational database. Here's the problem with that line of thought: The requirement that the same metrics are available in the same format causes the plan to fall apart. If there were any manipulations of any kind done outside of the database, they will need to be recreated inside the database to support the scoring process before the PMML code can be applied. PMML doesn't account for any of the data preparation tasks, just the scoring algorithm to be applied to the final data. PMML assumes the data is already complete.

 **DON'T MISUNDERSTAND PMML**

PMML actually reinforces the need and benefits of preparing analytic data within a database. If any data preparation steps are done in an analytics tool before developing a model, it is necessary to recreate those manipulations in the database for the PMML to work. Why build the data preparation steps twice in two environments? Just build them in the database to begin with.

PMML even further reinforces the necessity of maximizing in-database processing. For PMML to work at maximum efficiency it is necessary to point to data that is ready to be modeled with an analysis tool. The data shouldn't be changed, but simply fed into the modeling algorithms required. Then, the scoring code generated by the model's PMML code will work immediately without any re-engineering of data tasks in the deployment environment.

Newer versions of PMML have begun to incorporate the ability to specify some data preparation logic within the PMML, but it still has a long way to go to negate the points outlined here. Due to its limitations, PMML will remain an option used less frequently.

## Using MPP Systems for Data Preparation and Scoring Wrap-Up

Massively parallel processing (MPP) platforms are a growing and extremely valuable aspect of a modern analytic architecture. Most large organizations today have an enterprise data warehouse that houses a huge portion of important corporate data. Smaller companies often have relational data marts. More and more processing is being pushed into these data warehouse platforms, and this trend is going to continue.

Any organization that's looking to improve analytic scalability needs to look into the world of MPP. As data volumes continue to increase, it is no longer feasible to move data around as part of an analysis process except where absolutely necessary. The additional scalability also greatly expands the breadth and volume of analytic processes that can be deployed for an organization. These additional processes can use traditional data, big data, or a combination.

Before we end this section, we should discuss one last point. While enterprise data warehouses have been a big focus in the discussion, most MPP vendors today offer "appliances" that are scaled-back versions of their enterprise class systems. These appliances are meant specifically for targeted purposes such as an advanced analytics team that needs to crunch through a lot of data. Where appliances are often designed for one or two specific workloads, the enterprise data warehouse is designed to support many workloads.

Advanced analytics is one workload, albeit an important one. Be sure if planning to use an EDW for advanced analytic processes that it supports running such processes concurrently with other workloads like querying and reporting. If not, consider a separate appliance. Some vendors even market appliances targeted specifically to analytic professionals. They are affordable and follow all the same principles as enterprise MPP systems.

## CLOUD COMPUTING

The concept of cloud computing is getting a lot of attention these days. As with many technologies, cloud computing is going through a hype cycle. Let's start by defining what cloud computing is all about and how it can help with advanced analytics and big data. As with any new and emerging technology, there are conflicting definitions of what cloud computing is. We'll consider two that serve as a good foundation for our discussion. The first comes from a McKinsey and

Company paper from 2009.[3] The paper listed three criteria for a cloud environment:

1. Enterprises incur no infrastructure or capital costs, only operational costs. Those operational costs will be incurred on a pay-per-use basis with no contractual obligations.

2. Capacity can be scaled up or down dynamically, and immediately. This differentiates clouds from traditional hosting service providers where there may have been limits placed on scaling.

3. The underlying hardware can be anywhere geographically. The architectural specifics are abstracted from the user. In addition, the hardware will run in multi-tenancy mode where multiple users from multiple organizations can be accessing the exact same infrastructure simultaneously.

A true cloud is going to have to comply with all three of those criteria. It is going to have to mask the underlying infrastructure from the user, it is going to have to be elastic to scale on demand, and it has to be on a pay-per-use basis.

 **JUMP? HOW HIGH?**

A cloud takes away concern for resource constraints. Users can get whatever they need whenever they need it. They'll get charged, of course, but only for what they use. No more fighting with system administrators over resources. When a cloud is asked to jump, it will ask "How high?" instead of fighting about whether it will jump at all!

Another definition comes from the National Institute of Standards and Technology (NIST), which is a division of the U.S. Department of Commerce. They list five essential characteristics of a cloud environment.[4]

1. On-demand self-service

2. Broad network access

3. Resource pooling

4. Rapid elasticity

5. Measured service

Each of those criteria has to come into play. The similarities between the McKinsey definition and the NIST definition are easy to see. You can learn more about the work the NIST has done on the cloud on their web site.[5]

As with anything, there are good and bad points, pros and cons, strengths and weaknesses related to cloud computing. An organization needs to know enough to make an educated choice. Certainly the cloud is going to become more widely used for advanced analytics in the future. This is particularly true for development purposes. As we'll discuss, for production work the future is a little less clear. Let's explore the two primary types of cloud environments: (1) public clouds and (2) private clouds.

## Public Clouds

Public clouds have gotten the most hype and attention. With a public cloud users are basically loading their data onto a host system and they are then allocated resources as they need them to use that data. They will get charged according to their usage.

There are definitely some advantages to such a setup:

■ The bandwidth is as-needed and users only pay for what they use.

■ It isn't necessary to buy a system sized to handle the maximum capacity ever required and then risk having half of the capacity sitting idle much of the time.

■ If there are short bursts where a lot of processing is needed then it is possible to get it with no hassle. Simply pay for the extra resources.

■ There's typically very fast ramp-up. Once granted access to the cloud environment, users load their data and start analyzing.

■ It is easy to share data with others regardless of their location since a public cloud by definition is outside of a corporate firewall. Anyone can be given permission to log on to the environment created.

There are also some cons to a public cloud environment:

- Typically, there are few performance guarantees in a public cloud. By definition there can be any number of people making any number of large requests for the same resources at the same time. Of course, it is possible to pay extra for exclusive use of a cloud server.

- This can cause high variability in performance. How fast a job will run will not be known until it is submitted. There may be some indications based on past performance, but it isn't guaranteed the same will be seen again.

- There are concerns around the security of the data. While some may argue that the concerns aren't as valid in fact as they are in theory, the perception of security concerns is a big problem itself.

- It can get expensive if a cloud isn't used wisely since users will be charged for everything that they do. Bad queries that eat up a lot of system resources are annoying on your own system but have no real direct cost. In a cloud, you could have quite a big charge as a result of a bad query.

- If an audited trail of data and where it sits is required, it is not possible to have that in a public cloud. It may not even be possible to identify if data is all in the same country.

Given those pros and cons, what are the appropriate and inappropriate uses for a public cloud?

Cloud hardware resources are described as elastic, meaning they can grow and contract at any time fairly easily. This means it is easy to expand the CPUs, storage, and memory size on a server and have more compute power. It also means that it's easy to pay for and use 10 more servers at any time. But this kind of scalability is not the same as an MPP system. Most public cloud servers operate independent of each other. MPP systems are one big system. This means that if an organization has many, many small to medium processes, a cloud can be a great help. However, a cloud will not be of much help when it comes to running massive processes that go beyond the scale of the individual servers available in the cloud environment. While MPP software can run in the cloud, the fact that the underlying hardware is unknown and can change at any time creates numerous performance problems for MPP software.

Perhaps the best use for a public cloud is pure research and development work, where performance variability isn't something to worry about. If analytic professionals are experimenting with some new data to figure out what it offers, a cloud is a terrific environment to consider. A lot of times in exploratory analytical development work, performance isn't an issue. It doesn't become an issue until a process is deployed. For non-mission-critical analytical processes, the cloud is a potential long-term host even for deployed processes.

A public cloud can be problematic if data security is a big concern. It's necessary to apply good security protocols and tools to a public cloud and keep your environment highly secure. One thing out of your control are the employees at the cloud provider company. If they are hackers or thieves of any kind, they can do the same damage an employee within a company could do. The probability of this is extremely low, but the public outcry from a security breach would be much worse if caused by a cloud employee than a company's own employee. Putting sensitive data in a public cloud requires implementing a strong security plan. Otherwise, don't do it.

 ## ARE YOU SURE YOU'RE SAVING MONEY?

If an analytic professional only had himself to worry about, he could probably spend far less using a cloud than buying his own equipment. In a large organization there is a catch, however. Once many different people and departments start using the cloud, it is possible to quickly end up paying more in pay-per-use fees than what it would cost to own a system!

Another interesting caution on a public cloud is one that many people don't think about. While a cloud is cheap compared to buying a system, if only a few processes need to be run, a cloud can actually cost more than having an in-house system. Once there are many users leveraging a public cloud and paying on a per-use basis, it can be cheaper to buy an in-house system. On top of the cost savings, performance can improve on a system that is owned since the organization will have full control of the environment.

Over time, it is possible public cloud offerings will be able to handle enterprise-level, mission-critical functions at a good price. The vendors that offer a higher level of performance guarantee today charge much more for the premium service than base cloud offerings. It is possible that cloud offerings will be able to satisfactorily address security concerns, whether real or perceived. Until then, public clouds are largely going to be used sparingly by most companies, with a focus on process development work.

## Private Clouds

A private cloud has the same features of a public cloud, but it's owned exclusively by one organization and typically housed behind a corporate firewall. A private cloud is going to serve the exact same function as a public cloud, but just for the people or teams within a given organization. See Figure 4.5 for an illustration of a public versus a private cloud.

One huge advantage of an onsite private cloud is that the organization will have complete control over the data and system security. Data is never leaving the corporate firewall so there's absolutely no

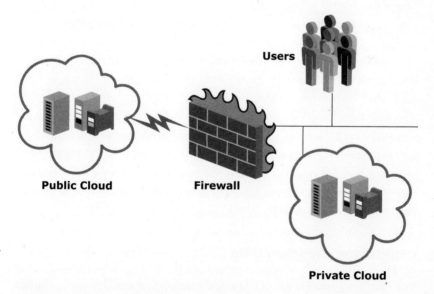

**Figure 4.5** Public Clouds versus Private Clouds

concern about where it's going. The data is at no more risk than it is on any other internal system.

One downside of an onsite private cloud is that it is necessary to purchase and own the entire cloud infrastructure before allocating it out to users, which could in the short term negate some of the cost savings. Capital outlaid this year will increase this year's expense relative to a public cloud. In the years that follow there will be lower cost than if everything had been done on a public cloud. In the long run, if a lot of groups and users will be using a cloud environment, it can be much cheaper to have a private cloud.

 ## SHORT-TERM VERSUS LONG-TERM COSTS

A private cloud can be much cheaper than a public cloud in the long run if many users are involved. However, the initial capital outlay and setup will cause higher costs in the short term when implementing a private could. Over time, the balance will shift.

A private cloud isn't dissimilar in concept to the analytical sandboxes that we're going to be discussing in Chapter 5. A primary difference is the fully self-service provisioning of a true private cloud versus a typically more controlled sandbox environment. However, the two concepts are very close and pragmatically virtually identical. For advanced analytics purposes, it is possible think of them as both achieving more or less the same thing. One difference is that if using a private cloud and strictly following the rules of a cloud, the dynamic workload could lead to some performance problems as users contend for resources. With a sandbox, it is possible to set it up so teams have a certain level of resources when they need it. Conversely, it requires more effort for users of a sandbox to gain access to additional resources than for users of a cloud.

## Cloud Computing Wrap-Up

The cloud is getting a lot of hype and attention these days, and there's certainly merit in cloud architectures. As with anything, organizations need to make sure they understand the appropriate uses for a cloud and the pros and cons of those uses.

In the near- to middle-term, public clouds will mainly be used for development work requiring data that isn't sensitive. Private clouds, or their close cousin the analytic sandbox, are going to continue to grow in usage and influence for all kinds of analytical work.

The bottom line is that it makes sense to have a flexible, more loosely structured, and less tightly controlled environment in an organization to facilitate research, innovation, and exploration. Clouds are one method of providing such an environment.

## GRID COMPUTING

There are some computations and algorithms that aren't cleanly converted to SQL or embedded in a user-defined function within a database. In these cases, it's necessary to pull data out into a more traditional analytics environment and run analytic tools against that data in the traditional way. Large servers have been utilized for such endeavors for quite some time. The problem is that as more analysts do more analytics, the servers continue to expand in size and number. This gets quite expensive, and analysts often still often overwhelm whatever capacity they have.

A grid configuration can help both cost and performance. It falls into the classification of "high-performance computing." Instead of having a single high-end server (or maybe a few of them), a large number of lower-cost machines are put in place. As opposed to having one server managing its CPU and resources across jobs, jobs are parceled out individually to the different machines to be processed in parallel. Each machine may only be able to handle a fraction of the work of the original server and can potentially handle only one job at a time. In aggregate, however, the grid can handle quite a bit. Grids can therefore be a cost-effective mechanism to improve overall throughput and capacity. Grid computing also helps organizations balance workloads, prioritize jobs, and offer high availability for analytic processing.

Using such a grid enables analytic professionals to scale an environment relatively cheaply and quickly. A grid won't make sense in all cases, however. When running several very, very intensive jobs, a grid may not be an optimal choice. Since each job goes to a single machine, big jobs won't run as quickly on the cheaper machines as on a larger server. But if a large organization has many processes being run and most of them are small to medium in size, a grid can be a huge boost.

A more recent innovation within grid environments are high-performance analytics architectures, where the various machines in the grid are aware of each other and can share information. This allows very large jobs to be handled quickly by leveraging all of the resources in the grid at the same time and it addresses the concern mentioned with the limitations of jobs being run on a single machine within the grid. This new breed of grid holds significant promise and will likely become an accepted option over time. As of this writing, an even newer option is evolving where the grid is directly attached to a database system so that performance of the grid will increase further. The SAS High-Performance Analytics offering is one example.

As more complicated modeling approaches evolve and methods like commodity modeling, which we'll discuss in Chapter 6, continue to gain acceptance, a grid can be one method to effectively handle the additional modeling workloads that result.

## MAPREDUCE

MapReduce is a parallel programming framework. It's neither a database nor a direct competitor to databases. This has not stopped some people from claiming it's going to replace databases and everything else under the sun. The reality is MapReduce is complementary to existing technologies. There are a lot of tasks that can be done in a MapReduce environment that can also be done in a relational database. What it comes down to is identifying which environment is better for the problem at hand. Being able to do something with a tool or technology isn't the same as being the best way to do something. By focusing on what MapReduce is best for instead of what theoretically can be done with it, it is possible to maximize the benefits received.

MapReduce consists of two primary processes that a programmer builds: the "map" step and the "reduce" step. Hence, the name MapReduce! These steps get passed to the MapReduce framework, which then runs the programs in parallel on a set of worker nodes. Recall that MPP database systems spread data out across nodes that can then be queried. In the case of MapReduce, there is a lot of commodity hardware to which data is being passed as needed to run a process. Each MapReduce worker runs the same code against its portion of the data. However, the workers do not interact or even have knowledge of each other.

If there is a steady stream of web logs coming in, it might be handed out in chunks to the various worker nodes. A simple method would be a round robin procedure where entries are passed to nodes sequentially over and over. Some sort of hashing is also common. In this case, records are passed to workers based on a formula so that similar records get sent to the same worker. For example, hashing on customer ID will send all records for a given customer to the same worker. This is critical if analysis by customer ID is planned.

Mapreduce.org defines MapReduce as a programming framework popularized by Google and used to simplify data processing across massive data sets. Hadoop is a popular open-source version of MapReduce supplied by the Apache organization. Hadoop is the best-known implementation of the MapReduce framework. We'll stick to the generic term MapReduce for this section, but all of the content applies regardless of which implementation of the MapReduce framework you use.

Organizations are finding that it's vital to quickly analyze the huge amounts of data they are generating to better make decisions. MapReduce is a tool that's helping those organizations handle the unstructured and semi-structured sources that are not easy to analyze with traditional tools. Most enterprises deal with multiple types of data in addition to relational data from a database. These include text, machine-generated data like web logs or sensor data, images, and so forth. Organizations need to process all that data quickly and efficiently to derive meaningful insights. With MapReduce, computational processing can occur on data stored in a file system without loading it into a database first. This is a key feature that we'll return to later.

A big distinction of a MapReduce environment is the specific ability to handle unstructured text. In a relational database, everything is already in tables and rows and columns. The data already has well-defined relationships. This is not always true with raw data streams. That's where MapReduce can really be powerful. Loading big chunks of text into a "blob" field in a database is possible, but it really isn't the best use of the database or the best way to handle such data. MapReduce can help.

## How MapReduce Works

Let's assume there are 20 terabytes of data and 20 MapReduce server nodes for a project. The first step is to distribute a terabyte to each of the 20 nodes using a simple file copy process. Note that this data has to be distributed prior to the MapReduce process being started. Also note that the data is in a file of some format determined by the user. There is no standard format like in a relational database.

Next, the programmer submits two programs to the scheduler. One is a map program; the other is the reduce program. In this two-step processing, the map program finds the data on disk and executes the logic it contains. This occurs independently on each of the 20 servers in our example. The results of the map step are then passed to the reduce process to summarize and aggregate the final answers. See Figure 4.6 for a visual of the process.

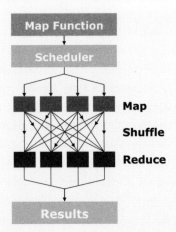

MapReduce breaks a job into many pieces and runs them independently.

**Figure 4.6** MapReduce Process

Let's look at an example where an organization has a bunch of text flowing in from online customer service chats taking place on its web site. An analytic professional creates a map step to parse out each word present in the chat text. In this example, the map function will simply find each word, parse it out of its paragraph, and associate a count of one with it. The end result of the map step is a set of value pairs such as "<my, 1>," "<product, 1>," "<broke, 1>." When each worker node is done executing the map step, it lets the scheduler know.

## SHARE THE WORK, PART 2!

The essence of MapReduce is to allow many machines to share the burden of working through a large amount of data. When the logic required can be run independently on different subsets of the data, the parallel nature of MapReduce makes it quite fast.

Once the map step is done, the reduce step is started. At this point, the goal is to figure out how many times each word appeared. What happens next is called shuffling. During shuffling the answers from the map steps are distributed through hashing so that the same key words end up on the same reduce node. For example, in a simple situation there would be 26 reduce nodes so that all the words beginning with A go to one node, all the B's go to another, all the C's go to another, and so on.

The reduce step will simply get the count by word. Based on our example, the process will end up with "<my, 10>," "<product, 25>," "<broke, 20>," where the numbers represent how many times the word was found. There would be 26 files emitted (one for each reduce node) with sorted counts by word. Note that another process is needed to combine the 26 output files. Multiple MapReduce processes are often required to get to a final answer set.

Once the word counts are computed, the results can be fed into an analysis. The frequency of certain product names can be identified. The frequency of words like "broken" or "angry" can be identified. The point is that a text stream that was totally unstructured has now been structured in a simple fashion so that it can be analyzed. The use of MapReduce is often a starting point in this way. The output of MapReduce is an input to another analysis process.

There can be thousands of map and reduce tasks running across thousands of machines. That's where MapReduce becomes so powerful. When there are huge streams of data and what has to be done against the data can be broken into pieces, that is the sweet spot for MapReduce. If one worker doesn't need to know what's happening with another worker to execute effectively, it is possible to achieve fully parallel processing. In our example, each word can be parsed by itself, and the contents of the other words are irrelevant for a given map worker task.

The preceding point cannot be missed, as it is crucial for understanding when and how to apply MapReduce. When data is handed out to the workers, each worker will only know of the data it sees. If the processing required involves awareness of data from other workers, then a framework other than MapReduce needs to be used. Luckily, there are many cases where data can be handled in this way. Parsing one web log or one RFID record into pieces doesn't depend on anything else. If text needs parsed by customer ID, then when handing out the data, it simply must be hashed so that all records for a given customer end up on the same worker.

Conceptually, MapReduce breaks up a problem like a parallel relational database does. But MapReduce is not a database. There is no defined structure. Each process is not aware of anything that's happened before or after it. There is some overlap in what you can do in MapReduce and in a database. A database can even provide input data to a MapReduce process, just as a MapReduce process can provide input to a database. The key is figuring out what's best for each task. Just because it is possible to do something with a given tool set doesn't mean it is the best way. Other tool sets may be much better suited. A database and MapReduce should be used for what they each do best.

## MapReduce Strengths and Weaknesses

MapReduce can run on commodity hardware. As a result, it can be very cheap to get up and running. It can also be very cheap to expand.

It is easy to expand the capacity because all that is required is to buy more servers and bolt them on to the platform.

We already talked about the fact that there are some problems that MapReduce can handle easily that a relational database is not as good at. Such tasks include things like parsing text, crunching through web logs, and reading in a huge raw data source. MapReduce is at its best when there is a large set of input data where much of the data isn't required for analysis. If only a small piece of the data is really going to be important, but it isn't clear up-front which pieces will be important, MapReduce can help. MapReduce can be a terrific way to sort through the masses of data and pull out the important parts.

 **SIPPING FROM THE HOSE**

Many large data streams such as web logs have a lot of data in them that has no long-term value. MapReduce allows you to take the sips you need out of the stream of data while letting the rest run past, just like how you drink a small part of the water flowing past when you take a drink from a hose.

The fact is that it doesn't make sense to waste a lot of time and space loading a bunch of raw data into an enterprise data warehouse if at the end of processing it, most of it is going to be thrown away. If data is only needed for a short time, there is no point to putting it into a more persistent location such as a data warehouse. MapReduce is perfect for these occasions. Trim off the excess data before loading it into a database.

On many occasions, MapReduce is used similarly to an extract, load, and transform (ETL) tool. ETL tools read a set of source data, perform a set of formatting or reorganization steps, and then load the results into a destination data source. To support analysis, ETL tools take data from operational systems and get it loaded into a relational database so that it can be accessed. MapReduce is similarly often used to process a source of big data, summarize it in a meaningful way, and pass the results into an analysis process or database. In the preceding example, the raw text is transformed into word counts that can be analyzed. The results of the process can be fed into a database so that the additional information can be combined with existing information.

MapReduce is not a database, so it has no built-in security, no indexing, no query or process optimizer, no historical perspective in terms of other jobs that have been run, and no knowledge of other data that exists. While it provides the ultimate flexibility to process different kinds of data, it also comes with the responsibility to define exactly what the data is in every process created. Everything is more or less going to be custom coded, including data structures. Every job is an entity in and of itself that does not have awareness of other things that may be going on.

MapReduce is still not very mature. There aren't many people who know how to use it well, how to configure it, or how to do the coding required. It is hard today to build a strong competency in MapReduce based on the resource constraints. This is going to change over time as MapReduce matures and more people become proficient with it. It is a big consideration as this book is written, however.

## MapReduce Wrap-Up

MapReduce is going to grow in influence and popularity as big data becomes a larger part of what organizations need to tackle. The ability to take a process and run it in parallel on commodity hardware is quite attractive when dealing with huge masses of data, much of which won't be of interest or value in the long term. By breaking the task into small pieces, it gets done faster and more cheaply than through other options.

MapReduce isn't a database, nor is it a replacement for one. It can, however, add a lot of value to an enterprise's databases. Once MapReduce processes and pulls out the important parts of a big data stream, those important pieces can be made available within a traditional database environment to facilitate further, deeper analysis, as well as broad query and reporting access. In some ways, MapReduce is like an ETL process on steroids.

Let's close this section with a quick example. Web logs are very large and contain a lot of useless data. MapReduce is useful for sifting through the haystack to find the valuable needles. Imagine a MapReduce process working through the logs in near real time in order to identify immediate actions that are needed. For example, find all customers who viewed a product and didn't buy it. A MapReduce process can identify the list of customers who need a follow up e-mail and that information can be sent immediately to a process to generate the e-mails. This can be done without the overhead of first loading the raw data into a relational database and running a query.

However, once the immediate task is done, the most important pieces of the data can be loaded into a database. That way, the data is alongside all of the other important customer history so that more strategic analysis across time and across business units can be executed. In this example, the list of customers identified is loaded into the database to record that they were sent an e-mail. This will allow the tracking and monitoring of e-mail history, just like is done with every e-mail campaign.

## IT ISN'T AN EITHER/OR CHOICE!

Massively parallel relational databases, clouds, and MapReduce all have roles to play in an analytic ecosystem that's going to effectively tame big data. All three can be used together to maximize results. There are many ways to combine these technologies:

- There are databases that run in the cloud.
- There are databases that embed MapReduce functionality. For example, Teradata's Aster platform has a patented SQL MapReduce implementation that allows MapReduce processes to be executed as part of an SQL query.
- As another way to use both a database and MapReduce, MapReduce can be run against data sourced from a database or it can feed a database.
- MapReduce can also run against data in the cloud.
- Taking it a step further, MapReduce can run against data in a database that is hosted on the cloud!

These three technologies can interact and work together. Each can enhance the others if it is used correctly. It's not an either/or situation.

These options can all be part of an analytic ecosystem, and many organizations will evolve to have all three. Grid computing configurations can also sit alongside any of the scenarios above as required.

## WRAP-UP

The most important lessons to take away from this chapter are:

- Analysts have been pushing the limits of scalability for decades. Big data is just the next generation of intimidating data to tame.

- Analytic and data management environments are converging. In-database processing is replacing much of the traditional offline analytic processing used to support advanced analytics.

- Massively parallel processing (MPP) databases, cloud architectures, and MapReduce are all powerful tools to aid in attacking big data.

- Analytic professionals can leverage MPP databases for data preparation and scoring using SQL, user defined functions (UDFs), embedded processes, and predictive modeling markup language (PMML).

- Clouds can be public or private and make it easy to get the resources you need. You only pay for what you use. Clouds can be terrific for uses such as research and development activities.

- In public clouds performance isn't guaranteed, security must be stringently addressed, and data is out of an organization's direct control.

- The cost of using a public cloud can exceed the cost of internally owned infrastructure if a public cloud gets used widely within an organization.

- Private clouds enable flexibility within a secure environment and make terrific sense for large organizations.

- Grid configurations can assist in scaling processes that can't be passed to a database. Grid options are expanding and becoming more powerful.

- The MapReduce framework is an up-and-coming technology that allows programs to be run in parallel.
- MapReduce can help tame big data by preprocessing it and passing important pieces on for further analysis.
- Relational databases, clouds, and MapReduce all add value in taming big data. The three technologies can integrate and work together to make each better and more effective than it would be on its own.

## NOTES

1. The comment column is based on information from the web site http://whatsabyte.com.
2. You can find out more information at www.DMG.org.
3. McKinsey and Company, "Clearing the Air on Cloud Computing," March 2009.
4. National Institute of Standards and Technology, Draft, "NIST Working Definition of Cloud Computing," 8-21-09, version 15. http://csrc.nist.gov/publications/drafts/800-146/Draft-NIST -SP800-146.pdf.
5. National Institute of Standards and Technology, www.nist.gov/itl/ cloud/index.cfm.

CHAPTER **5**

# The Evolution of Analytic Processes

What does the increased scalability discussed in Chapter 4 buy an organization? Not much, if it isn't put to use. Upgrading technologies to today's scalable options won't provide a lot of value if the same old analytical processes remain in place. It will be a lot like buying a new 3-D TV with all the bells and whistles, and then simply connecting it to an antenna, grabbing local TV signals from the air. The picture might be improved over your old TV, but you certainly won't be changing your viewing experience very much compared to what is possible with the new TV.

Similarly, as the options practitioners of advanced analytics have in terms of scalability evolve, so, too, must the processes used to generate and deploy analytics. Legacy processes for deploying analytic routines simply aren't able to take advantage of the current state of the world. Without changing key aspects of existing analytical processes, organizations will not realize more than a fraction of the gains in power and productivity that are possible with the new levels of scalability available today. It isn't possible to tame big data using only traditional approaches to developing analytical processes.

One process that needs to be changed is the process of configuring and maintaining workspace for analytic professionals. Traditionally, this workspace was on a separate server dedicated to analytical processing. As already discussed, in-database processing is becoming the new standard. However, in order to take advantage of the scalable in-database approach, it is necessary for analysts to have a workspace, or "sandbox," residing directly within the database system. In the big data world, a MapReduce environment will often be an addition to the traditional sandbox. The first part of this chapter will discuss what an analytical sandbox is, why it is important, and how to use it.

As analytic professionals begin consistently leveraging a database platform for their work through a sandbox, they will be doing some tasks repeatedly. For example, each individual analyst will need certain core metrics on customers regardless of the specific analysis he or she is building. Enterprise analytic data sets are key tools to help drive consistency and productivity, and lower risk into an organization's advanced analytics processes. The second part of the chapter will start with an overview of what a basic analytic data set is. Then, we'll cover what an enterprise analytic data set (EADS) is, what the benefits of an EADS are, and how an EADS can be utilized by other users or applications beyond the analytic professionals it is developed for.

Many analyses lead to "scoring routines" that need to be deployed and applied on a regular basis. For example, a customer propensity model scoring routine might provide the likelihood that any given customer will purchase a certain product in the next month. Historically, updating scores for each customer was a time-consuming and infrequent task. In today's world, it is often necessary to keep scores up to date on a daily, if not real-time, basis. The third part of the chapter will discuss how to embed scoring routines within the database environment, as well as how to effectively track and manage the models and processes that are developed through model management.

## THE ANALYTIC SANDBOX

In Chapter 4, we discussed the power of massively parallel database systems. One of the uses of such a database system is to facilitate the building and deployment of advanced analytic processes. In order for analytic professionals to utilize an enterprise data warehouse or data mart more effectively, however, they need the correct permissions and access to do so. An analytic sandbox is the mechanism for achieving this. If used appropriately, an analytic sandbox can be one of the primary drivers of value in the world of big data.

The term "sandbox" originates from the sandboxes that many children play in. Within a sandbox, children can create anything they like. They can reshape the sand at will, depending on their desires at the time. Similarly, a sandbox in the analytics context is a set of resources that enable analytic professionals to experiment and reshape data in whatever fashion they need to. Other terms used for the sandbox concept include an agile analytics cloud and a data lab, among others. Which term you apply to the concept isn't important. What is important is that you embrace the concept.

## The Analytic Sandbox: Definition and Scope

An analytic sandbox provides a set of resources with which in-depth analysis can be done to answer critical business questions. An analytic sandbox is ideal for data exploration, development of analytical processes, proof of concepts, and prototyping. Once things progress into ongoing, user-managed processes or production processes, then the sandbox should not be involved.

A sandbox is going to be leveraged by a fairly small set of users. There will be data created within the sandbox that is segregated from the production database. Sandbox users will also be allowed to load data of their own for brief time periods as part of a project, even if that data is not part of the official enterprise data model.

Data in a sandbox will have a limited shelf life. The idea isn't to build up a bunch of permanent data. During a project, build the data needed for the project. When that project is done, delete the data. If used appropriately, a sandbox has the capability to be a major driver of analytic value for an organization.

## Analytic Sandbox Benefits

What are the benefits of an analytic sandbox? Let's explore the topic from both an analytic professional's view and IT's view.

Benefits from the view of an analytic professional:

- **Independence.** Analytic professionals will be able to work independently on the database system without needing to continually go back and ask for permissions for specific projects.
- **Flexibility.** Analytic professionals will have the flexibility to use whatever business intelligence, statistical analysis, or visualization tools that they need to use.
- **Efficiency.** Analytic professionals will be able to leverage the existing enterprise data warehouse or data mart, without having to move or migrate data.
- **Freedom.** Analytic professionals can reduce focus on the administration of systems and babysitting of production processes by shifting those maintenance tasks to IT.
- **Speed.** Massive speed improvement will be realized with the move to parallel processing. This also enables rapid iteration and the ability to "fail fast" and take more risks to innovate.

 **A SANDBOX IS GOOD FOR EVERYONE!**

There are distinct advantages tied to a sandbox environment for both analytic professionals and IT. It isn't something that hurts one group at the expense of the other. People on both sides are often afraid of the concept at first since they don't understand it. It may take some time to educate people and get past that initial reaction. The effort will be worth it.

Benefits from the view of IT:

- **Centralization.** IT will be able to centrally manage a sandbox environment just as every other database environment on the system is managed.
- **Streamlining.** A sandbox will greatly simplify the promotion of analytic processes into production since there will be a consistent platform for both development and deployment.
- **Simplicity.** There will be no more processes built during development that have to be totally rewritten to run in the production environment.

- **Control.** IT will be able to control the sandbox environment, balancing sandbox needs and the needs of other users. The production environment is safe from an experiment gone wrong in the sandbox.

- **Costs:** Big cost savings can be realized by consolidating many analytic data marts into one central system.

## An Internal Sandbox

For an internal sandbox, a portion of an enterprise data warehouse or data mart is carved out to serve as the analytic sandbox. In this case, the sandbox is physically located on the production system. However, the sandbox database itself is not a part of the production database. The sandbox is a separate database container within the system. See Figure 5.1 for an illustration.

Note that with big data, it will be wise to also add a MapReduce environment into the mix. This would typically be installed alongside the database platform unless you're using a system that can combine the two environments together. The MapReduce environment will require access to the internal sandbox. Data can be shared between the two environments as required. We talked about MapReduce in Chapter 4.

One strength of an internal sandbox is that it will leverage existing hardware resources and infrastructure already in place. This makes it very easy to set up. From an administration perspective, there's no difference in setting up a sandbox than in setting up any other database container on the system. What's different about the sandbox are some of the permissions that will be granted to its users and how it is used.

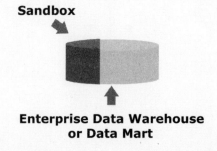

**Sandbox**

**Enterprise Data Warehouse or Data Mart**

**Figure 5.1** An Internal Sandbox

Perhaps the biggest strength of an internal sandbox is the ability to directly join production data with sandbox data. Since all of the production data and all of the sandbox data are within the production system, it's very easy to link those sources to one another and work with all the data together. See Figure 5.2 for an illustration of how this is possible.

An internal sandbox is very cost-effective since no new hardware is needed. The production system is already in place. It is just being used in a new way. The elimination of any and all cross-platform data movement also lowers costs. The one exception is any data movement required between the database and the MapReduce environment.

There are a few weaknesses of an internal sandbox. One such weakness is that there will be an additional load on the existing enterprise data warehouse or data mart. The sandbox will use both space and CPU resources (potentially a lot of resources). Another weakness is that an internal sandbox can be constrained by production policies and procedures. For example, if on Monday morning virtually all the system resources are needed for Monday morning reports, sandbox users may not have many resources available to them.

## An External Sandbox

For an external sandbox, a physically separate analytic sandbox is created for testing and development of analytic processes. It's relatively rare to have an environment that's purely external. Internal or

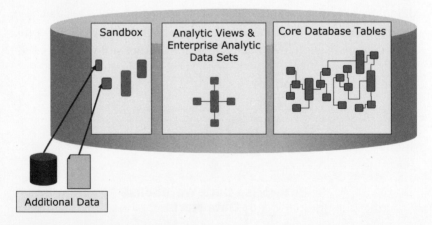

**Figure 5.2** Detailed Internal Sandbox View

hybrid sandboxes, which we'll talk about next, are more common. It is important to understand what the external sandbox is, however, as it is a component of a hybrid sandbox environment. See Figure 5.3 for an illustration.

The biggest strength of an external sandbox is its simplicity. The sandbox is a stand-alone environment, dedicated to advanced analytics development. It will have no impact on other processes, which allows for flexibility in design and usage. For example, different database settings can be explored or an upgrade to a newer version of the database can be done to test new features. This is similar to what is often done on traditional test and development systems used for building applications.

One common question that often arises is "Isn't this external system completely violating this concept of keeping the data in-database when analyzing it?" The answer is no if you consider it an analytics development environment. Most organizations have a test and/or development environment, independent of their production system, for application and business intelligence work. It's a necessary component to help build, test, and debug new processes. An external sandbox is exactly the same concept for the exact same reasons, only it's dedicated to analytic initiatives.

Another strength of an external sandbox is reduced workload management. When only analytic professionals are using the system, it isn't necessary to worry much about tuning and balancing. There will be predictable, stable performance in both the sandbox and production environments. For example, sandbox users won't have a Monday morning downgrade to their resources due to reporting needs. They'll have a steady level of access to the sandbox.

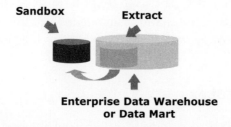

**Figure 5.3** An External Sandbox

## AN EXTERNAL SANDBOX DOESN'T VIOLATE THE RULES

An external sandbox does not violate the rules of in-database processing. View an external sandbox as a test and development environment for analytics. There are many valid and compelling justifications for such environments, and they are ubiquitous for application and report development.

An external sandbox is preferably a relational database of the exact same nature as the production system. This way, moving processes from the sandbox to the production environment is simply a matter of copying things over. If data extracts sent to the sandbox are kept in the same structure as on production, migrating will be easy to do.

When it comes to working with big data, a MapReduce environment should be included as part of an external sandbox environment. In this case, the external sandbox environment will have a relational database and a MapReduce component. In some cases, one system can handle both responsibilities, in other cases there will be two physical platforms required.

A major weakness of an external sandbox is the additional cost of the stand-alone system that serves as the sandbox platform. To mitigate these costs, many organizations will take older equipment and shift it to the sandbox environment when they upgrade their production systems. This makes use of equipment that would otherwise be discarded and saves any costs associated with hardware for the sandbox.

Another weakness is that there will be some data movement. It will be necessary to move data from the production system into the sandbox before developing a new analysis. The data feeds will also need to be maintained. The feeds don't have to be too complicated, but it is an extra set of tasks to maintain and execute. Any data feeds should be scoped very tightly and should focus only on what is absolutely needed.

### A Hybrid Sandbox

A hybrid sandbox environment is the combination of an internal sandbox and an external sandbox. It allows analytic professionals the flexibility to use the power of the production system when needed, but also the flexibility of the external system for deep exploration or tasks that aren't as friendly to the database. See Figure 5.4 for an illustration.

The strengths of a hybrid sandbox environment are similar to the strengths of the internal and external options, plus having ultimate flexibility in the approach taken for an analysis. It is easy to avoid production impacts during early testing if work is done on the external sandbox. When it comes time for final testing and pre-deployment work, the production sandbox can be used. A single MapReduce environment might augment the hybrid sandbox by supporting both the internal and external sandboxes.

Another advantage is if an analytic process has been built and it has to be run in a "pseudo-production" mode temporarily while the full production system process is being deployed. Such processes can be run out of the internal sandbox easily.

The weaknesses of a hybrid environment are similar to the weaknesses of the other two options, but with a few additions. One weakness is the need to maintain both an internal and external sandbox environment. Not only will it be necessary to keep the external sandbox consistent with the production environment in this case, but the external sandbox will also need to be kept consistent with the internal sandbox.

It will also be necessary to establish some guidelines on when each sandbox option is used. There ought to be certain types of activities that are earmarked for the external sandbox and certain activities earmarked for the internal sandbox. It can't be a matter of analytic

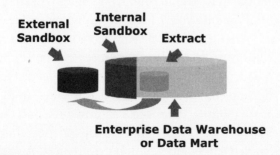

**Figure 5.4** A Hybrid Sandbox

professionals arbitrarily using one or the other. The analytics team is going to have to develop guidelines and stick to them.

### DON'T OVERFILL A SANDBOX

Only the minimum data needed for analysis efforts should be copied to an external sandbox environment. The sandbox should host only a small portion of the data stored in the production environment. The specific data will change over time depending on current analytical needs. Don't replicate more than absolutely necessary.

The last weakness is that some two-way data feeds may be required, which adds complexity. There must be some consistency in the data available to the internal sandbox and the external sandbox. As new data is developed in one of the sandbox environments, it may need to be replicated it in the other.

### Don't Just Use Data. Evolve It!

One of the best uses for a sandbox environment is to identify new data sources that should be added into an organization's systems and processes on an ongoing basis. Perhaps you purchase a feed of social media data, or a household demographic file, or you get a feed of a new big data source. How will analytic professionals explore and experiment with this new data?

Imagine the folly of the typical approach of setting up a process to formally get the new data in production before it can be explored. What would that entail? You'll have to justify and scope the project to load the data. Then there will be a project commissioned to develop the extract, transform, and load (ETL) processes to load the data into the system. A data model to put the data into will need to be designed, approved, and implemented. Then all of the above must be tested. After three or six months, the process is turned on, and the data is in there and ready for use. At that point, perhaps analysis shows the data doesn't have much value and you don't really need it. What a waste of resources it was to get it formally added to the system!

**TASTE A SAMPLE FIRST**

When people aren't sure they'll like an ice cream flavor, they ask to try a taste. If they like it, they order a whole serving. If not, they move on to another flavor. Follow the same logic with new data sources, especially big data sources. Don't go for a whole serving until you know it is something you want. Experiment and try the data first in your sandbox.

The way a sandbox is used to avoid the preceding scenario is to get a onetime feed of the new data, load it up in the sandbox, and test it out. If it doesn't work out very well, move on. If it does, that is the time to kick off the lengthy and expensive process to get the data formally loaded on an ongoing basis. Using an analytical sandbox to explore and prove the value of new data sources is a vastly faster and cheaper way to go than traditional paths.

## Workload Management and Capacity Planning

As analytic professionals start to use a sandbox, there are a lot of built-in components of database systems that will enable it to work smoothly. Sandbox users can be assigned to a group that has permissions that make sense for the purpose of developing new advanced analytics processes. For example, it is possible to limit how much of the CPU a given sandbox user can absorb at one time. Enterprise class systems are flexible enough to let users get only 10 percent of resources if the system is in demand, but if it is nighttime and no one else is active, a user can use the entire system.

It is possible to control the number of concurrent queries or even the types of queries that users can make. Perhaps individuals are only allowed five concurrent jobs at a time. There can also be processes to identify poorly formed queries, such as a query that includes a cross-join of two large tables, and terminate such queries.

One of the important things to do is to limit disk space usage through data retention policies. When a data set is in a sandbox and it hasn't been touched in a couple of months, the default should be that it is deleted. A sandbox should not just continuously build up data sets, as often happens in traditional environments.

I've literally seen clients who have five terabytes of distinct corporate data, yet their analytic environment has 30 to 50 terabytes. The reason is that each analyst has made a copy of much of the five terabytes. Each analyst may even have multiple copies for different projects. This causes a huge proliferation of replicated, redundant data. That same approach should not be replicated within the sandbox environment. Within the sandbox, unless someone requests something be kept for a specific purpose, it needs to be deleted.

Especially with an internal sandbox, as more analytics are implemented, it will change the mix and level of resource usage in both the sandbox environment and the production environment. That's okay. Since the environments are on a single standardized platform, then the analytic processing can be accounted for in projections of usage just the same as everything else. Capacity plans should be discussed before getting started, but there is nothing special about sandbox processing that changes what the people who develop capacity plans need to do. Sandbox activity simply folds in. The system administrators know how to take care of this.

 **THE OPPOSITE OF WHAT MANY ASSUME IS TRUE!**

A sandbox environment can drive additional value from current investments rather than adding costs. It doesn't inherently cause the need for new equipment. Nor does a sandbox inherently cause problems with other processes. It can drive more value from existing investments without any negative impacts. Once you understand a sandbox and how it works, you will find that the opposite of what many assume is true!

There's one really big, common misnomer. People often think that an analytic sandbox is going to "destroy" the system, use up all the resources, and cause a lot of mayhem. That's not true at all. In fact, very big analytic jobs usually need to be run once or twice at the beginning of a project. They are not being run again and again. Big jobs can be easily scheduled to run at night, for example, when the system would otherwise be underutilized. As opposed to the use of an analytic sandbox somehow eating up all system resources, and pushing it over a cliff, it can actually lead to the opposite. The analytics being run in a sandbox can use resources that would otherwise be sitting idle. This helps drive even more value out of the investments made in the infrastructure without necessitating any increases to it. That's a great thing!

This leads to a final, related point. Adding analytics into an environment with a sandbox does not inherently, in and of itself, require any new capacity. If a system is 95 or 99 percent utilized today, then putting an internal sandbox on it is probably going to require upgrading that system. That's not an inherent impact of the analytic sandbox, however. That's a function of the fact that the system is so busy that any new application or process placed on it is going to require adding more capacity. Similarly, if older equipment is used for an external sandbox, there are no new costs. In fact, new value will be driven from equipment that would have been thrown away and not producing any value at all.

## WHAT IS AN ANALYTIC DATA SET?

An analytic data set (ADS) is the data that is pulled together in order to create an analysis or model. It is data in the format required for the specific analysis at hand. An ADS is generated by transforming, aggregating, and combining data. It is going to mimic a denormalized, or flat file, structure. What this means is that there will be one record per customer, location, product, or whatever type of entity is being analyzed. The analytic data set helps to bridge the gap between efficient storage and ease of use.

Most data in relational databases is stored in what is known as third normal form. This is a method of storing data that eliminates data redundancy but makes queries more complex. Third normal form table structures are very efficient for storing and retrieving data, but they cannot be directly used for most advanced analytics efforts. Getting into the details of what third normal form is all about is out of the scope of this book. What matters is that analytic tools usually require data in a simple, denormalized, flat file format. The sophistication in advanced analytics is in the algorithms and methods applied to the data, not in the structure of the data itself. Such data sets can take several forms, which we'll discuss next.

## Development versus Production Analytic Data Sets

There are two primary kinds of analytic data sets, which Figure 5.5 illustrates. A development ADS is going to be the data set used to build an analytic process. It will have all the candidate variables that may be needed to solve a problem and will be very wide. A development ADS might have hundreds or even thousands of variables or metrics within it. However, it's also fairly shallow, meaning that many times development work can be done on just a sample of data. This makes a development ADS very wide but not very deep.

A production analytic data set, however, is what is needed for scoring and deployment. It's going to contain only the specific metrics that were actually in the final solution. Typically, most processes only need a small fraction of the metrics explored during development. A big difference here is that the scores need to be applied to every entity, not just a sample. Every customer, every location, every product will

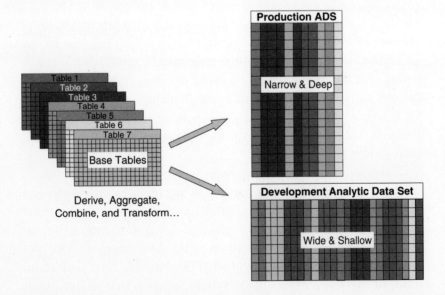

**Figure 5.5** Development versus Production Analytic Data Sets

need to be scored. Therefore, a production ADS is not going to be very wide, but it will be very deep.

For example, when developing a customer model, an analytic professional might explore 500 candidate metrics for a sample of 100,000 customers. The development ADS is therefore wide but shallow. When it comes time to apply scores to customers in production, perhaps only 12 metrics are needed but they are needed for all 30,000,000 customers. The production ADS is therefore narrow but deep.

## Traditional Analytic Data Sets

In a traditional environment, all analytic data sets are created outside of the database, as illustrated in Figure 5.6. Each analytic professional creates his or her own analytic data sets independently. This is done by every analytic professional, which means that there are possibly hundreds of people generating their own independent views of corporate data. It gets worse! An ADS is usually generated from scratch for each individual project. The problem is not just that each analytic professional has a single copy the production data. Each analytic professional often makes a new ADS, and therefore a new copy of the data, for every project.

As mentioned earlier, there are cases where companies with a given amount of data end up with 10 or 20 times that much data in their analytic environment. As an organization migrates to a modern, scalable process, it doesn't want to carry over the model of having all of these different copies of the data for each of the users. An alternative method is required, which we'll get to in a moment.

One of the big issues people don't think about with traditional ADS processes is the risk of inconsistencies. Perhaps an analytic professional has ended up over time defining sales as gross sales net of returns and discounts. At the same time, the person in the next cube has been defining sales as gross sales net of discounts, but not returns. It is not that either of them is wrong in any absolute sense, but each has a slightly different definition. If they are doing work for the same business partners, they will have inconsistencies in how they do their analysis and report their results back to their partners. This can cause problems.

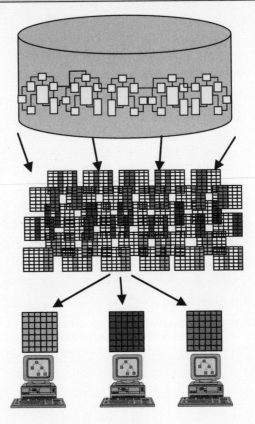

**Figure 5.6** Traditional Analytic Data Set Process

Another huge issue with the traditional approach to analytic data set generation is the repetitious work. If analytic professionals are creating very similar data sets again and again, it's not just the space and system resources they are using, but it's their time. They have to set up the ADS processes, they have to run them, and they have to babysit them and make sure they are complete. This extends all of their time lines and adds costs to all of their projects.

**INCONSISTENCY CAN HURT MORE THAN REDUNDANCY**

While it is true that a traditional analytic data set generation process leads to a lot of redundant data, this isn't the biggest problem. Often overlooked is the fact that different analytic professionals may develop slightly different definitions of key metrics over time. Their results will therefore be inconsistent. These inconsistencies are often not acknowledged or even known.

There is one last area of wasted energy and resources. Once an ADS process is created for a project, the work is not done. When the process is ready for production, an analytic professional is going to have to reverse engineer it to push it back up into production. If, as is typical historically, the production environment is not the same platform as the development environment, that will involve rewriting the entire process to work in the production environment. For example, it may be necessary to translate code from an analytic tool into SQL or a UDF. This is a very costly and error-prone step. Some companies spend more time and money deploying a ready-to-go analytic process than they did creating the process to begin with!

## ENTERPRISE ANALYTIC DATA SETS

Let's talk about a way to streamline the analytic data set creation process through an enterprise analytic data set, or EADS. An EADS is a shared and reusable set of centralized, standardized analytic data sets for use in analytics.

What an EADS does is to condense hundreds or thousands of variables into a handful of tables and views. These tables and views will be available to all analytic professionals, applications, and users. The structure of an EADS can be literally one wide table, or it may be a number of tables that can be joined together.

An EADS is collaborative in that all of the various analytic processes can share the same, consistent set of metrics. An EADS is going to greatly simplify access to data by making many metrics available directly to analytic professionals without further effort. They no longer have to go and navigate the raw third normal form tables and derive all the metrics themselves. An EADS is going to greatly reduce time to results and it is a "build once, use many" endeavor. See Figure 5.7 for an illustration.

One of the most important benefits of an EADS, which isn't often the first that people think about, is the consistency across analytic efforts. With greater consistency in the metrics feeding an organization's analytics, people can be comfortable that metrics feeding different processes were computed identically. Enterprise analytic data sets, if used appropriately, can help reduce data preparation time from 60 to 80 percent of total project effort to a much lower percentage. A

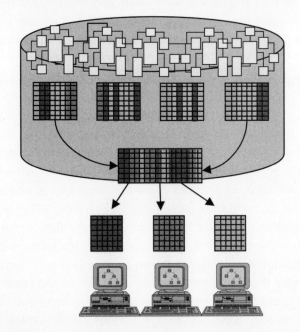

**Figure 5.7** Enterprise Analytic Data Set Process

goal might be to get as low as 20 to 30 percent. Key features of an enterprise analytic data set include:

- A standardized view of data to support multiple analysis efforts.
- A method to greatly streamline the data preparation process.
- A way to provide greater consistency, accuracy, and visibility to analytics processes.
- A way to open new views of data to applications and users outside of the advanced analytics space.
- Something that will allow analytic professionals to spend much more time on analysis!

## When to Create an Enterprise Analytic Data Set

When should you create an enterprise analytic data set? You should create an EADS when you're doing a lot of analysis in a given area and you expect to do a lot more of it. You can create an EADS for any entity on which you focus your analysis. Such entities include customers, products, locations, employees, and suppliers. Anything analyzed on a regular basis is a candidate for an EADS. An EADS will evolve over time. If a new source of big data is identified, additional metrics can be added to an EADS to account for the new information.

There will be time and cost associated with creating enterprise analytic data sets. Don't let that scare you. The costs will be more than made up over time through the cost savings of both man-hours and equipment. The commodity modeling concept discussed in Chapter 6 is a perfect example of a type of analysis that would not be feasible without an enterprise analytic data set to support it.

It requires a cross-functional team to build an effective enterprise analytic data set. Business team members will have to help define the metrics that they want to study about the business. Analytics team members are going to build out the logic to generate those metrics. IT is going to have to maintain the enterprise analytic data set structures and processes within the environment where it will be deployed. Only by having all three teams contributing will the maximum benefit from the effort be realized. The next few sections will dig deeper into how the process works.

## What Goes in an Enterprise Analytic Data Set?

Designing an enterprise analytic data set is actually a fairly simple process. The process starts by taking an inventory of all the metrics that are commonly used by all of the analytic professionals. If there are multiple versions of the same metric in use, incorporate them all. For example, perhaps some analytic professionals use total sales, net of discounts and returns, and some use total sales, net only of discounts. Include both versions in the EADS so that total gross sales net of discounts *and* total gross sales net of both returns and discounts are present. There is no need to choose just one! Over time, if more metrics are developed that are of importance, add them. An enterprise analytic data set should always be evolving. An EADS might start with a specific set of metrics today, but more metrics will be added over time.

 **CHOOSE THEM ALL!**

There aren't many situations in life where you are presented with choices and can answer with "I'll take them all!" An enterprise analytic data set is one of those situations. Include every metric definition in use so that all needs are covered. The extra effort to include variations of a metric is trivial. Save the argument about which metrics are better for which uses for another day. You'll be covered no matter who wins that argument!

It is important to understand that the goal of an enterprise analytic data set is not to give analytic professionals 100 percent of the data required for every project. While it will hopefully approach 90 percent, any given project may need some custom metrics that aren't typically required and therefore aren't covered by the EADS. That's okay.

For example, perhaps deep analysis is desired on the top-selling products of the holiday season. An EADS likely contains data only at a product group level. In this case, a handful of specific products are the target of the analysis. Metrics for those products will have to be computed to augment the group-level data already present in the EADS. However, analyzing these individual products isn't a common need, so it doesn't make sense to add the product metrics to the EADS.

If the enterprise analytic data set has 80 to 90 percent of needed metrics sitting there waiting, analytic professionals can focus on the extra 10 to 20 percent that need to be computed and then move on to their analysis. They can also leverage the logic utilized to create the EADS metrics. Over time, however, analytic professionals may see consistent, repetitious patterns in some of the extra metrics they are adding in. If so, then add those metrics to the EADS. There will need to be a governance process to handle adding the new metrics.

## Logical versus Physical Structures

As we've discussed, an enterprise analytic data set is logically one row per entity, with dozens, hundreds, or thousands of metrics. If you are familiar with "old school" flat files, that's basically what we are talking about. Physically, as you can see in Figure 5.8, an EADS may not be stored in a way that matches that logical view.

While it may be logical to view a customer EADS as a customer table with sales, demographics, and direct marketing response information, it could very well be stored differently. The EADS might be

**EADS Logical View:**

Customer ADS Table

| Customer | Total Sales | Total Purchases | Home-owner | Gender | Mail Responder | E-mail Opt In |
|----------|-------------|-----------------|------------|--------|----------------|---------------|

**EADS Potential Physical View:**

Customer Sales

| Customer | Total Sales | Total Purchases |
|----------|-------------|-----------------|

Customer Demographics

| Customer | Home-owner | Gender |
|----------|------------|--------|

Customer Direct Marketing

| Customer | Mail Responder | E-mail Opt In |
|----------|----------------|---------------|

**Figure 5.8** Logical versus Physical View of an EADS

physically stored so there is one table or view that has the sales metrics, one that has the demographic metrics, and one that has the direct marketing metrics.

Users don't have to worry about this. Once the right metrics are defined, the people who manage the database can figure out the ideal way to actually store it. Then, views can be added to provide users with the view they desire based on the physical tables.

## Updating an Enterprise Analytic Data Set

Updating an enterprise analytic data set is one big driver of why there might be physically separate tables. Different types of data such as survey data, sales data, and demographics data can require updating with different frequencies. Maybe sales metrics need to be updated every day. Demographics may be updated quarterly. Survey information may never get updated once it is loaded. If a new survey is done, its data is loaded when the survey happens, but then it isn't touched again.

Based on that, it may be easier to have different types of data in different physical tables so that they can be updated independently. It will save system resources by not having the overhead of a lot of extra metrics in a table when updating only a few. In addition, by having those separate tables or views, it makes it easy for analytic professionals to go and pull the specific types of data that they want. Last, many databases have a limit to how many columns can be in one table. For a large EADS, multiple tables may be required to accommodate column limits if for no other reason.

Note that no matter how an EADS is physically stored, views can be placed on top to pull together different pieces as needed. One view might have just the sales and survey metrics, while another view has just the survey and demographic metrics, and another view has all three. Over time, if a new data source is added, such as social media data or web data, metrics based on it can be added into the enterprise analytic data set as well. An appropriate way to store the new data as well as an updated set of views to leverage the new data can be identified.

## Summary Tables or Views?

One option for an enterprise data set is to have it be a set of summary tables that are updated via a scheduled process. There are benefits to a table-based enterprise analytic data set.

First, you have a true "compute once, use many" scenario. The total system load from analytic professionals is going to be vastly reduced. This is because instead of having each person repetitiously running the same type of process to do big joins and aggregations, it's going to be run one time in batch and then shared.

Another advantage is that most advanced analytics efforts involve a heavy use of historical data. Having slightly out-of-date data isn't going to make a big difference. Perhaps an organization is updating its EADS sales information nightly, or even just weekly. For most advanced analytics projects, that's fine. When many metrics are cumulative, they won't be impacted much either. For example, average market basket size by customer won't change much if a sale from today is missed given that there is a year of other history entering the computation.

A final benefit is that the analytic professionals are going to have very low latency in getting their data. Since the EADS tables are sitting there waiting, the analytic professionals can get right to it. No more waiting for big queries to run. They are going to be able to get straight to their analysis.

There are a few downsides to a table-based EADS. First is that the enterprise analytic data set tables will not be fully up-to-date with the latest data. Second is that they will use disk space on the system, potentially a whole lot of it. Last, an appropriate update schedule for the various components will have to be determined and appropriate processes put in place.

A second option is to make the enterprise analytic data set a series of views that are run on demand. There are several benefits to this approach.

First, the enterprise analytic data sets are always going to be completely fresh and updated. Next, if real-time or near-real-time analysis is important, analytic professionals will be fine since they're always getting the latest data. Last, if any changes are made to the enterprise data set, they will be immediately available. The second the views are updated, anyone who next queries the view will get the updates included.

 **DO WHAT IS NEEDED**

You'll need to decide how frequently to update your enterprise analytic data sets. You'll also need to decide whether to store your EADS as physical tables, logical views, or both. Let the facts guide you to the answer. The requirements gathered should make it clear what direction to go. In most cases, there will be a combination of tables and views.

Downsides to view-based enterprise analytic data sets exist as well. First, the system load won't necessarily be reduced that much. This is because of the fact that even though the analytic professionals are leveraging the same view, it's still going to be running the process each time that someone queries it. However, while the system load won't be reduced a lot, there is still the huge benefit of the consistency and transparency of the computations. Last, analytic professionals will have to wait longer to get their data back since the data will be generated from the detailed data on demand instead of being precomputed.

In many cases, it will make sense to have a combination of both tables and views included in EADS structures. Some of the data may need to be fully up-to-date, while other data can be a bit stale. Do what's appropriate for each specific data source. Deciding whether to use a table or a view should be based on the requirements, performance needs, and space constraints.

Also be sure to look for ways to limit storage when tables are used. Don't store ratios or other similarly derived metrics. Use a view on top of a base table to compute such things. For example, if an EADS has total sales and total transactions, there's no reason to store sales per transaction. Put a view on top that divides sales by number of transactions. It uses virtually no extra system resources to compute that on demand, but will save a lot of space.

## Spread the Wealth!

Once an organization has deployed an enterprise analytic data set, it needs to make maximum use of it. The EADS should not be something utilized only by analytic professionals. There is no reason why business intelligence and reporting environments, as well as their users, can't leverage the EADS structures as well. Why build a lot of logic to compute metrics within a reporting environment if the metrics are already available and waiting in an EADS?

Similarly, any application that would benefit from the contents of an EADS should leverage it. One common example is a CRM tool leveraging a customer EADS to facilitate segmentation efforts. In this case, customer metrics from an EADS are made available to the CRM application. Then, users are able to select customers based on the metrics without computing them within the CRM tool. Another example would be a call center application utilizing a customer EADS to provide customer metrics to call center reps. In this case, when a customer calls, the rep may see a variety of metrics about the customer on the screen. These metrics, such as recent purchases, can help the rep determine how to best handle the call.

The point is that there is a wealth of information compiled within an EADS. It will help eliminate redundant efforts, greatly increase transparency, and improve consistency. It will provide more speed and scalability. Equally important is the fact that an EADS opens up a wide range of information directly to other users and applications that would otherwise not have direct access to it.

## EMBEDDED SCORING

Once an organization has an analytic sandbox set up and has implemented enterprise analytic data sets, it will be able to develop analytic processes and models more quickly and consistently. Analytic processes will also be much more scalable. What's next? How is value driven from the new processes to take the organization to the next level? One way is through embedded scoring processes that enable analytic results to be used.

Embedded scoring involves enabling scoring routines to run in the database so that users can leverage the models built in an effective, scalable fashion. Successfully implementing embedded scoring will include not just deploying each individual scoring routine, but also a process to manage and track the various scoring routines that are deployed. Note that a "score" can be something generated from a predictive model, or it can be any other type of output from an analytic process.

Just to review, analytic processes often result in the outputting of a new piece of information. Examples include a customer's likelihood to purchase a product, the optimal price point for a product, or the expected lift in sales that a specific location will see during a promotion. When the analytics developed are applied with current data, this is called scoring. For example, before determining who to send an e-mail to, the likelihood of each customer to respond is needed based on the most current data available. The process of updating those likelihoods is the scoring process, and it should be as automated and streamlined as possible. Getting scoring processes embedded within a database environment leads to a number of benefits. Let's explore them.

First, scores run in batches will be available on demand. If regularly scheduled batch updates to a set of scores are done, then when a user needs to access a score it will be there waiting. It's also possible to do a batch update only when needed. For example, an organization may update the scores for the customers being added to a mail list only at the time the mail list is created.

Next, embedded scoring enables real-time scoring. This is especially important for situations such as web offers. If someone's on a site now, he must be scored based on what is known about him right now, including what he just did on the site, to get the right offer to him when he browses the next page. Similarly, perhaps someone is on the phone with a call center. As the customer has a conversation with a call center rep, the rep inputs any new information he or she has learned. The inputting of that information might warrant an update to the customer's score so the rep knows the right path to go down next.

Next, embedded scoring will abstract complexity from users. It's very easy for both individual users and applications to ask for a score. The system handles the heavy lifting. As a result, embedded scoring will make scores accessible to less technical people.

A final benefit is having all the models contained in a centralized repository so they are all in one place. If an inventory of models and scores created is kept through a model management process, it is possible to keep track of what has been created more easily. No longer will analytic professionals across an organization keep the scoring processes they create within their specific control. Rather, they will be managed centrally and deployed for wider use.

## Embedded Scoring Integration

Once scoring routines are deployed, the scores generated can be utilized very easily by users and applications. CRM applications, for example, can point to segmentation and propensity scores. All that a user of the CRM application has to do is click in the CRM tool to access the scores. Operational applications can also leverage scores. For example, perhaps a model is predicting probable out of stocks based on sales rates. When a high-risk situation is found, it is necessary to send an alert to a local manager. Or perhaps an airline has models looking at the probability of delays based on the weather. Those scores are updated by flight and are passed to the application used to track and manage those delays. Any user can also directly access the scores via an ad hoc query.

## ANALYTIC RESULTS MUST BE USED TO DRIVE VALUE

In order to benefit from the analytic processes it builds, an organization must use the results. Without making the use of the analytics easy, the organization won't leverage them to the full extent possible. Embedded scoring processes are critical to enabling ease of use, which leads to scores being utilized by a wide range of users and applications.

In Chapter 4, we talked about options for leveraging parallel database systems. Those same methods apply for developing embedded scoring processes.

- SQL, the native language of the database, is one option. This is especially true for models like decision trees, linear regression, or logistic regression. Even to hand code a scoring routine in SQL is fairly simple for such models.

■ User-defined functions make things a little fancier. They truly embed a scoring routine in the database as a native function.

■ Predictive modeling markup language (PMML), as discussed, is a way to build a model in one system and pass information about the model to another system. The information passed enables the receiving system to generate scoring code automatically.

■ Finally, embedded processes allow analytic tools to run in the database directly so that no translation from the analytic tool's language into other languages is necessary at all.

Review Chapter 4 for more information on each of these options. The important thing for our purpose here is that all of the options apply when implementing embedded scoring processes.

## Model and Score Management

There are four primary components required to effectively manage all of the analytic processes an enterprise develops. They can be seen visually in Figure 5.9. The components include analytic data set

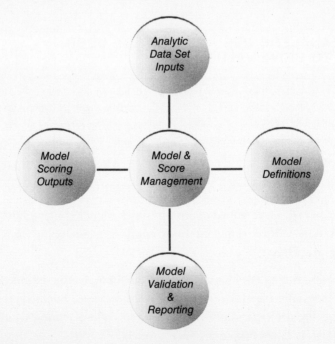

**Figure 5.9** Model and Score Management Components

inputs, model definitions, model validation and reporting, and model scoring output. There are commercially available tools to help with model and score management, or a custom solution can be built to address an organization's specific needs. Let's review what each component is.

### Analytic Data Set Inputs

It is necessary to track the details for each analytic data set or enterprise analytic data set that feeds into an analytics process. What needs to be tracked is a variety of information about the data sets, in addition to the technical facts needed to create and store them. This component of a model and scoring management system will manage information on the analytic data sets themselves. Note that these data sets may be enterprise analytic data sets, custom data sets for the process, or a combination of both. Information tracked includes:

- The name of the SQL script, stored procedure, user-defined function, embedded process, table, or view that will provide the data set to the user.
- The parameters that need to be entered to run the analytic data set process. Users might have to specify a date range or a product filter, for example.
- The output table(s) and/or view(s) that the process will create, along with the metrics they contain.
- The relationship between each analytic data set and the analytic processes that have been created. Any given analytic data set can feed into one or more models or processes. A given model or process might also require more than one analytic data set input.

### Model Definitions

It is necessary to track a variety of information about each model or process. Note that a model in this case can be a true predictive model, or it can be some other analytic process, such as a ranking of customers by sales, that needs to be utilized on a regular basis. A model or process is registered with the model management system at the time it's created. Information tracked includes:

■ The intended usage for the model. What business issue does it address? What are the appropriate business scenarios where it should be used?

■ The history of the model. When was it created? Who created it? What revisions has it gone through?

■ The status of the model. Is it still in development? Is it active and in production? Is it retired?

■ The type of model. What algorithm was utilized? What methods were applied?

■ The scoring function for the model. What is the name of the SQL script, stored procedure, embedded process, or user-defined function that will provide scores back to the user? Note that scoring functions assume that the required analytic data set tables are available.

■ Information on the model input variables. What are the specific variables from the input analytic data set(s) that are used in the model or process? A given model or process might require metrics from just one ADS or it might require metrics from several.

## Model Validation and Reporting

It is typically necessary to have a series of reports that help manage the models and processes over time. These reports can cover a range of topics and purposes. Information tracked includes:

■ Reports that show how a specific run of scores compares to the development baselines.

■ Specific summary statistics or validations, such as a lift or gains chart, that need to be reviewed after every scoring run.

■ Model comparisons or variable distribution summaries.

Report output can be generated automatically when scores are updated or only upon request. Such reports are often used for the critical step of monitoring the performance of a model over time. All models will degrade as time passes and business situations evolve. Reports will help identify when it's time to revisit a model.

**DON'T LOSE CONTROL**

Without a concerted effort to track models and analytic processes, an organization runs the risk of models being used incorrectly due to confusion over what they are, or even models being totally forgotten about. A model and score management system will help ensure this does not happen. It also ensures that if one process is updated, it is easy to identify what other processes will be impacted.

### Model Scoring Output

The final items it is necessary to track are the model scores that are output from the scoring process. These are the actual scores generated for every entity such as customer, location, or product. Information tracked includes:

- What is the score value? Where it is stored? What is the identifier of the customer, product, etc. that the score is for?
- The timestamp marking when a score was created.
- If desired, historical scores, as well as current scores. Some organizations keep historical scores for an extended period; others don't. In your organization, you can decide what makes sense.

## WRAP-UP

The most important lessons to take away from this chapter are:

- Legacy processes for deploying analytical processes and models aren't designed to take advantage of the current state of the world. To tame big data, it is crucial that processes are updated to take full advantage of the scalability available.
- Analytic professionals need permissions beyond those that are typical. An analytic sandbox is a mechanism to give them the freedom they need while allowing IT to keep resources in balance.
- A sandbox is ideal for data exploration, analytic development, and prototyping. It should not be used for ongoing or production processes.

- There are several types of sandbox environments, including internal, external, and hybrid sandboxes. Each can be augmented with a MapReduce environment to help handle big data sources.

- An analytic data set (ADS) is a set of data at the level of analysis. Examples include customer, location, product, and supplier.

- Don't simply migrate traditional, project based ADS approaches to an in-database architecture. Instead, upgrade to a formal enterprise analytic data set (EADS) structure.

- An EADS is a set of predefined tables and views that provides easy access to hundreds or thousands of common metrics needed for analysis.

- An EADS improves performance, removes redundancy, increases transparency, and drives consistency across analytic initiatives.

- Open an EADS to applications and users in general, not just analytic professionals and analytic applications. An EADS has important information and should be shared widely.

- Embedded scoring builds on both the sandbox and EADS structures to provide scoring routines that are easily accessible by users and applications.

- Scoring can be embedded via SQL, user-defined function, embedded process, or PMML.

- Model and score management procedures will need to be in place to truly scale the use of models by an organization.

- The four primary components of a model and score management system are analytic data set inputs, model definitions, model validation and reporting, and model scoring output.

# CHAPTER 6

# The Evolution of Analytic Tools and Methods

I s it possible to build a house using nothing but hand tools and following blueprints from decades ago? Sure. But very few people would want to do that given the modern power tools and updated blueprints available today. Similarly, analytic professionals can continue to build analytic processes using nothing but custom code and traditional methodologies. However, if time is taken to understand the options now available, few would choose to do so. Just as a home can be built with less manual effort and more features than a generation ago, so, too, can analytic processes be.

Analytic professionals have used a range of tools over the years that enabled them to prepare data for analysis, execute analytic algorithms, and assess the results. It's no surprise that the depth and functionality of these tools have increased. In addition to much richer user interfaces, tools now automate or streamline common tasks. As a result, analytic professionals end up with more time to focus on analysis. When combining new tools and methods with the evolved scalability and processes discussed in Chapters 4 and 5, organizations will be well positioned to tame big data.

In this chapter, we'll cover several topics related to how analytic professionals have changed their approaches to building analytic processes to better leverage the advances in tools and scalability available to them. Topics will include ensemble models, commodity models, and text analysis. We'll also cover several ways that the analytic tool space has evolved and how such advances will continue to change how analytics professionals do their jobs. Topics will include the rise of visual point-and-click interfaces, open source tools, and data visualization tools.

## THE EVOLUTION OF ANALYTIC METHODS

Many of the commonly used analytical and modeling approaches have been in use for many years. Some, such as linear regression or decision trees, are effective and relevant, but relatively simplistic to implement. Simplicity was necessary historically, given tight limits on both tool availability and scalability, but today much more is possible.

Until the advent of computers, it really wasn't feasible to run many iterations of a model or to try highly advanced methods. Just as the technologies used to process data have grown massively in scale, so have the tools and techniques used to analyze the data. Today it is possible to run many iterations of many algorithms against large and robust data sets.

Often, analytic professionals will simply do a lot more of the same long-standing methods as a result of today's new scalability. However, many have also started to put into practice new and different methodologies that make better use of the evolved tools, processes, and scalability available to them. Many of these newer methods were defined in theory long ago but simply weren't practical until recently. While methods will continue to evolve, we're going to discuss a few worth considering today. These include ensemble methods, commodity modeling, and analysis of text data.

### Ensemble Methods

Ensemble approaches are fairly straightforward conceptually. Instead of building a single model with a single technique, multiple models are built using multiple techniques. Once the results from all of the models are known, all of the results are combined together to come up with a final answer. The process of combining the various results can be anything from a simple average of each model's predictions to a much more complex formula. It is important to note that ensemble models go beyond picking the best individual performer from a set of models. They actually combine the results of multiple models in order to get to a single, final answer.

The power of ensemble models stems from the fact that different techniques have different strengths and weaknesses. Certain types of customers, for example, may be scored poorly by one technique but very well by another. By combining intelligence from multiple models, a scoring algorithm becomes better in aggregate, if not literally for every individual customer, product, or store location scored.

For example, perhaps linear regression, logistic regression, a decision tree, and a neural network are all created to predict the likelihood of a customer purchasing a given product. The scores from each model would be combined into a final score in an ensemble approach. Often, that combination can beat the individual models at predicting the purchases.

A terrific technical book on ensemble models is *Ensemble Methods in Data Mining* by John Elder and Giovanni Seni.[1] The evolution of analytic tools has enabled the use of ensemble approaches to grow. Without a good way to manage workflow and tie the results of multiple models together, ensemble modeling is a cumbersome process. Imagine having to manually start a process for every one of the methods that will be experimented with. When each process completes, imagine manually combining the output of all those methods to examine how they each turned out. Imagine finally having to manually decide how to combine them. Today, analytic tools will do most or all of the tedious work for you.

 ## THE WISDOM OF CROWDS

Every individual modeling approach will have strengths and weaknesses. By combining various results together, the blended answer can be better than any of the individual models that fed it. This is similar to how many people making a prediction can produce an average answer that is very close to correct. This phenomenon is often called the wisdom of crowds.

One reason ensemble models are gaining traction is that the theory behind them is easy to understand. The wisdom of crowds under the right conditions in everyday life has been discussed widely (see the book *The Wisdom of Crowds* by James Surowiecki[2]). The University of Iowa's Iowa Electronic Market has for years demonstrated that many people making educated guesses will often on average come very, very close to the right answer. In fact, the group average can be closer to the right answer than any of the individuals that contributed to that average.

An ensemble method is putting the same concepts discussed in *The Wisdom of Crowds* to work in analytics. Many models making educated guesses at the relationships being quantified will on average come very, very close to the right answer. Will ensemble modeling solve all of an organization's analytical problems? Of course not. But organizations should add them to the mix of methods utilized.

## Commodity Models

One trend that has been increasing is the use of what might be called commodity models. We'll define a commodity model as one that has been produced rapidly and with less concern for squeezing out every ounce of lift or predictive power. Commodity models might be done via a simple stepwise analysis procedure, for example, on a mostly automated basis. The goal of a commodity model is not to get the best model, but to quickly get a model that will lead to a better result than if there had been no model at all.

Used appropriately, commodity models can be quite useful and can extend the impact of analytics within an organization. Traditionally, building models was a time-intensive task. As a result, it was expensive. Analysts would spend weeks or months just getting data together and then more time running models against the data. This necessitated building models sparingly and only for very high-value problems. If you had a 30- to 40-million piece mailing upcoming, then it was absolutely worth the investment to build a model. If you had an upcoming mailing of 30,000 pieces for a fairly inexpensive product, there was no way it was worth investing in a model.

If analytic professionals are making use of a modern environment including a scalable sandbox, as well as modern processes including enterprise analytic datasets, then building models does not need to be as time-intensive as it used to be. We discussed these topics in Chapters 4 and 5. The more that standard variables are available and processing horsepower can be applied to them, the easier it is to go through the mechanics of building models.

Always remember that making it easier to go through the mechanics doesn't remove the need to be diligent and to make sure the correct mechanics are done. But if a good analytics professional is driving the process, it is possible to get things done much faster.

 ## SOMETIMES "GOOD ENOUGH" REALLY IS!

Commodity models aim to improve over where you'd end up without any model at all. That is a lower bar to cross than most models have historically attempted to clear. A commodity modeling process stops when something good enough is found. Such a process makes a lot of sense for low-value problems or situations where too many models are required to pragmatically make each the best it can be.

In evaluating a commodity model, the primary concern is that there's a benefit being achieved by using it. There may be much room for improvement if more effort was put in. But, if a quick model can help in a situation that otherwise wouldn't have a model, it is utilized.

Let's explore an analogy. If you own a home, there are some improvements where you put in only the best. Renovating a visible room like a kitchen, for example, is one area that often warrants a top-notch job. For some other improvements, you just get the job done. Perhaps when remodeling the guest bathroom you're willing to settle for mediocre materials and fixtures. The guest bathroom just isn't worth a huge investment. Commodity models help in similar situations for a business and have a wide range of uses. Let's explore a few.

### Uses for Commodity Models

Commodity models enable the application of advanced analytics to a much wider breadth of problems and a much wider scale within an organization than is possible via the path of having analytic professionals manually building model after model.

For example, retailers often build "propensity to buy" models for important product categories. It doesn't make sense to have a custom model built for slower-moving, less frequently promoted categories. For a grocery chain, having a propensity model for products like bathroom cleaning supplies and carbonated beverages makes perfect sense. Having models for slower-moving products such as shoe polish or sardines doesn't make sense.

But what happens when there is a need to promote less important items? Perhaps a sardine manufacturer is willing to sponsor a promotion for its sardine products. Some retailers now have models for all of their several hundred product categories. Many of the category models are generated in a commodity model fashion. Those models are simply available for the rare cases when they're needed, and they can add some value in those situations. Important categories like carbonated beverages or bathroom cleaning supplies still get special treatment, and highly customized models will be built for them. However, by using commodity models, at least there's an option for the smaller categories to have some type of model available as well.

Analytic tools today have evolved to more easily enable such models. They've added in capabilities to automatically attempt multiple algorithms, with multiple combinations of metrics, using multiple automated validation techniques. This helps get to a reasonably decent model quickly. Lower-value problems necessitate a change in method. What has to be accepted is that there's nothing wrong with aiming for a good-enough model, instead of the best model, when the business conditions dictate that it makes sense.

Let's look at another application of commodity models in the area of forecasting. Imagine a manufacturer. A manufacturer certainly needs to put a big effort into making sure it has accurate forecasts of demand at high levels such as by quarter, by product, and by country. What if it wanted to forecast demand at every single store or distribution point, for every single week, for every single product? There just won't be enough man-hours to build highly robust custom forecasts. At these lower levels of granularity, a good-enough forecast that can be automated makes sense. If the high-level forecasts are accurate and the low-level forecasts are built to match to those high-level forecasts in aggregate, the manufacturer will be fine. Certainly it will be ahead of where it would have been had it been trying to work without any detailed forecasts at all.

The most important consideration is to make sure that you build a process that will generate good-enough models and not junk. It is necessary to revalidate that a commodity modeling process is working on a regular basis, and people still need to sanity check the results. It is a very bad idea to turn a commodity process loose and let it run rampant without any intervention at all.

## Text Analysis

One of the most rapidly growing methods utilized by organizations today is the analysis of text and other unstructured data sources. A lot of big data falls into these classifications. Text analysis, as the name implies, takes some sort of text as input. This text can be written material like an e-mail, transcribed material such as a medical dictation, or even text that has been scanned from a hard copy and converted to electric form like old courthouse records. The reason text analysis has grown in prominence is because of the wealth of new sources of text data.

In recent years, everything from e-mails, to social media commentary from sites like Facebook and Twitter, to online inquiries, to text messages, to call center conversations is captured in bulk. Making sense of all this text is no easy task. There are issues to address when parsing it, issues to address when identifying context, and issues with defining meaningful patterns. Organizations are starting to have more text and unstructured data available to them than they do traditional, structured data. This type of data cannot be ignored.

Text is a very common type of big data and text analysis tools and methods have come a long way. Today there are tools that will help you parse text into its component words and phrases and then assist in determining the meaning of those words and phrases. Popular commercial text analysis tools include those offered by Attensity, Clarabridge, SAS, and SPSS.

Once the text is parsed into its components, there are methods that will help identify the sentiment or meaning of those components and find trends within them. It is also common to take parsed text and feed summary statistics about it into other models. For example, how many of a given customer's e-mails were positive or negative in tone? How often did a given customer focus on a specific product line in his or her communications? This is essentially creating some structured information out of the raw, unstructured data. This process of parsing and structuring text is often called information extraction.

Note an important theme here. Typically, unstructured data itself isn't analyzed. Rather, unstructured data is processed in a way that applies some sort of structure to it. Then, those structured results are what is analyzed. Think about a television show when detectives are seeking out a criminal. There is a common visual of a fingerprint that is shown. Then, various dots are placed on the fingerprint and connected. Finally, a match is found and they identify the criminal. In this case, the unstructured fingerprint isn't actually matched. What is matched is the structured shape that was created from patterns in the unstructured fingerprint. This is a recurrent theme with the analysis of big, unstructured data sources.

 **ANALYZING UNSTRUCTURED DATA**

Typically, unstructured data itself isn't analyzed. Rather, unstructured data is processed in a way that applies some sort of structure to it. Then, those structured results are what is analyzed. Very few analytical processes analyze and draw inferences directly from data in an unstructured form.

Applying context to the text is no easy task. There are methodologies to do so, but there will always be some art included. The fact is that the same words can mean different things. For example, if I call you a wicked person, I just insulted you. But if I say I just went down a wicked ski slope, I'm actually expressing how awesome the ski slope was. The waters of text analysis can get even muddier since words alone often don't tell the whole story, but also how the words are said. The inflection and tone used can totally change the meaning of a statement.

A terrific example I have seen used many times in the past is in Table 6.1. As each different word within the sentence is stressed, the entire meaning changes. When you see and hear someone speaking, it is easy to know what he or she meant. When you just have the text itself, there is no way to tell using only the statement itself. Sentences that surround a given statement might help identify what the speaker intended, but it gets much more complex to start going to that level of analysis. Nuances like those in Table 6.1 will help keep text analysis a challenging endeavor for some time to come.

Text analysis methods are something that most organizations absolutely must embrace. Text analysis has begun a major move from niche technique to having increasing importance and impact across a wide range of industries and problems. Text analysis is also just one example of the new types of methodologies that have to continue to develop and evolve to handle big data sources that are unstructured.

## Keeping Up with the Expanding Pool of Methods

New methods to address new business problems are continuously popping up. A concerted effort must be made to keep your organization's skills up-to-date and to not let your approaches stagnate. If a new method or approach applies to your business, someone needs to

**Table 6.1** How Emphasis Can Change Meaning

| Varying the Emphasis . . . | . . . Changes the Meaning |
|---|---|
| *I* didn't say Bill's book stinks. | But my buddy Bob did! |
| I **didn't** say Bill's book stinks. | How dare you accuse me of such a thing? |
| I didn't **say** Bill's book stinks. | But I admit that I did write it in an e-mail. |
| I didn't say **Bill's** book stinks. | It's that other guy's book that stinks. |
| I didn't say Bill's **book** stinks. | I said his blog stinks! |
| I didn't say Bill's book **stinks.** | I simply said it wasn't my favorite. |

be on top of it. Let's look at a couple of examples of methods that went from rarely used to ubiquitous. These examples are meant to illustrate how quickly a method that is rare can expand to broad usage.

Collaborative filtering is similar in purpose to an affinity analysis. Like affinity analysis, collaborative filtering is used to identify what a given customer might be interested in, based on what other "similar" customers are interested in. Collaborative filtering is used today by web sites across the globe, and it is a fairly fast, robust way to get a decent recommendation. In fact, the way collaborative filtering is typically implemented is a form of commodity model. A basic approach can be deployed easily and recommendations of reasonable quality can be generated quickly. With the rise of the web, collaborative filtering suddenly became quite common and important. It was not nearly as well known or widely used prior to the last 10 to 15 years.

Page rank is a methodology that underpins everything Google does. It is what Google uses to determine what links are most relevant out of all the possible links that can be provided to users when they execute a search query. Every other major search engine has its own variation on page rank. In fact, most individual web sites today have a version of this approach incorporated into their site to help whenever you ask for a search within the site. These techniques were developed very recently and weren't even really relevant until the Internet age.

Most of the general population still has never heard of collaborative filtering or page ranking methods. A generation ago, most people would never have been exposed to either in their entire life. In the last few years however, they've become ubiquitous. Millions of people interact with such analytics every day, whether they realize it or not, as they navigate the web. While many people haven't heard of the techniques, they use them all the time unknowingly. In the coming years, other methods that are currently obscure will explode in use. Every organization needs to ensure it has people on the lookout for what the next big methods are so that it can make use of them. This can be done by attending analytics conferences; reading analytics journals, articles, and blogs; or even good old-fashioned networking with analytic professionals from other companies.

## THE EVOLUTION OF ANALYTIC TOOLS

When I first started doing analytics in the late 1980s, user-friendly wasn't how I would describe the tools or systems available. All analytics work was done against a mainframe. Not only was there no choice but to directly program code to do analytics, but it was also necessary to use the dreaded job control language (JCL). Anyone reading this who has ever had to use JCL understands the pain!

As server and PC packages became common, they initially were mostly the same old coding interfaces migrated to new platforms. Graphics and output in those days were highly rudimentary. Initially, graphs were literally generated by printing text characters to make bar charts and using dashes to make grids. Output was more or less nothing but a lot of text summarizing what happened.

Over time, additional graphical interfaces were developed that enabled users to do a lot through point-and-click environments, rather than coding. Virtually all commercially available analytic tools had such interfaces available by the late 1990s. User interfaces have since improved to include more robust graphics, visual workflow diagrams, and applications focused on specific point solutions. Workflow diagrams are one of the nicest new features because they allow analytic professionals to have individual steps in a process laid out in a visual map where the tasks are all connected. It makes it easy to track the steps in a process visually.

As tools continue to evolve, so has their scope. There are now tools to manage deployment of analysis, to manage and administer the analytic servers and software that analytic professionals utilize, and to convert code from one language to another. There are also a number of commercial analytics packages available today. While the market leaders are SAS and SPSS, many other analytic software tools are also available. Many are niche tools that address certain specific areas. In addition, there are now open source analytic tools as well. We'll address all of this as we proceed.

## The Rise of Graphical User Interfaces

As we've discussed, before the mid- to late-1990s, the only option for doing statistical analysis was to write code. Many people, especially "old school" analysts, still like to write code. However, user interfaces are becoming more of the norm, and analytic professionals no longer have to be knee-deep in code in order to be effective. The graphical user interfaces available today help generate a lot of code "under the hood" on users' behalf.

There is often heated debate as to whether "real" men or "real" women use graphical interfaces or whether they only write code. In fact, nobody should have any issue using a graphical user interface as long as that interface is robust and allows analytic process development at a pace that equals or exceeds hand coding. Real analytic professionals do whatever is best to get a job done as accurately and efficiently as possible. In addition, software packages today offer robust solutions that not only generate code quickly, but can help guide users through a predefined process aimed at solving specific problems.

An additional benefit of a user interface is that if code is being automatically generated, it will be bug-free and optimized. This is distinct from hand coding, where typos are common, debugging is par for the course, and a piece of code's level of performance optimization is totally variable based on who wrote it. Early versions of analytical user interfaces were quite cumbersome, and it was literally faster to write code than to use the interface if you knew how to code well. This has really changed as newer user interfaces effectively automate the generation of a lot of mundane code on a user's behalf. This allows more focus on the analysis itself and the methodologies required and less on brute force coding.

 ## DON'T BE AN OLD FOGEY

Many user interfaces today can truly accelerate the generation of code while ensuring it is bug-free and optimized. All analytic professionals should give today's interfaces a chance. The results may be a surprise! This is especially true for those who have been coding for decades and are resistant to anything but direct coding. Tools can help analytic professionals be more efficient while freeing up time to focus on analysis methods instead of writing code.

One big risk with user interfaces overlaps with one of their key strengths: They make it easy to generate code. That sounds great, but the ability to generate code quickly also makes it easy to generate bad code quickly. This is something we'll discuss further when we talk about what makes a great analytic professional in Chapter 8. If a user isn't proficient, he or she can accidentally create code through a user interface that is doing something totally different from what was intended. Without the ability to understand the code generated, a user won't be able to identify such situations, and that can lead to incorrect and inaccurate processes being developed.

Users of a graphical user interface should understand coding and should be able to review the code the tools have generated for them to validate that the code generated is doing what was intended. Often, when working with a user interface, you will click a few options and expect a certain result. However, when you look at the code the tool generated, you realize a different result has been created. Modern user interfaces should be productivity enhancers that help analytic professionals to be more efficient and to spend more time doing analysis and less time coding. The tools should not be a replacement for knowledge, diligence, and effort.

## The Explosion of Point Solutions

A trend that has accelerated in the past decade is the availability of analytic point solutions. Analytic point solutions are software packages that address a very specific, narrow set of problems. Typically they focus on a set of related business issues, and they often sit on top of analytical tool suites.

Examples of point solutions include price optimization applications, fraud applications, and demand forecasting applications, among others. Point solutions built on tool suites, such as SAS, will utilize some of the generic functionality of the underlying toolset. However, the user interface will be geared specifically to a targeted set of problems. There may be many man-years of development work that go into a point solution. Organizations can consider purchasing one as an alternative to building their own solution. It can save both money and time.

A money-laundering detection application for a financial institution, for example, will have a set of algorithms and business rules that look for suspicious patterns in the movement of money. The interfaces of such a tool will be centered on identifying cases that look suspicious and providing additional information as needed to aid an investigation into the case. Such a tool can help an organization get started quickly without having to build a bunch of processes from scratch.

Analytic point solutions have gained traction as a way to allow specific departments within an organization to utilize higher analytics in their daily business processes. These tools typically require a very high level of knowledge to install, configure, and initially set up the parameters of the analytics to be run. Over time, there's a lower bar for how much knowledge is required for ongoing maintenance and usage of the solution. This opens point solutions to a wider user base. Note that this does not violate the previous point about people not using tools if they don't understand code. Point solutions are built and configured to constrain a user to actions that are appropriate.

Users of analytic point solutions are typically going to be power users, relative to average businesspeople. But, they're not going to be as advanced in their skill sets as analytic professionals. Once the solutions are configured and set up by experts, they enable automation of many tasks so that a power user is able to effectively monitor the tool's output and make sure everything is working okay. The beauty of this approach is it leads to a wider level of adoption of analytics within an organization and an additional level of scale. No organization is ever going to have enough analytic professionals to handle all required analytics in a manual fashion. Analytic point solutions remove some of that burden.

 **GET TO THE POINT (SOLUTION, THAT IS)!**

Analytic point solutions can be a terrific way to address specific business issues. Such tools often enable a wider user base to get involved in the analytics process. Implementing a commercial point solution can also be much faster than building a custom solution. Just be prepared for the sticker shock you may experience when you see the pricing of some of the tools available.

One big downside of point solutions is they can be quite expensive. Some point solutions have been known to cost $10 million or more for an enterprise license. If the financial return is there to justify such an expense, then that's okay. But a typical organization won't be able to fund and absorb the setup time and effort, nor the setup costs, to implement a lot of point solutions at once. Point solutions will more typically be implemented in a serial fashion. As one implementation is completed, another will begin.

Point solutions will certainly be developed in coming years to address common aspects of analyzing big data. Some of those new solutions may be exactly what an organization requires to get started. It is worth exploring the marketplace so that you'll be aware of what is out there as you plan your efforts.

## The History of Open Source

Open-source software packages have been around for some time. Open-source packages are available to the public for free via download. In addition, the actual source code is also available so that users can customize and add on to the software as desired.

There are examples of widely adopted and highly successful open-source applications. Firefox, the web browser, is one example. Other examples are the Linux operating system, and Apache web server software. The rise of the Internet drove a lot of open-source activity, as the prior examples illustrate. Given all the innovation that has occurred in the Internet space, it is natural that there would be a lot of open-source innovation along with it.

There seem to be open-source packages for just about anything these days. There are open-source databases, open-source business intelligence and reporting tools, open-source data integration tools, open source office productivity suites, and so forth. There are a few cases, such as Linux and Apache, where an open-source toolset has become a fully accepted option, if not a leader, within the space that it plays. In many more cases, open-source products are outside the mainstream and primarily fill specific niches. Office productivity tools would be an example of this scenario. In general, large and/or well-established corporations have been slower to widely adopt open-source tools than startups or academic environments.

One compelling feature of open-source tools is the fact that thousands of individuals are contributing to improving the functionality of that tool. If a bug is found, it can be patched fairly quickly by a motivated pool of developers working in their spare time. Major open-source projects have a formal organization that supports them. In some cases those organizations will be completely volunteer-based. In other cases, there will be full-time employees working for a non-profit established to manage the open-source project. Through donations, the nonprofit is able to fund some salaries, but the goal isn't to make money from the software itself. The goal is simply to make enough money through donations to pay a few people to make sure the open-source project is managed effectively. Open source is certainly going to continue having impacts over time, including in the field of analytics. This brings us to the R project.

## The R Project for Statistical Computing

Open-source has come to the world of advanced analytics in the form of the R Project for Statistical Computing, also known simply as "R." R is a free, open-source analytics package that competes directly with, as well as complements, commercial analytic tools. R is a descendent from the original "S." S was an early language for statistical analysis that was developed decades ago. The name R appears to be derived both due to the software being an update to S and also because the original authors names (Robert Gentleman and Ross Ihaka) began with R.[3]

R has picked up a lot of steam and is now used by a large number of analytic professionals. This is especially true in the academic and research environments. Within a corporate environment today, if there's a large team of analytics talent, it's often the case that at least a few members of the team are using R in some way.

Commercial tools are still far more prominent, but R is growing in influence. While R is making huge gains in the number of users it has, as of today it isn't as deeply entrenched in large enterprises as it is in places like academia. It tends to be used for research and development activities rather than large-scale, critical production analytic processes. That could change over time, but that's where things stand as this is written.

R does have a wide range of capabilities. It is more object-oriented than many other analytics tool sets. It can be linked with common programming platforms like C++ and Java, which makes it possible to embed R within applications. In fact, commercial analytic tools have even enabled R to be executed within their toolsets. That's a compelling feature. Details on such topics are beyond the scope of this book.

Perhaps the biggest advantage of R is that as soon as a new modeling or analysis approach is developed, someone will get it into R. R will have new functionality much faster than commercial tools, and this makes perfect sense once you think about it. A commercial tool vendor isn't going to bother to integrate a new algorithm until that algorithm has been proven to have a market demand. Then they'll have to get it added into their release schedule, code it, and put in a future release. That can take years in total. With R, as soon as a few people think an algorithm is worthwhile, they'll go and code it.

 **ARE YOU USING R?**

R is an up-and-coming open-source analytics toolset. It has made a lot of progress in recent years and has become widely used. R has its advantages and disadvantages, and it won't be appropriate for every organization or every problem within an organization. But, it very well could have a role in yours.

The fact that R is free is also a positive to many people. However, as with any other open-source projects, there are companies that offer proprietary add-ons and/or services for a fee. These companies can help you implement R, help you develop processes in R, and in some cases they have add-ons that enhance the functionality of the underlying open-source package. One negative aspect of the software being free is that support isn't available as it would be with a commercial tool. You are more or less on your own to find answers. While there is a large community to reach out to for answers, there is no single, accountable person or team to put on the spot.

One of the big downsides of R is that programming is a fairly intensive process. While there are some graphical interfaces that sit on top of R, many users today still primarily write code. Plus, R interfaces are much less mature than the similar interfaces for commercial tools. Of course, this may change over time as R matures.

Perhaps the biggest disadvantage of R is its scalability. There have been some improvements made recently, but R still isn't able to scale to the level of other commercial tools and databases. The base R software runs in memory as opposed to running against files. This means it can only handle data sets the size of the memory available on a machine. The amount of memory in even a very expensive machine is far less than required for handling enterprise-level data sets, let alone big data. If a large organization wants to tame big data, R can be a piece of the solution, but it won't realistically be the only piece of the solution based on where it sits today.

More and more tools are developing connectors to R, including commercial analytic software packages. Will it become a leader like Apache or Linux? Or will it remain a niche product like open source office productivity suites? Only time will tell how much of a player R will become in the advanced analytics space.

## The History of Data Visualization

The visualization of data is as old as data itself. Recently it's become an entire industry. People such as Edward Tufte make their livings discussing, researching, and evaluating visualization techniques. Tufte has written multiple books, including the classic *A Visual Display of Quantitative Information*.[4]

Charles Joseph Menard's depiction of how Napoleon's troops were decimated on their march to Moscow in 1812 is considered one of the best visualizations of all time.[5] If you take a look at his picture by following the link in the endnote, you can clearly imagine what those troops went through.

In the world of analytics, visualization refers to charts, graphs, and tables that display data. Until the age of computers, graphs were drawn by hand. Computers revolutionized the methods and ease of creating visualizations. I recall my first color printer. It was for my Radio Shack Color Computer. It literally had small, colored, ballpoint pens that would move and draw on a piece of paper that looked like a wide receipt tape. I could create some very basic, low-resolution bar charts but not much more.

Early analytic software was actually quite ingenious in the way it used keyboard characters to create graphics that perhaps weren't beautiful, but did manage to get the point across very well. Each bar in a bar chart might be made up of rows of Xs, as in Figure 6.1. A pie chart might be made up of periods, commas, and dashes. A table would be framed with dashes ("-") and pipe ("|") characters.

By the time desktop office productivity applications became ubiquitous, almost anyone could make a nice, colorful chart or graph complete with labels, legends, and axes. Analytic tools also upgraded their graphics capabilities to move far beyond text-based charts.

Until recently, however, most visualizations were static. A chart created in a desktop presentation or spreadsheet tool was static until it was updated. Typically, updating was done in a manual fashion. Today there are visualization tools that allow interaction

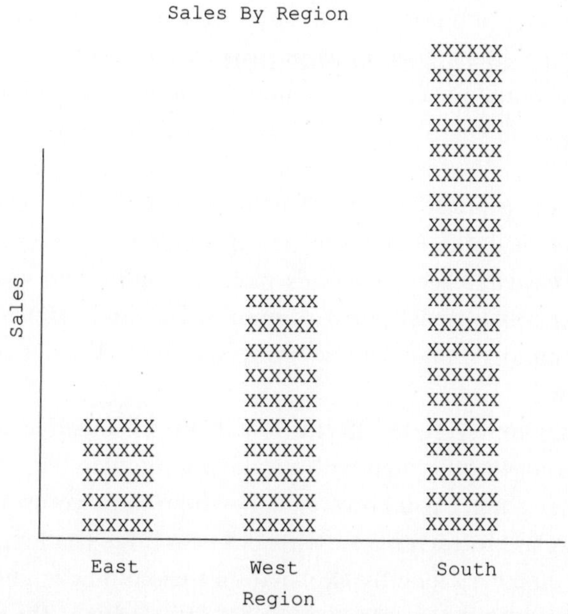

```
                       Sales By Region
                                        XXXXXX
                                        XXXXXX
                                        XXXXXX
                                        XXXXXX
                                        XXXXXX
                  |                     XXXXXX
                  |                     XXXXXX
                  |                     XXXXXX
                  |                     XXXXXX
                  |                     XXXXXX
      s           |          XXXXXX     XXXXXX
      e           |          XXXXXX     XXXXXX
      l           |          XXXXXX     XXXXXX
      a           |          XXXXXX     XXXXXX
      S           |          XXXXXX     XXXXXX
                  |  XXXXXX  XXXXXX     XXXXXX
                  |  XXXXXX  XXXXXX     XXXXXX
                  |  XXXXXX  XXXXXX     XXXXXX
                  |  XXXXXX  XXXXXX     XXXXXX
                  |  XXXXXX  XXXXXX     XXXXXX
                  |_____

                     East      West      South
                              Region
```

**Figure 6.1** Early, Rudimentary Bar Chart Style

with graphics to explore and analyze data in new and powerful ways. Let's explore them.

## Modern Visualization Tools

Visualization tools have evolved so far that many people don't realize the capabilities that exist. Tools like Tableau, JMP, Advizor, and Spot-fire help analytic professionals and business users move beyond graphics that simply illustrate a story that has already been developed. Visualization tools enable the analytic professional or business user to develop a new story in an interactive, visual paradigm.

Today's visualization tools allow multiple tabs of graphs and charts to be linked to the underlying data. Even more important, the tabs, graphs, and charts can be linked to each other. If a user clicks on the bar for the Northeast region, all the other graphs will instantaneously adjust and show only Northeast data as well.

These new tools might be thought of as presentation and spread-sheet software "on steroids." Not only do some visualization tools have the equivalent pivoting and data manipulation capabilities that a spreadsheet program might have, but they also have the charting and graphing capabilities that rival or exceed those of a presentation program. Now add the ability to connect to large databases, intertwine the visuals, and explore and drill down at will. It results in something powerful.

The whole premise of data visualization is that it's very hard for humans to look at large tables or sets of numbers and identify trends. It's far, far easier to see the trends with an appropriate visual. Some visualizations, like social network graphs, transmit information that would be almost impossible to understand or describe without a visualization.

Just imagine trying to effectively explain to someone how countries are arranged on a map without having the map itself as a guide. Once you see a map, you know exactly where those countries are and how they relate to each other. It would be a huge challenge to come up with even a very lengthy explanation that could even begin to get across the same amount of information and clarity as the visual of a map does.

**DON'T SAY IT; SHOW IT**

Human brains are wired to be very sophisticated in interpreting visual input. An effective visualization can quite literally make a pattern or trend jump right off the page at you. Looking at traditional spreadsheets or reports, it can be quite difficult to see what you're looking for and easy to miss important trends. A picture in the form of an effective data visualization really can say more than a thousand words.

A new idea not yet available in a commercial tool is the idea of immersive intelligence.[6] The concept of immersive intelligence is to borrow the graphics capability behind 3-D, immersive online worlds such as Second Life, and sophisticated visual tools like those used in genetic research. These technologies are then used to provide a robust, interactive view of data. Are there ways to navigate through data in an interactive, 3-D environment to gain new insights? Time will tell.

Visualizations can literally enable insights that are not otherwise possible to discern. Analytic professionals now use these tools to help develop analysis and explore data. Some analytic professionals now also use visualization tools exclusively for their graphics and presentations. They find the tools to be faster and more robust than traditional charting tools. Plus, if someone asks a question during a presentation, they are able to drill down and get the answer while they're presenting. They won't have to do the usual approach of promising they'll generate a new chart and send it out in the morning. Any organization looking to tame big data is going to need to consider adding visualization tools to their toolbox.

## Why Visualization Is Important to Advanced Analytics

In Chapter 8, we're going to discuss in detail how important the communication and delivery of results is to the success of an analysis. An analytic professional will routinely need to explain complex analytical results to non-technical businesspeople. Anything that can help that to be done more effectively is a good thing. Data visualization falls into this category.

Why go into all the details of logistic regression if there is no need to? Including all the parameter estimates, decile statistics, and model assessment statistics is overkill if a simple gains or lift chart will tell a business sponsor everything he or she really needs to know. The details will be needed as backup, but business sponsors shouldn't be worrying about technical details. They trust their analytic professionals to take care of those.

Not many people would rather see a long list of business rules than a visual depiction of a decision tree model. What if a casino or retailer wants to understand what parts of a casino floor or retail store are busiest? One option is to create a bunch of spreadsheets, lay them out on a table, and try to figure out the patterns in your head. Alternatively, you can simply produce a heat map of the casino or store floor plan where color represents the level of activity. The answer will then be instantly obvious.

 **IMPACTFUL, NOT PRETTY**

It is important to focus on visualizations with impact that make a point easier to see and comprehend. Too many people get caught up in using flashy graphics just because they can. Simple is best. Only get fancy or complex when there is a specific need.

Note that graphics for graphics' sake are not what we're talking about here. Many people routinely overuse or over-complicate graphics just because they are easy to generate. A fancy looking 3-D bar chart doesn't add any analytical value over a 2-D bar chart and can actually be harder to read and interpret. The focus should be on effective, impactful visualizations that help illustrate a point more clearly than can otherwise be done. A pretty graphic that serves no point can detract from a message and cause confusion.

Sometimes a simple table will be all that is needed. There are other cases, however, where an appropriate visualization will increase an audience's comprehension of the point being made by orders of magnitude. Think back to our example of a map. Understanding how to visualize data and results effectively will help analytic professionals become better, more effective, and more successful at their jobs. The impact of visualization tools is only starting. Such tools are going to be used more and more in the future both in doing an analysis and in communicating the results.

 **NEW DATA WILL TRUMP NEW TOOLS AND METHODS EVERY TIME**

New data inputs will impact a model more than a new tool or method. Adding new data to a traditional process will increase lift more than applying new tools and methods to the same old data. This is why it is important to pursue big data and not simply upgrade how you handle what you have.

As a final note, this chapter has focused on advances in tools and methods. In the end, the availability of new data will have bigger impacts on the quality and power of analytics than the tools and methods themselves. For example, having detailed web data on customers when it wasn't previously available will increase the quality and power of a propensity model far more than advancement in a logistic regression or ensemble procedure used to build the model. Tool advances help to get the most out of new data sources, but the data itself is the bigger driver of value. This is why it is critical for organizations to pursue the capture and use of the big data sources available to them.

## WRAP-UP

The most important lessons to take away from this chapter are:

- Ensemble methods leverage the concept of the wisdom of the crowd. Combining estimates from many approaches can lead to a better answer than the individual approaches alone.
- Commodity models aim for a good-enough model quickly and in a mostly automated fashion. Squeezing out every last ounce of power isn't a concern.
- Commodity models allow the expansion of modeling to lower-value problems, as well as problems where too many models are needed to manually intervene on them all.
- Text analysis has become a very important topic in the era of big data, and methods for addressing text data are advancing rapidly and being applied widely.

■ A huge challenge in text analysis is the fact that words alone don't tell the entire story. Emphasis, tone, and inflection all come into play yet are not captured in text.

■ User interfaces have evolved to include robust graphics, visual workflow diagrams, and focused point solutions.

■ User interfaces should be used as productivity enhancers for analytic professionals who know what they are doing and can ensure that the tools are doing what is expected "under the hood." It is easy to do things wrong with a friendly interface.

■ Analytic point solutions focus on only a narrow area of analytics, such as fraud or pricing, but go very deep within that area. Such tools have been growing in influence.

■ R is an open-source analytic tool that has experienced increased adoption in recent years. An advantage of R is the speed with which new algorithms are added to the software. A disadvantage of R is its current lack of enterprise-level scalability.

■ It is far easier to see a pattern than it is to explain it or pull it out of a bunch of spreadsheet data. Modern visualization tools allow database connections, intertwined and interactive graphics, and more visualization options than traditional charting tools.

■ Data visualization is not about fancy looking graphics. It is about displaying data in a way that allows greater comprehension of the point being made.

## NOTES

1. Giovanni Seni and John Elder, *Ensemble Methods in Data Mining: Improving Accuracy through Combining Predictions* (Morgan and Claypool Publishers, 2010).

2. James Surowiecki, *The Wisdom of Crowds* (Anchor Books, 2005).

3. The Comprehensive R Network (CRAN), http://cran.r-project.org/doc/FAQ/R-FAQ.html#Why-is-R-named-R_003f.

4. Edward R. Tufte, www.edwardtufte.com/tufte/books_vdqi.

5. Edward T. Tufte, www.edwardtufte.com/tufte/minard.

6. Immersive Intelligence Colleagues, http://im-tel.org/.

# PART THREE

# Taming Big Data: The People and Approaches

# CHAPTER 7

# What Makes a Great Analysis?

Computing statistics, writing a report, and applying a modeling algorithm are each only one step of many required for generating a great analysis. There is no "easy" button that lets you take one simple step and get a solid result. Not understanding and focusing on what is required to do an analysis right can cause a lot of pain, lead to wrong decisions, and generate enormous levels of extra work.

This chapter will explore several themes. We'll start by clarifying a few definitions, and then we'll discuss a variety of themes that relate to creating a great analysis. Each theme will contain a lesson in the nuances that separate reporting or statistic generation from analysis, as well as meaningful analysis from useless analysis.

The principles discussed apply broadly and are not specific to big data. However, with big data adding even more complexity to the mix than organizations are used to dealing with, it's more crucial than ever to keep the principles in mind. Your organization won't be able to tame the big data tidal wave by reports alone. Nor will you be able to tame it through substandard analytics.

## ANALYSIS VERSUS REPORTING

Too many organizations mistakenly equate reporting with analysis. That may seem harsh at first glance, so let's clarify what is meant by the statement. Reports are important and can be valuable. Reports used correctly will add value. But reports have their limits, and it is important to understand what they are.

In the end, an organization will need both reporting and analysis to succeed in taming big data, just as both reporting and analysis have been utilized to tame every other data source that's come along in the past. The key is to understand the difference between a report and an analysis. It is also critical to understand how they both fit together. Without that understanding, your organization won't get it right.

 ## THOUGHT IS WHAT CREATES AN ANALYSIS

An analysis can lead to reports, and reports can lead to an analysis. It is even possible to have an analysis based entirely off of reports. For example, you might run 10 reports, line them up on the desk, identify the key things you see in each, and write a summary of what you found and what it means. That's an analysis. It is the thought that a person puts into the business implications of data or statistics that makes an analysis. Data and statistics without any interpretation are useless.

## Reporting

Let's start by defining "reporting." A reporting environment, as we will define it here, is also often called a business intelligence (BI) environment. Such an environment is where users go to select the reports they want to run, get the reports executed, and view the results. The reports may contain tables, graphs, and charts in any combination. The key factors that define a report include:

- A report will provide back to the user the data that was asked for.
- That data will be provided in a standardized, predefined format.
- There is no person involved in generating a report outside of the user who requested the report through his or her reporting interface. (This assumes the report template itself has already been created and deployed.)
- As a result, reports are fairly inflexible.

Let's clarify that last point. Complicated report templates can be created with a variety of prompts and filters. There may be many options in such reports, but within the constraints of those pre-defined options they are fairly inflexible. The average user is not typically able to generate a completely new report or overhaul how the predefined prompts and filters work. The user can simply fill in the prompts and filters that are already in place.

One way that reports are often misused is when having a bunch of reports available is mistaken for having a lot of analysis available. There is a common phenomenon that can be found in many organizations. The person in IT who is in charge of the business intelligence environment will say, "We have a world-class BI environment. We've got 500 reports available that cover every possible aspect of the business that anybody could want. Our businesspeople have everything they need."

At the same time, a business user will say, "I am so frustrated! We spent a year or two building this reporting system and I still don't have what I need." If the businesspeople get in a room with the IT people, the conversation often starts with the businesspeople complaining they don't have what they need. The IT people will tell them they are crazy since there are 500 reports available. It can devolve into an argument of finger pointing and accusation.

The disconnect stems from the fact that buried somewhere within those 500 reports probably is more or less what the business users want. But when they are overwhelmed with 500 reports it's very difficult for them to find what they need. In addition, any two people might want to look at things just a little bit differently. Each business user might want to have one extra metric on a report or to have it organized in a different manner. There may be 500 reports out there, but none of them are exactly what any given businessperson wants.

 **IN REPORTING, SIZE DOESN'T MATTER!**

Many IT organizations focus on building as many reports that cover as many topics as possible. This can be driven by business users who submit requirements that cover anything they may ever possibly want, rather than what they actually need and will use. As a result, huge suites of reports often overwhelm users and they don't get what they need. Focus on providing a more limited set of relevant reports. Don't fall into the trap of assuming whoever has the most reports available wins!

It's far better to produce a handful of reports that are exactly what end users want than it is to create an all-encompassing suite of 500 reports. It isn't the number of reports, but the relevance of the reports, that matters. Too often, the number of reports gets the focus (with more being assumed to be better, of course!) rather than the relevance. As we'll discuss next, even having the perfect mix of reports for every business user still doesn't provide analysis. It simply makes a lot of data available to feed into the analysis process.

There are times where further analysis of a report really isn't required. For example, assume you have a report of sales by product by week and you want to know if your products hit their sales target last week. By running the report, the answer is right in front of you, and no further work or analysis is required to get your answer. This is one way that reports can add a lot of value. They can be configured to answer common questions quickly and simply. If everything looks good, there isn't a need for any further work. If something is seen that doesn't match expectations, then further analysis to determine why will be necessary.

## Analysis

Now that we've defined reporting, let's define analysis. From there, it will be possible to compare and contrast the two. The key points that define an analysis are:

- An analysis provides answers to the questions being asked.
- An analysis process takes any steps needed to get the answers to those questions.
- An analysis is therefore customized to the specific questions being addressed.
- An analysis involves a person who guides the process.
- By its very nature, the analysis process is flexible.

An analysis is really about saying: "I've heard the problem. I'm going to put together what is needed to address the problem." It's an interactive process of a person tackling a problem, finding the data required to get an answer, analyzing that data, and interpreting the results in order to provide a recommendation for action. The differences between analysis and reporting are summarized in Table 7.1.

Interplay between reporting and analysis is common and necessary. In fact, each makes the other more effective. For example, consider a sales manager with a basic sales summary report showing monthly sales by region. It is a very simple report that he looks at every day so he can get a feel for whether or not the business is on track. One day he sees something incredibly unusual that he doesn't understand. As a result, he walks down the hall and alerts the analytics team that there's something weird on the sales summary report. He asks them to dig in and find out what's going on. His request based on that report just spawned an analysis, which is exactly what it should be doing.

On the flip side, consider the analytic professional assigned to investigate that problem. She goes through and identifies what some of the underlying causes are. She comes back and shows the sales manager what she found. The manager may comment that the data she just put together is very, very useful. While she generated it to identify what caused this specific issue today, he'd like to see the same information on an ongoing basis, even if things do look to be on track.

What just happened? Her analysis of a problem today has led to a new standard report. She automates what she did, and it becomes a standard report moving forward.

One thing to keep in mind as your organization attempts to tame big data is that a great analysis can be created by simply piecing

**Table 7.1** Summary of Analysis versus Reporting

| Reporting . . . | Analysis . . . |
| --- | --- |
| Provides data | Provides answers |
| Provides what is asked for | Provides what is needed |
| Is typically standardized | Is typically customized |
| Does not involve a person | Involves a person |
| Is fairly inflexible | Is extremely flexible |

together information you already have in different ways for a new purpose. It's looking at the business in a way that hasn't been done before. As much as analytics professionals love to talk about all the fancy stuff they do, a huge portion of what any of them do isn't that exciting. It is getting the data ready for their analysis and often doing a lot of simplistic computations as a starting point.

 ## THE VALUE OF ANALYSIS IS IN LOOKING AT DATA DIFFERENTLY

The point of analysis is to not make a problem harder than it needs to be. Sometimes a simple analysis will do the trick and provide all the answers needed. Just looking at data differently can often yield powerful insights. If there isn't a need to get fancy, then don't. Instead, be happy a simple solution was found and move on to the next problem.

It often isn't necessary to get too fancy before an answer becomes clear. The value is in doing things in a different way more than doing something fancy. For example, perhaps some anomalies in sales are noted at a retail chain. One solution would be to build a complex predictive model that attempts to determine what drivers went into creating those anomalies. However, a first step might be to look at whether there were any supply-chain issues. Perhaps a shipment was delayed or a major weather event kept customers home. If it is possible to identify such a cause, there is no need to build a fancy model. You've found your explanation via a simple analysis and can stop there.

## ANALYSIS: MAKE IT G.R.E.A.T.!

For analysis to have an impact, it has to be done well. There are a number of factors that need to come together for an analysis to truly add value. What separates a great analysis from a poor analysis? A great analysis will meet the G.R.E.A.T. criteria! Let's briefly cover what those are.

## Guided

A great analysis will be guided by a business need. It won't be an analysis done just because it is interesting or fun. With big data in particular, it is easy to get drawn into a lot of interesting but irrelevant work. A great analysis is one that starts through the identification of a specific business problem. Once underway, the analysis is guided by what is required to solve that problem. Every step of the analysis should be guided by the needs of the problem being addressed.

## Relevant

Clearly, any great analysis has to be relevant to the business. This means more than just choosing an arbitrary business problem. The problem needs to be one that the business feels needs a solution, and it has to be a problem that the business has an ability to address There is no point to figuring out how sensitive different segments of customers are to the price point of a product if the product is being discontinued. It just isn't relevant.

## Explainable

A great analysis will need to be explained effectively to those tasked with acting on it. It is possible to get carried away with formulas, algorithms, and statistics. While technical details may be the proof required behind the scenes that an analysis is valid, the results need to be explained in terms that decision makers can understand and digest. A great analysis will be explainable and easy for them to make use of.

## Actionable

A great analysis will be actionable. It will point to specific steps that can be taken to leverage the results to improve a business. There is no point to an analysis showing that moving a few stores a mile down the road will increase sales if there is no way the company would ever actually move the stores. Without providing the ability to be acted upon, an analysis is just noise.

## Timely

A great analysis will be delivered in a timely fashion so that it is available when decisions need to be made. Having the answer to a question next month doesn't do any good if the decision needs to be made next week. It is possible for an analysis to be great in every aspect, but it just can't be completed in time for the decision it supports. If so, look for another problem to focus effort on. A late analysis isn't great.

## CORE ANALYTICS VERSUS ADVANCED ANALYTICS

This book talks a lot about advanced analytics. This raises the question of how "advanced" analytics are different from other analytics. Let's refer to nonadvanced analytics as core analytics to keep it simple. Core analytics tend to ask simple questions and provide simple answers. A core analytics process is going to investigate what happened, when it happened, and what the impact was.

Let's illustrate with an example. A product manager needs to know how a sales promotion performed last month. Did the company get a lot of new subscribers to sign up as planned? How would a core analysis look into this question? A core analysis might look at how many subscribers signed up. That's what happened. How did the sign-ups occur by day? That's when it happened. How much money did the new subscribers bring in, and how did that compare to the baseline? That's the impact.

Note that all the data for the core analysis in this case can be provided by standardized reports. The analysis itself is the process of examining those reports, making inferences, and suggesting action. In this case, the analysis will consist of looking at the numbers and determining if the goals were met or not. The product manager can then determine whether or not the promotion can be considered to be a success.

The problem is that a core analysis such as this leaves a couple of questions unanswered. Specifically, why did the promotion produce these results, and what can be done about it in the future?

**ADVANCED ANALYTICS GOES DEEPER**

Advanced analytics goes beyond what happened, when it happened, and what the impact was. It also tries to identify what caused it to happen and what can be done about it in the future. Advanced analytics encompasses a range of activities including complex ad hoc SQL, predictive modeling, data mining, forecasting, optimization, and other similar activities.

Advanced analytics goes further than core analytics. Advanced analytics includes everything from complex ad hoc SQL, to forecasting, to data mining, to predictive modeling. One question that often arises is how advanced analytics is different from data mining, forecasting, or predictive modeling. The answer is that everything you would think about when you think of those activities is encompassed within advanced analytics. However, advanced analytics also includes other processes that aren't necessarily algorithm-intensive, such as ad hoc SQL—not basic everyday SQL queries, but highly complex SQL queries that involve combining data sources in complex ways.

The reason activities like advanced SQL are included in the definition is that the main goal of advanced analytics is to quantify the cause of events, predict when they might happen again, and identify how to influence those events in the future. Sometimes it doesn't require a fancy model to get the insights you require to answer those questions.

As an example, imagine a company is doing an initial exploration of customer web activity. An analysis is commissioned to identify if viewing a product on the web increases the likelihood of purchase or not. It will take quite a bit of work to parse the web data and combine it with other customer data since the web data is new. A starting point can be as simple as a correlation analysis. For the first effort, there isn't a need to build a fancier model and process. If a strong correlation is found between browsing and sales, then the company can be comfortable marketing to people who browsed but did not buy. Perhaps later they'll want to quantify the relationship more precisely. But in the short term, they're confident they've found a pattern that they can profit from, so they use it.

Advanced analytics is an important part of an organization's overall analytical strategy. It can help take an organization to the next level. Advanced analytics involves very complex SQL or data manipulation along with modeling, forecasting, data mining, and similar disciplines. While an organization won't have as many people with the skills to do advanced analytics, those people can provide very powerful insights that would not otherwise be possible.

## LISTEN TO YOUR ANALYSIS

No analysis is great unless it is taken seriously. One common trap to be aware of is the trap of "cherry picking" analysis findings. Often there is an executive who has been around for a very long time. He or she is from back in the days when there was no choice but to make decisions based largely on gut feel. That executive's guess is probably usually very good. It's hard to find a high-level person in an organization who isn't pretty good at getting it right with his or her gut. Such executives get where they are because their gut has been good at making the right choices. The goal of analysis isn't to completely replace executives' gut instincts, but to enhance it with facts.

There are many cases where executives like those described in the preceding paragraph are resistant to letting numbers and data tell them what to do. Some executives will request an analysis to see whether the data supports an action being considered. When the analysis comes back and supports the action, the analysis is proudly used to further justify the decision and show that the decision is backed by the data. The analytic professionals who generated it are thanked profusely. That sounds like a terrific outcome, doesn't it?

The problem comes into play when the analysis comes back and suggests that perhaps the executive's plan isn't looking so good. If a company and an executive are committed to analytics and fact-based decisions, it is necessary to heavily reconsider that plan. What sometimes happens, however, is that the results are swept under the table. The recommendation to proceed is made anyway. There is no mention of the analysis when explaining the decision, but there is mention of all the other reasons why the company should proceed.

The preceding example is cherry picking. It's only using analytics when the results serve your purpose. If you're going to use analysis, you've got to use it across the board and consistently. Cherry picking and using the results only when they bolster your case isn't using analytics to make your business any better whatsoever. It's simply doing what you always would have done and using an analysis as extra justification in those cases where it supports you. Since no decisions will actually be changed by the analytics performed, there really is no point to doing the analysis and no benefit from it.

 ## DON'T SUPPORT CHERRY PICKING!

One of the worst abuses of analytics is to cherry pick results. Cherry pickers tout analysis findings when the results serve the purpose at hand. But, they ignore the findings when the results conflict with the original plan. An organization claiming it uses analytics to make decisions when cherry picking is standard practice is dishonest. Nothing will change or improve in such an environment. There will just be a lot of extra time and money spent on analysis efforts that change nothing.

## FRAMING THE PROBLEM CORRECTLY

In order to have a great analysis, it is necessary to ask the right question, gather the right data to address it, and design the right analysis to answer it. Perhaps the most important part of all of the distinctions between a great analysis and something less is framing the problem correctly up front. We need to start at the beginning, before the analysis process begins.

Framing the problem means ensuring that important questions have been asked and critical assumptions have been laid out up front. For example, is the goal of a new initiative to drive more revenue or more profit? The choice made leads to a huge difference in the analysis and actions that follow. Is all the data required available, or is it necessary to collect some more data? Have alternatives been considered in terms of how to design an analysis to address the problem? Without framing the problem, all the rest of the work is junk. It will result in a classic garbage in, garbage out scenario.

Consider the example of a team of consultants building a customer segmentation model for a client. The client had a business-to-business component and a business-to-consumer component. While the consultants were aware that the client had a business-to-business component, it was relatively small and had never been mentioned in any of the meetings leading up to the project.

The client sent the consultants data for the project. The consultants started struggling with the models because there were customers that were very extreme in their behavior. The consultants informed the client that something unusual was going on, as they were seeing very odd patterns that they couldn't explain. The client immediately said, "That's our business-to-business customers." The client acknowledged that only consumers had been discussed, but as it ends up, they provided all the data for both businesses and consumers in the data feed.

## FRAMING IS EVERYTHING

The way you frame your problem and design your analysis are more important than anything done after that. An analysis can't be accurate and useful if the problem is poorly framed and a poor analysis is designed. Place the proper emphasis on the framing and design process to make sure it is done right. Otherwise the result won't be a great analysis.

The inclusion of businesses is an important thing to know to say the least! The consultants had not framed and designed the analysis appropriately to account for the business customers, and those customers were messing up the models. The consultants ended up building the client two models: one for businesses and one for consumers. It was necessary to have the business-to-business customers separated because they had such totally different patterns of behavior. In order to frame the problem correctly, it was necessary to either focus on only one type of customer, or to build a model for each type of customer.

Great analysis starts with framing the problem correctly. This includes assessing the data correctly, developing a solid analysis plan, and taking into account the various technical and practical considerations that are in play. Arguably, framing the problem is the most critical step of an analysis, because if it isn't done right, neither will be anything that follows.

## STATISTICAL SIGNIFICANCE VERSUS BUSINESS IMPORTANCE

Analytic professionals put a lot of focus on statistical significance, and that's not a bad thing. The key is that statistical significance is only part of the story in delivering a great analysis. Statistical significance testing takes a set of assumptions and determines the probability that the results seen would happen if the assumptions are correct.

For example, if it is assumed that a coin is fair, then it will land heads and tails each 50% of the time. With a fair coin, the odds of getting 10 tails in a row are very small. If 10 tails in a row are seen, there are only two possibilities. The first is that a streak of luck that occurs in only one in 1,024 attempts was just witnessed. The second is that the coin isn't really fair after all. A significance test related to a run of 10 tails would say that you can be 99.9 percent or so confident that the coin isn't fair. This is because a fair coin will only yield such a result 0.1 percent of the time. Such a computation is what statistical significance is all about.

It is necessary to differentiate between statistical significance and business importance. They are not the same. Let's examine why.

### Statistical Significance

Statistical significance is used frequently for averages and percentages. It's also used to evaluate the parameter estimates that come out of statistical models. Statistical significance testing can be very, very valuable for helping make sure that data doesn't fool you. It will say from a mathematical perspective whether a difference is large enough to be of merit or not. There are times when differences that appear to be significant will not be and times that differences that appear small will be found significant. A statistical test will make sure the right conclusions are reached.

There is an entire discipline built around testing. A common term in the business world for this discipline is test and learn. Test and learn is really just the basic experimental design concepts taught in statistics classes in college. In a test and learn environment, an experiment is designed so that it is possible to specifically measure the effects of one or more options and identify which of the options is going to work best.

Businesses have to be diligent in making sure they follow the correct approach and don't simply run with the "obvious" answer. One of my favorite examples of something completely counterintuitive is from a problem in graduate school. Take a look at Table 7.2. There are two baseball players who played together for five seasons. What can be seen is that Joe had a higher batting average than Tom in every single one of those five seasons. So a very simple question to ask is: "Who has the higher batting average across those five seasons?" Take a moment, think about it, and lock in your answer.

And the answer is . . . This may surprise you: We don't know who has the best overall batting average! There is not enough information in Table 7.2 to know who had the best batting average across all five seasons. How can that be? If we knew that Joe and Tom had the same number of at bats in each season, then the answer is as simple as it seems. Joe would be the winner. But what if they had different numbers of at bats? What if, in the season when both Joe and Tom had their best average Joe was hurt for a few months and had only a fraction of the at bats as Tom? Similarly, what if Tom was injured in

**Table 7.2** Baseball Batting Averages by Season

| Season | Tom | Joe | Winner |
|--------|------|------|--------|
| 1 | .252 | .255 | Joe |
| 2 | .259 | .266 | Joe |
| 3 | .237 | .241 | Joe |
| 4 | .253 | .255 | Joe |
| 5 | .256 | .257 | Joe |

the season with the lowest averages so Joe had a lot more at bats? It ends up that Tom can have a higher aggregate batting average than Joe even though Tom was beaten in every single season! It's not going to be the most common scenario, but it is absolutely possible.

 ## NEVER TAKE SHORTCUTS

When you are given only part of the story, it is possible to be completely wrong in the conclusions you reach. Never take the easy way out and decide that results are so compelling that it isn't necessary to go through the formality of proving their statistical significance. Always ensure you have all the data you need and do all the tests required against that data before reaching your conclusions.

Without knowing the number of at bats, it isn't possible to say who did better overall. Take a look at Table 7.3 to see an example of how Tom can be the winner across the five-year period in total. The difference between Tom's and Joe's averages are not statistically significant in this case based on a t-test. So instead of what appears to be the obvious answer that Joe beat Tom, we find that Tom actually beat Joe. But it isn't that simple, either. Even though Tom won, the

**Table 7.3** Full Comparison of Batting Averages

| Year | Tom: Avg. | Tom: At Bats | Tom: Hits | Joe: Avg. | Joe: At Bats | Joe: Hits | Winner |
|------|-----------|--------------|-----------|-----------|--------------|-----------|--------|
| 1 | .252 | 123 | 31 | .255 | 341 | 87 | Joe |
| 2 | .259 | 355 | 92 | .266 | 109 | 29 | Joe |
| 3 | .237 | 139 | 33 | .241 | 377 | 91 | Joe |
| 4 | .253 | 304 | 77 | .255 | 294 | 75 | Joe |
| 5 | .256 | 363 | 93 | .257 | 206 | 53 | Joe |
| **Total** | **.254** | **1,284** | **326** | **.252** | **1,327** | **335** | **Tom!!!** * |

* Tom did win, but by an amount that is not statistically significant. From a statistical perspective, Tom and Joe are tied.

margin of victory is not statistically significant. They are tied from a statistical perspective. The answer is more nuanced than it appears.

Most people would see Table 7.2 and not bother giving the question any more thought. They would go with what appeared to be the obvious answer that Joe had a better overall average. Never do that. Always make sure you test and validate.

There is one last point to cover related to statistical significance. Most people start to feel pretty comfortable when they're 95 percent or 99 percent certain that their experiment crossed a given hurdle. The thing to keep in mind is that when you're 95 percent certain you are right, there is still a 5 percent chance you are wrong. That means that one out of every 20 times you do a similar experiment, you can expect to be wrong when you accept the results.

Make sure that the level of certainty tested for matches the level of risk that can be taken comfortably and affordably. For example, if a company would go completely bankrupt with an incorrect decision, then 95 percent certainty doesn't seem so great. Perhaps 99.9 percent or higher would be a better level of certainty to aim for.

Over a large a series of actions, the chances of being wrong at least once begin to get quite large. You have to be ready to absorb those mistakes. Or, you need to set your significance bar very, very high to keep the risk very, very low. Clinical trials for new drugs utilize a very high bar because the impacts of a bad drug are so large, including even death. The bar for deciding if a company should put Image A or Image B at the top of a web page for the rest of the day can be much lower.

## Business Importance

We've covered how statistical significance is meaningful, how it is necessary to be careful to get complete data and do the right tests, and that nobody can ever be 100 percent sure the right decision is being made. The story doesn't end there. The final step is to assess the importance of a statistically significant finding to the business.

Let's assume statistical significance is found in an analysis. There is another layer of equally important, or even more important, questions to ask. There is a statistically significant result, which is terrific. But is it important to the business? How is the business going to use and take action on the statistically significant results? A real effect has been found, but is it large enough to have a meaningful impact?

Always put the results in a business context as part of the final validation process. Maybe it is possible to be 99 percent confident that the lift in response from a given change to an offer is at least 10 percent. That's good. But what if the baseline is a basic offer and the change tested is a bonus offer that costs twice as much? In that case, getting an extra 10 percent of response may not cover the extra costs. The fact that the response rate is significantly higher doesn't actually matter. It still isn't important from a business perspective.

Look beyond significance tests and take into account the bigger picture. What are the costs associated with making the recommended changes? How much additional revenue might be generated over time? Is the new approach consistent with the overall corporate strategy? Are people and man-hours available to make the process changes that will be required? Statistical significance is critically important, but it only matters to the extent that it can be validated to be something that is important from a business perspective.

## A GREAT ANALYSIS PROVIDES VALUE, NOT NOISE

It is crucial to understand the difference between statistical significance and business importance. This is especially true as big data comes of age. Analytic professionals are going to find some really interesting things in big data. As numbers geeks, they may say, "Wow! This is cool!" But it is important to ask whether or not the business will care about it. Part of an analysis is to ask if what has been found just happens to exist, or if it's also relevant and actionable. Otherwise, it is just noise.

## SAMPLES VERSUS POPULATIONS

It used to be that sampling was a necessary and common practice. A huge concern was often whether or not there would be enough sample size for the problem at hand. With big data, having enough data for a sufficient sample is certainly not an issue. Using today's scalable systems, it's often possible to work with an entire population. It is no longer necessary to take a 10 percent sample of customers because that's all that can be handled. There are some areas, such as clinical trials, where small sample sizes can still cause trouble. Those areas are the exceptions rather than the rule today. However, it is still important to consider when sampling should be a part of an analysis plan. When a sampling process is needed, it needs to be done correctly.

The next time you're reading a newspaper, look at the surveys that are invariably contained within it. What you'll see at the bottom of any survey result is a stated margin of error. This is typically in the plus or minus 3 to 5 percent range. You'll also see the size of the random sample used, which is typically in the 800 to 1,200 person range. These margins of error and sample sizes are going to be very consistent regardless of the question, regardless of the topic, and regardless of the size of the population being sampled. All that is needed to be within a few percentage points is around 1,000 responses.

The bigger a sample is made, the tighter the margin of error will be and the higher the certainty that the "real" answer is pretty darn close to what was seen in the sample. Big data can yield sample sizes so large that common summary statistics end up showing high, high levels of statistical significance. These differences can be extremely tiny, and irrelevant from a business perspective.

Perhaps a sample of hundreds of millions of web sessions is explored to study how many people clicked on link A or link B. It very well might be found that 2.5235 percent click A and 2.5237 percent click B. That difference of .0002 percent can be statistically significant if the sample is big enough. However, it is such a small difference that even if it's statistically significant, it doesn't matter. It doesn't meet the business importance or relevance criteria we've discussed. As an old statistical guideline simply states, "A difference is a difference only if it makes a difference."

It used to be that analysts would stress over having enough sample. The concern was that the margin of error of the analysis would be too big with a small sample. When a sample is too small, differences need to be relatively large to be found statistically significant. Many analyses would be effectively pointless under those conditions. These days it is almost necessary to make sure that too big of a sample isn't used. Having too much sample seems an odd concept. But it is a concept to consider.

If there is a specific problem that only requires exploring 200,000 random customers to get the precision needed, processing 20 million just because it is possible is a waste of time and resources. Consider choosing a sample size so that it will start to find a statistically significant difference at the same time the difference becomes important and relevant. If a 1 percent difference must be found to take action, choose a sample size where 1 percent is going to be where statistical significance will start to be found. Using a huge sample may lead to finding differences of small fractions of a percent to be significant. This leads to a lot of extra processing for no practical gain. Ensure there is a large enough sample, but not one that is vastly larger than required. Taming big data will require trimming data down to the essential pieces.

There are times when 100 percent of the data is absolutely needed. One of the most common examples is where it is necessary to find a "Top N" list based on some criterion. For example, it may be necessary to identify the 100 highest-spending customers. By definition, any random customer sample won't have all the top 100 customers, but only a random subset of them. It is necessary to search all the customers to get the full top 100. As before, the problem will dictate if a sample is needed, and what size the sample should be. Make good use of samples when possible.

Another common misconception is that a single sample will work for many different problems. A marketing department may only need a 10 percent sample of customers for their work. So, marketing takes a sample of 10 percent of customers and then gets all of the activity for that 10 percent of customers. This sample won't work for other departments. Why? Let's explore.

 **YOU NEED ALL YOUR DATA!**

As many different samples are pulled for many different problems, you will eventually touch 100 percent of the underlying data. Don't make the shortsighted mistake of throwing away data not needed for a specific problem. Sampling doesn't negate the need to collect and store all of the relevant data that you can. An enterprise data environment is not built from a sample. Samples are pulled from an enterprise data environment!

Consider a telecommunications company. A 10 percent customer sample works great for the customer relationship management (CRM) team. Soon, however, the retail team needs to analyze performance of retail locations. What that group needs is a 10 percent sample of locations and all of the transactions tied to those locations. It's a sample striped a whole different way. They might not have all the information on any given customer, but they'll have every piece of information for a given store. Similarly, a product manager may need a 10 percent sample of all of the transactions that included their product. This sample won't necessarily have all the transactions for any given customer or any given store. All three departments need a different type of sample.

The point is that any given problem may require just a 10 percent sample. But every problem might require a *different* 10 percent sample from the last, as Figure 7.1 shows. Over time, as different samples are pulled for all sorts of different problems, 100 percent of the data will be required at some point. Therefore, all data must be kept and made available, even if never more than 10 percent of it is used at once!

## MAKING INFERENCES VERSUS COMPUTING STATISTICS

This topic is the heart of the difference between analysis and reporting, and between great analysis and poor analysis. Imagine that an analysis

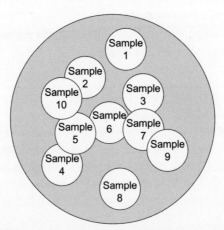

Any given problem may require only a small sample of the data. However, over many samples chosen for many problems all of the data will be needed.

**Figure 7.1** Different Samples Require Different Data

has uncovered statistics that are significant. The analytic professional behind it has also validated that the findings are important and relevant to the business. Now he has to infer what might be done as a result. To produce a great analysis, it is necessary to infer potential actions that can be taken and to provide some guideposts about what can be done as a result of the findings. In addition, if there are actions that the analysis doesn't support, then those too need to be documented.

A great analysis makes the decision process for a decision maker as easy as possible. The decision maker is going to have to make the final call. The important thing is that an analysis summary provides suggestions as a starting point. A great analysis needs to make initial inferences and not just compute statistics. Just as a report isn't an analysis, simply providing statistics or other technical information isn't an analysis, either.

 ## YOU NEED ANALYTIC PROFESSIONALS, NOT REPORTERS!

The job of an analytic professional is to provide analysis and recommendations, not reports, data, and statistics. Just as there is value in reports, there is value in someone who can analyze data and provide the output necessary to address a problem. The big value, however, is added when those results are interpreted and an action plan is generated. That is what turns reports into analysis and reporters into analytic professionals.

It isn't enough to point out that option #1 outperformed option #2 by 10 percent. Given all of the results, what decision should be made? A great analysis will include recommended steps. If option #2 outperformed option #1 by 10 percent, then include the statement that option #2 should be implemented. In a simple case like this, that is pretty obvious. Many analyses will be more complex, however. In those cases, guidance on what action the results imply will be immensely helpful. The decision maker shouldn't need to figure out the options on his or her own. He or she should be given options to accept or reject.

## WRAP-UP

The most important lessons to take away from this chapter are:

- Reporting is not analysis. Generating a report is only the starting point for an analysis. Analysis and reporting both help make the other more effective when used appropriately.

- Analysis is about doing whatever it takes to enable a fact-based decision to address a business issue. Anything from reports to predictive models can play a role in the analysis process.

- A G.R.E.A.T. analysis is Guided by a business problem, Relevant, Explainable, Actionable, and Timely.

- Advanced analytics goes beyond the simple questions of what happened, when it happened, and what the impact was. It also looks into why it happened and what can be done about it.

- One of the worst ways to pursue analytics in an organization is to cherry pick positive results and ignore negative results. Such behaviors negate the purpose and value of analysis.

- The most important part of any analysis happens before it begins. The way the problem is framed up-front can determine the success or failure of the analysis.

- Statistical significance is not the same as business importance! Do not rely exclusively on statistical measures to determine what the important findings of an analysis are.

- Statistical significance tests provide only a probability of being correct. Tie the significance level tested for to the ramifications of the rare cases where the wrong call will be made.

- Even if it is possible to work with an entire population, it may add expense and effort without practical benefit. Sampling is a good strategy in many cases, including with big data.

- A great analysis involves offering inferences and potential actions, not simply reporting statistics and facts.

CHAPTER **8**

# What Makes a Great Analytic Professional?

Before we get into the chapter, you're going to take a little quiz. It's a very simple quiz, so don't stress out. What you need to do is sit back and think for a few minutes about what the most important traits are in a world-class advanced analytics professional. We'll call such a person an analytic professional for our discussion. Think of the kind of person who will be capable of creating the great analysis discussed in Chapter 7 and taming big data. These are the highly skilled, trained professionals who build predictive models, create forecasts, and similar activities, as opposed to those who mainly build complex spreadsheets or reports. Develop a list of the three to five traits that you would consider most important. What are they? Your list can contain anything you think is important. Once you've got your list together, continue reading.

Most of the readers of this book probably got the answer at least partially wrong. The reason for that is that there are some very common assumptions made about what's most important in a great analytic professional, and many of those assumptions are incomplete, if not just plain wrong! This chapter will delve into why this is true, and will discuss the traits that differentiate a great analytic professional from the rest of the pack. First, let's define in more detail what we mean by the term analytic professional.

## WHO IS THE ANALYTIC PROFESSIONAL?

The people who fall under the umbrella of analytic professional go by a variety of names. The most common names used traditionally include those such as analyst, data miner, predictive modeler, and statistician, among others. Recently, the term data scientist has become quite common, especially among those who spend a lot of time analyzing big data and using tools like MapReduce. For our purposes here, we will consider all of these people to be analytic professionals.

The fact of the matter is that there are many more similarities than there are differences in the underlying skill sets of people who use the various preceding titles. On a day-to-day basis, each type of professional is leveraging data to solve a business problem. There may be some different tools or algorithms used by different types of analytic professionals, but a great analytic professional that works in one area should be able to transfer those skills to another if desired. As we'll show in this chapter, the things that differentiate a great analytic professional from the rest of the pack really have nothing to do with the tools, algorithms, or data that he or she typically works with.

Most pointedly, the new community of data scientists isn't too different from the community of traditional analysts. Just as analysts have always focused on finding new and useful ways to leverage data to solve business problems, data scientists are focused on finding new ways to leverage data to solve business problems. The fact that the data scientists tend to use different toolsets, programming languages, and data sets doesn't make their underlying goals and purpose different. The same underlying skills and competencies come into play.

The only thing stopping a great traditional analyst from becoming a great data scientist is some training and study. The same goes in reverse as well. Any great analytic professional will have no problem picking up a new programming language or tool on top of those already used. And, every great analytic professional will jump at the chance to learn about a new data source and how it can be applied.

Those who consider themselves analytic professionals, whether they use the term data scientist, analyst, or something else, should agree with all of the points made in this chapter. Those who interact with these professionals should agree as well. It is important that analytic professionals understand how much more similar they are to each other than some may think. The same traits and behaviors are the hallmark of any great analytic professional.

## THE COMMON MISCONCEPTIONS ABOUT ANALYTIC PROFESSIONALS

Most people asked to produce a list of important traits for analytic professionals will include some sort of specific degree. It is usually assumed that a great analytic professional is going to need a statistics, math, computer science, operations research, or similar degree. Often, it is assumed that success will require a master's or PhD degree. Another area people tend to focus on heavily is programming experience. They'll say that a great analytic professional needs to know how to program in any of a variety of languages that are used for analysis. The logic behind this criterion is that there are tools such people use, and a great analytic professional must be able to use those tools well.

Here's why those two broad areas just mentioned, which are almost universally selected, miss the mark. The fact is that a great analytic professional *will* need a strong base of knowledge in math and statistics. A formal degree? Not necessarily. It is possible to learn on the job and through other means than a formal degree. A great analytic professional will also need programming skills since all the major analytical tools require some level of programming knowledge to use them optimally. However, those programming skills don't guarantee success, either.

The reason these answers aren't correct ties to a phrase used in mathematical proofs: *necessary, but not sufficient*. Having skills in statistics, math, and programming is certainly necessary to be a great analytic professional, but they are not sufficient to make a person a great analytic professional. More is required beyond those basics. Having the base math and programming skills is a given. While those skills are important, they are not the most important factors in distinguishing a great analytic professional from a not-so-great one. They are just the starting point.

If a hiring manager focuses too much on technical skills and academic knowledge, he or she will too often end up with an employee who's focused on those things rather than the big picture of generating a meaningful analysis. It is important that an organization include other criteria in the search for great analytic professionals. After all, nobody needs a "statistics geek" sitting in the corner running fancy algorithms day and night. That won't lead to success.

What is needed is an analytic professional who's going to be part of the team. Who will understand the business problems an organization is trying to solve. Who will understand how to generate the analysis needed to address the organization's business problems effectively. You can't tame big data without some top-notch talent. Let's now discuss some of the criteria to consider when finding that talent.

## EVERY GREAT ANALYTIC PROFESSIONAL IS AN EXCEPTION

One thing that's surprised me over the years is how virtually every great analytic professional that I know is an exception to the rules in some way. I know others in the field who have had the same experience. What does it mean that great analytic professionals tend to be the exceptions? If working from a list of what are commonly considered the prime traits of a great analytic professional, most of the great ones will violate one or more of those traits! Let's start with some discussion on why some traits aren't as important as they seem before we move on to the more important traits.

### Education

There's a gentleman I worked with years ago who is one of the best analytic professionals I've ever known. Let's call him Bart. Bart joined our then-employer before I was hired, so I didn't know what his background was when I started. What I did realize pretty quickly was that this guy really knew his stuff. I could go to him and he could help me with programming questions, he could help me with statistics questions, and he could help me understand the company's business, which I was trying to learn as a new employee. Most important, he could help me understand our clients' businesses.

Over time I found out that he had "only" an undergraduate business degree. Bart didn't have any advanced degrees. He didn't have any formal statistics or math degrees. He had an undergrad business degree along with the associated basic statistics classes that came with it. He also hadn't had any formal training in programming. He had taught himself how to program.

When Bart got on the job, he took some courses and learned the fundamentals he needed to know about statistics from the experienced people he worked with. He also picked up some books. Bart learned how to do the programming he needed to do by jumping in and figuring it out. He turned himself into one of the best analytic professionals I've ever known. But technically, he had none of the formal educational and technical training that would be expected. It didn't matter. He is exactly the kind of person you'd want taming big data for you. Don't focus exclusively on formal education. Focus on whether an analytic professional has learned what is required to do the job.

## Industry Experience

It's very common for companies and hiring managers to worry about what industry an analytic professional, or anyone else, has experience in. If there is an analytic professional in telecom, many assume that there's no way he or she can add value in banking. If the analytic professional is in banking, many assume there's no way he or she can add value in manufacturing. If the analytic professional is in manufacturing, they won't even think about having him or her work in retail.

That's not really fair. Given the choice between two equally qualified candidates, one who knows an industry and one who doesn't, of course it can make sense to take the one who knows the industry. The choice is rarely that clean, however. Consider a choice between two people. One is a mediocre analytic professional who knows an industry in and out. The other is a phenomenal analytic professional in another industry who knows nothing about the industry in question. Take the latter any day. A great analytic professional in one industry can learn about another and become great there, too. A mediocre analytic professional is likely to stay that way. In addition, getting some outside perspectives from another industry can be quite beneficial. Every industry has certain ways of doing things. A team can learn a lot from somebody outside the industry.

 **LOOK OUTSIDE**

Now and then, look outside your industry when hiring an analytic professional. If people are great analytic professionals, they'll pick up your business pretty quickly. They'll also cross-pollinate your team with all of the ideas and approaches they bring from their background. Hiring a person from a competitor who already does exactly what you want him or her to do isn't always a bad thing, but you do need to mix it up over time.

Let's illustrate the pitfalls of an unbending industry requirement through the true story of a gentleman named Mark. Mark had been focused primarily on the banking industry for several decades. Our team was under a resource crunch, and we really needed help on a project at a retail account. One thing that everyone agreed upon was that Mark was a very, very good analytic professional. But could he succeed in a retail project given his banking background?

Great analytic professionals will agree that if someone "gets it" in one industry, he or she can get it in another. He or she may have to change his or her thinking somewhat, learn some new terminology, and compute some different metrics, but he or she can succeed. That's a true statement about many other disciplines as well. Mark was given the opportunity to work on the retail project. He agreed to put in the extra time required to learn about the industry and also agreed to work closely with the retail experts assigned. Even that first project was a success, and within months, Mark was meeting with other retail customers who thought that he had been doing retail for years! This was because Mark "got" the underlying business concepts and was able to translate everything he knew from his past in banking into the retail environment. He was motivated, creative, and smart. That's what really mattered.

## Beware "The List"

A few years ago, my company's human resources (HR) department came to me and said, "We have some new rules, so you need to update the list of required and preferred traits for your job openings. From now on anything you put down as required will be absolutely required." In other words, if the position description says a candidate has to have a bachelor's or better in statistics, it would not be possible to interview or hire anybody that didn't have it.

I thought about it and I sent back to HR my revised list with a long list of preferred attributes. My required attribute list had only one item: a bachelor's degree with no specification of discipline. The only reason a bachelor's degree was listed was to ensure that candidates had some level of higher education. Honestly, the list may have been too harsh even with that single requirement.

HR called and said, "Hey, Bill, did you make a mistake? You've basically got nothing required here. Aren't there some things that are important and that you're going to have to have?" I told them what I just discussed. I said, "Honestly, every person on my team violates at least one or two of the things that I would normally put as required. If I put something as required, and I won't be able to make an exception, then I can't list it. I can't take the risk that I have to pass over a good person because the job description is set in stone. I'd rather have an ambiguous job description and be able to get the right person."

## HIRE KNOWLEDGE AND SKILLS, NOT CHECK BOXES

When hiring analytic professionals, it is fine to start with a laundry list of experiences and education as a starting point. Having some, but not necessarily all, of the boxes checked is a reasonable first pass. But it isn't sufficient. Many aspects of a great analytic professional involve factors that aren't technical in nature at all. In fact, great analytic professionals are distinguished from the pack based less on technical skills than on other factors such as those we'll discuss next.

## THE OFTEN UNDERRATED TRAITS OF A GREAT ANALYTIC PROFESSIONAL

Let's talk about a handful of traits that are absolutely critical in a great analytic professional. While these traits are also valuable for a range of other disciplines, it doesn't negate the importance of them to analytics. Each of the following are of higher importance than any of the traits we've already discussed. While a lower bar exists for maintaining established analytic processes, recruiting and retaining the right talent are paramount when an organization is looking to break new ground and build new analytic processes. A higher bar must be crossed to tame big data and create the new, innovative, business-changing analytic processes that big data enables.

### Commitment

Commitment is a trait that benefits every profession. There are people who will do whatever it takes to hit a deadline or make a project succeed. However, there are people who are willing to put in only so much effort. Within your organization, you can probably identify the people you can count on and those you can't. Any great analytic professional is going to be committed. Luckily, this trait tends to come across in an interview based on how the candidate describes his or her past work and successes. Listen carefully to ensure you pick up on a candidate's level of commitment.

There really isn't much more that needs to be said about commitment. It is universally understood to be important across fields. This includes the field of analytics.

### Creativity

Creativity isn't something that most people consider when thinking about an analytic professional. Most people think that an analytic professional is running statistical formulas that are pretty well defined. He or she is going to go by the book, and there's nothing creative about it. Is that true?

Well, not really. The bottom line is that every business problem is different, and the data available to address each problem is often complex and incomplete. An analytic professional has to figure out how he or she is going to put the data together in new ways to solve the latest problem. That takes a good bit of creativity. There's no book or set of rules that says how to make a lot of those decisions and how to do it correctly.

Additionally, every single time an analytic professional is going through an analysis, he or she is going to hit some unforeseen issues. Sometimes they're minor bumps. Sometimes they're pretty major snags. Those "Oh, @#%$&*!!!" moments pop up and make the analytic professionals realize that they've got a big problem. Creativity is what allows someone to come up with a novel solution to such problems. The problem might be with the data, or it might be that there is an aspect of the business that wasn't understood until getting into the weeds of the analysis. Creativity is how to get around those barriers and still get to an end result that hits the mark.

Don't underestimate the importance of creativity in an analytic professional. It is not the most common of traits among those who will call themselves analytic professionals, either. Creativity is a huge filter. If you talk to 10 people, you'll be lucky if a couple of them even begin to meet the bar for creativity. Some organizations utilize personality tests or have candidates solve seemingly random problems in order to evaluate creativity. One way I like to gauge creativity is to ask candidates about some past analysis "Oh, @#%$&*!!!" moments that they had to overcome. A creative analytic professional will have a good story to tell you. An analytic professional who isn't creative will simply supply a list of steps he or she took to try to overcome the problem.

### Clean Data Is Only in Textbooks

Does the topic of clean data really fit in a section on how creativity helps define a great analytic professional? It does. This is because analytic professionals often have to get quite creative in how they handle data. The fact is that data is never, ever as clean as they want it to be, and it is often not as clean as it really needs to be. The data always has gaps, inconsistencies, and just plain errors. It also almost always violates some of the assumptions being made as part of an analysis plan.

In school, it is wonderful to have data that is accurate, clean, and complete. If there are any data points that don't fit, it is possible to identify why and adjust for them. Everyone in school gets this crazy idea that the textbook examples reflect what they'll come across in the business world. Well, in business, it doesn't work that way. The data is never as nice as it is in class. A gender code will contain something random like an "H" in addition to the expected "M," "F," and "U" (for unknown). A customer will have sales of $10,000,000 at a grocery store. A product will be sold that has a product code that does not exist.

These situations pose a serious problem. Namely, what can be done when the data isn't really what is wanted and needed? Should the customer with unrealistic sales be ignored? Should the "H" be changed to a "U"? Can the correct product code be identified? Figuring out how to make the best of the data an analysis has available is one of the hardest parts of any analytics effort, and it can require quite a bit of creativity. Once an analytic professional finds that the data isn't complete enough to fully answer what was hoped, it is time to get creative in figuring out ways to get the most possible from it. This involves ignoring or correcting some data. It may be necessary to identify some small wins and make them happen quickly, then direct focus to improving those wins.

 ## GO FOR IMPROVEMENT, NOT PERFECTION

You've got to go after business problems with the goal of improving results, not perfection. This is critical. It is easy to get hung up on the fact that with a little more work, a little more lift can be achieved by getting the data a little cleaner. Great analytic professionals focus on improving results and squeezing out what they can from subpar data. Results may not be perfect, but if they enable an improved decision then that is okay.

Analysis of loyalty card data is one area where data is never perfect. Even the best customers don't remember to use their card every time. What this means is that the "complete" picture of each customer's spending really isn't complete at all. However, all is not lost. Really good customers will tend to use their card most of the time. There will still be enough data to understand them. The fact that some data is missing isn't going to ruin the analysis. Sure, some cus-

tomers may be slightly misunderstood based on the partial information, but the data is complete enough to make good decisions. Great
analytic professionals understand this.

### Clean-Enough Data

One important question great analytic professionals ask about data,
no matter how dirty it is or how much it violates assumptions, is
whether or not it is clean enough. Can they get results that they can
believe in? Can they get results using the data that are solid enough
that they can have confidence that real gains are possible? If the
answer is yes, then they go for it. The data doesn't need to be perfect.
It needs to be good enough to get to a decision point. Great analytic
professionals are very good at getting creative in the ways in which
they validate that data is clean enough.

Let's consider a data source that is widely used, but that is full of
error. Household demographic files have been available for decades.
On average, the demographic data providers do a good job of getting
accurate information on households. However, the data on any specific household may be incorrect since there are assumptions that are
made throughout the process of compiling the data. This doesn't stop
the data from being useful. High-level patterns and trends can be
believed, even if specific households within those trends may have
problems. Marketers have used such data to great advantage even
though it isn't perfect. There are creative ways to adjust for known
biases and issues. If the data was ignored due to the errors within it,
a lot of value would be left on the table.

Within a corporate environment, a great analytic professional will
similarly be able to get creative and figure out how to use corporate
data sources to drive value. It is a matter of looking at the data available as a glass half full of value rather than as a glass half empty of
value. This skill is even more valuable when dealing with big data due
to facts discussed in Chapter 1. Big data often isn't clean and often
contains extraneous information that must be filtered out.

## Business Savvy

Great analytic professionals have the ability to understand the business model that they're working within, and how analytics can address

that business's problems. Great analytic professionals are going to be able to focus on what the important metrics and outcomes from the business perspective are, as well as the important metrics from a technical perspective. They're going to take the time and make the effort to achieve that level of understanding. Regardless of a person's innate talents in the area of business savvy, it requires interest and focus to develop it well. If someone doesn't have the interest and desire to understand your business, he or she won't become a great analytic professional for you.

Note that business savvy and industry experience are not the same thing. Industry experience is more a set of facts and knowledge. Business savvy is a softer set of skills. A person who is very business savvy in general will not have trouble picking up a new industry. Great analytic professionals such as Mark, who we discussed earlier, are able to apply their underlying savvy to a wide range of situations and problems. As you interview analytic professionals, probe into why they made the decisions they made during past projects. If they are business savvy, they will mention some practical business considerations along with the technical considerations. Discussion will also include comments on why certain concerns were more or less relevant given the business issues being addressed. An analytic professional without business savvy will focus primarily on the technical requirements and assumptions.

 **AN ODD HYBRID**

Great analytic professionals are an odd hybrid. In some aspects of their job, they need to be as technical as a pure IT person. In others aspects, they need to be as business savvy as a pure businessperson. Straddling both those worlds is difficult, which why it is hard to find really great analytic professionals.

### The Right Level of Granularity

One aspect of business savvy is being able to tie analysis results to the granularity of the decision to be made. What does that mean? Let's say a businessperson comes to an analytic professional to improve a marketing campaign. If a model can be built that will perform 2 percent better than the current approach, it will be a winner. In this case, the analytic professional has been given a bar to cross. He or she needs to be confident that the current results can be beaten by at least 2 percent.

When presenting the results, is he or she going to say that the model beat the baseline performance by 5.32526 percent? Hopefully not. This is particularly true if the margin of error is plus or minus 2 percent. Who cares that the point estimate is 5.32526 percent when the margin of error is plus or minus 2 percent? Going to the level of thousandths of a percent is a distraction. The key is to communicate that results can be improved a little over 5 percent, plus or minus 2 percent. The worst case is somewhere north of 3 percent, so the model is a clear winner given the bar of 2 percent. That's all that the business people need to worry about. A great analytic professional won't confuse the business team with more detail than is needed and adds value. They'll use their business savvy to determine what to provide and how to position it.

One additional example relates to demand forecasts. A few years ago, a vendor was able to prove that its demand forecasts were much more accurate than the competition's. On average, the vendor showed that the organization only needed three extra units on hand, rather than the four extra units that the competition recommended. The project sponsors were pleased, but then threw out a question that brought the excitement down a bit. The sponsors pointed out that they had to order in minimum increments of six units! Given that, how could they address either of the forecasts effectively? When the granularity of action is six units, anything pointing to a finer level of action is useless. An analytic professional who has a high level of business savvy and is focused on framing their problems correctly will identify and account for such a constraint up front.

### Focusing on the Important

Data often violates assumptions. A lot of models require the assumption of a normal distribution, for example. Theoretically, there are big concerns when such assumptions are violated. In practice, however, if there's a strong relationship between two factors, that relationship is typically going to show up in some fashion regardless of what method is used. Does that mean that the parameter estimates and the projections of impact will be identical across various modeling options if the assumptions are badly violated? No. But it does mean that an important factor will usually be found to be important across the various methods even if assumptions are violated. If a high level of granularity is not needed, a rough read can be just fine.

Is it possible to have a scenario with a perfect U-shaped curve that violates the linear relationship assumption so perfectly that a linear regression will say there is no association at all between two variables? Yes, it's possible. The point is that it's not probable, and in most cases the fact that a relationship is present will be identified. If the sponsor of an analysis is looking for a rough read on a yes/no decision, the data and models need to be accurate enough to say yes or no. A great analytic professional knows when to dial up or down the precision of a result based on what is required. See Figure 8.1 for an example of some data that totally violates the assumption of a linear relationship. However, a regression line still captures the essence of the relationship effectively if all that is required is to understand if the two factors tend to vary together.

## Cultural Awareness

The use of offshore resources, typically from a developing country, is a huge trend across industries. For better or worse, it's hit the analytics

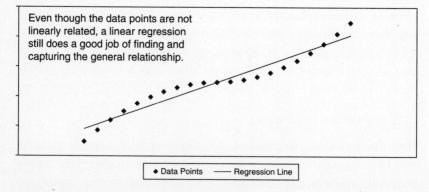

**Figure 8.1** Linear Fit of a Non-Linear Relationship

industry as well. We are not going to cover the political and philo-sophical arguments about whether offshoring is good or bad from an economic or moral perspective. Those arguments are for another day. What we do want to address is whether offshoring, as it's offered today, can meet the needs of business analytics.

Most offshore providers as of this writing focus on technical skill sets, and on providing a technically trained team. They will stress how they've got 25 PhD's in statistics armed with every software package in use today. Just supply them with a problem and they'll crank out an answer. The problem is that we've already discussed how technical skills are only a starting point for a great analytic professional. In addi-tion, it is very hard to be business savvy if you've never even seen the businesses you are analyzing in action.

Skills offshore providers offer can be helpful in assisting to solve well-defined analytical problems. But there are huge pitfalls when relying on offshore resources to supply end-to-end analytics support. Consider the typical situation where there is somebody half a world away, many time zones away, and a language barrier. These issues can be difficult by themselves. Now consider the huge cultural differences the offshore providers have and their lack of experience with how things work in the country they are working with.

Note that the same hazards apply regardless of who is providing the remote support. Americans will have just as much trouble provid-ing meaningful analysis to a business in India that they have never seen as analytic professionals in India will have providing meaningful analysis on an American business they've never seen.

A colleague told me a great story about an organization in the grocery industry that hired offshore resources to do analysis of their pet food category. As we start the story, picture in your head dog food cans and bags, some of which have a picture of a happy dog on the label. The analysis came back, and it was clear from the verbiage in the analysis documentation, as well as the verbal presentation, that the analytic professionals had completely misinterpreted what pet food products were. The results were not about pet food. The results were about—wait for it—canned dog meat! Do you see where this is going yet? The offshore team had interpreted that the smiling dog on the package wasn't happy to get the pet food that was in the can waiting for him. Rather, he was put in that can so we could have him for dinner!

Again, a similar issue could just as easily have arisen if the roles were reversed. It is very hard to have the right level of business savvy when totally unfamiliar with the business and the culture in which the business operates. Can offshore resources help? Yes, if they are used appropriately. Don't toss a business analysis problem over the wall and expect an offshore team with a purely technical background to set the analytic strategy, interpret the results, and spoon-feed you their findings. You need to have some really good, business-savvy analytic professionals guiding the process from your home base if it's going to succeed.

## Presentation and Communication Skills

Presentation and communication skills are critical to many jobs, including analytic professionals. No matter how good an analytic professional is at getting to the right results, if he or she has moved beyond an entry-level job, it will be necessary to not only produce strong analytic results, but also be able to tie the results together in a compelling, succinct story. A great analytic professional is going to be able to engage non-technical people and get them interested and excited about findings in terms that they can understand. He or she will weave an interesting story rather than recite statistics and facts.

An analytic professional can't come into the room talking about collinearity diagnostics, detailed model summary statistics, and other highly technical details to a business audience. He or she needs to come in and say, "Here's what we found, here's why it's important, and here's what you should consider doing as a result." There should also be discussion of exactly how the businesspeople will benefit from taking action. Will sales of their products increase? Will profit margins widen? At the end of the day, businesspeople care about how an analysis will help them, not all the technical points of how it was generated.

The communication of the results needs to be done in a short, to-the-point fashion. There's a large component of written communication skills involved, whether the analytic professional is putting together a slide show or a written document. There's also a large component of verbal communication and presentation skills, whether the analytic professional is doing a formal presentation or simply having an informal discussion in an office.

 **TAKE A TEST DRIVE**

A terrific way to assess the presentation and communication skills of an analytic professional is to require him or her to give a presentation as part of the interview process. You'll see what the person is made of and will be able to tell if you're looking at someone with potential to be a great analytic professional within your organization or not.

Not every analytic professional has to be comfortable getting in front of an auditorium full of people at a conference, or in front of an executive committee meeting. Not in the early stages of a career, at least. But every great analytic professional will need to be able to get in front of project sponsors and/or his or her own management in an office or conference room and walk through his or her results. One terrific way to assess candidates' presentation skills is to require a presentation as part of the interview process. You can either assign them a general topic or allow them to pick something of their choice. You will see them in action and under pressure. Where a candidate's communication skills stand will be clear within a few minutes.

### Results Aren't the Most Important Aspect of Success

This claim may be a surprise. However, the most important factor in determining if a given analytics project will succeed or fail is not the quality of the analytic results. In an ideal world, that would be the case. But, it isn't true in the real world that we live in. First of all, let's make clear that absolutely, positively getting results correct is important. It's crucially important and every analytic professional must ensure that results are accurate every time. At the end of the day, however, from the viewpoint of the people who sponsor analysis projects, the results themselves are at most 50 percent of the criteria that will determine if they view the project a success. So what else could possibly matter so much?

At least 50 percent of the success of a project will be how well an analytic professional is able to put together a presentation and document the results. Is he or she able to position his or her results effectively? Is the analytic professional able to interpret things in a way that makes sense to his or her audience so they will be comfortable taking action? This is something that can't be stressed enough. A great analytic professional can't just focus on the right analytics, however tempting that may be. He or she also has to leave time to focus on the right interpretation, positioning, and selling of the results to the businesspeople who asked for the analysis.

 ## IT'S THE DELIVERY, STUPID!

It takes hard work and practice to develop the ability to distill a lengthy and complex set of results down to digestible sound bites. At times, analytic professionals will feel they are watering things down too much. While it is necessary to have the details and defense of findings available, they shouldn't be brought out until necessary. The business team's eyes will glaze over, they'll tune out, and they won't use the results if discussion goes too deep. A great analytic professional will deliver results in a way that keeps the sponsors engaged and interested.

A business team won't care about the 10 weeks of effort and all the gory details waded through to get to the results. They care about the results. Analytic professionals must get the results across to them effectively, or the results may as well not exist. Again, producing great results is necessary, but not sufficient to have the project viewed as a success. Great analytic professionals understand this and put the appropriate focus on the delivery process.

### A Lesson from the Advertising Industry

Analytic professionals like to measure things. They like to do things in such a way that it can be proven if efforts are working or not. In the direct marketing industry, it's very clean-cut. Analytic professionals run a model and generate a list of people who should be e-mailed, called, or otherwise contacted. On the back end, it can be measured very exactly what the lift was from those efforts. If it worked, more of the same can be done. If it didn't work, the team can stop and try something else.

One of the biggest budgets on a lot of companies' books is mass advertising in the form of TV, radio, newspapers, and so on. Such media do have a role and can have an impact. However, it is nearly impossible to get a highly accurate measure of the impact of such efforts. To assess the impacts of advertising is notoriously tricky. Methodologies that try to estimate market level lift in sales due to market level TV, radio, and print campaigns are dicey at best. Methodologies at a lower level, such as a store level, aren't a lot better. Yet advertising is still pervasive, even when there are other, more measurable options available that budgets could shift to. Why is that?

One reason is because when a direct marketer comes in to talk about building analytics to do better targeted marketing, there's nothing overly sexy or exciting about it. A direct marketing analysis will identify who is statistically most likely to respond, and then an organization targets them to (hopefully!) drive more sales. Sure, the drive-more-sales part gets people's eyes lit up, but there's nothing really exciting about the storyline.

What do ad agencies do when they pitch their plans? They show up with a multimedia presentation. They'll have music. They'll have video. They'll have new catch phrases. They're going to get the audience so pumped up about their plans that they're ready to sign up. Even the fact that it can't be measured cleanly on the back end doesn't matter so much, because the audience has bought into the vision and the excitement of what that ad agency is suggesting they do.

The intention is not to pick on ad agencies (please don't send the nasty letters). Rather, the intent is to compliment them! The point is that advertising is not nearly as measurable as some other activities, yet it has maintained a huge share of expenditures. That is in part because of the advertising industry's ability to make what they do compelling to their sponsors. Advertising agencies fully understand and leverage the power of presentation and communication. An analytic professional who wants to be great can learn some lessons by studying how the ad agencies do things. Imagine how powerful a project can be if highly measurable actions and associated analytics are paired with the excitement level that advertising activities instill in the business community.

## Intuition

Intuition is probably the hardest to define of the traits we'll discuss. It is certainly the hardest to assess in someone until you see him or her in action. For our purposes, intuition is the ability for an analytic professional to somehow just see or feel what needs to be done next. When a barrier is hit, the analytic professional sits and thinks it through. He or she determines that any of paths A, B, C, or D can be taken, given the situation. How well does he or she choose? Does he or she seem to have a great intuitive feel for which of those directions is going to pay off? Can he or she pick an option and be successful most of the time? Or does he or she fumble through stops and starts across various options before finally coming up with a plan? Great analytic professionals have an uncanny ability to pick a good path more often than not.

There's a good book I recommend you consider reading. It is called *A Whole New Mind* by Daniel H. Pink (Riverhead Trade, 2006). It has some very interesting perspectives on the general, ongoing migration from a largely technical focus in terms of what will help people succeed in the world, to having more of a focus on the traits we have been talking about. Pink's book may help drive some of the themes we've discussed home for you on a broader scale.

In many ways, intuition is an inherent skill. But it can also be tuned and groomed. Ultimately, intuition is a blend of a problem-solving approach and experience from having hit similar situations and worked through them in the past. Building on those experiences and approaches, it is necessary to be smart enough to recognize when to apply previous learnings again and when to tweak them to a new situation.

A good intuition is a big factor in determining a great analytic professional, but it is very difficult to assess someone's intuition level during an interview. Some of the criteria that might seem relevant may not pass muster with human resources since they are too subjective and "squishy." Over time, you will be able to identify if an analytic professional has good intuition or not based on his or her performance and handling of problems.

### Art versus Science

One of the primary themes to grasp that has been under the surface of this chapter is that analytics isn't just about science. It is about art, too. A great analysis has a combination of solid science combined with a strong dose of artistry. The artistry in an analysis is figuring out how to deal with unusual problems, how to put together a compelling presentation, and how to best interpret the findings. A great analytic professional must be able to provide both the science and the art components. A great analytic professional isn't just a scientist but an artist as well!

Consider the example of cluster analysis, a common set of algorithms used for segmentation models. There are no simple, widely accepted metrics that identify the right answer. Segmentation modeling is actually pretty artistic. Analytic professionals who do a lot of segmentation models all have their own guidelines for what they look for. For example, I have a process I go through when assessing such models. I know when I'm doing it where I'm heading and what patterns I'm looking for; I'd have a very hard time explaining some of it effectively to someone else, however. Similarly, others have had trouble explaining their methods to me. Everyone has their own twist to how they assess segmentation models, and those twists have a large component of art to them.

If trust is an important factor in the work of an analytic professional being accepted in general, it is even more important when dealing with analytics that involve a large artistic component. When there aren't clear metrics that point to one choice or another, business sponsors will have to trust their analytic professionals' intuition and how they apply the art of analytics. This is a fairly big leap of faith, and one that takes time to build up to. A great analytic professional will build this trust over time and will become a true trusted advisor to his or her business partners.

**ANALYTIC PROFESSIONALS AS ARTISTS**

Just as two different painters can interpret a scene in totally different ways yet both yield very compelling artwork, so can two different people doing an analysis come up with different approaches that are very compelling in different ways. That's the artistry of analytics. Some algorithms leave less room for artistry, but artistry always underlies the decisions on how to best define a problem, design an analysis, and work through the available data to arrive at a solution. Great analytic professional are artists as much as scientists.

A big discussion topic recently in the analytics community has been that of a data scientist role within organizations. As we discussed at the start of the chapter, there isn't a big difference between what a data scientist does, as it's being defined today, and what advanced analytics professionals have always done. There may be a few different tools, such as MapReduce, that a long-time analyst needs to learn to meet the definition of data scientist, but learning new tools isn't anything new to such people. Does a data scientist have some new tools in the toolbox? Yes. Does he or she have a whole new purpose? No.

Equally important to the concept of a data scientist is looking at analytic professionals as data artists. These are the people who are going to dig into corporate data. They're going to create something out of it that helps solve a problem in an elegant and compelling fashion. Just as a painter will convert paints into a painting to hang in a house, data artists are going to convert data into a solution to a business problem.

Great analytic professionals will be artists as much as scientists. It is the combination of those two sets of skills that makes them great more than either alone. If you are skeptical of this claim, ask some great analytic professionals you know about their other skills or hobbies. You'll find surprisingly many also have a very strong talent for music, art, or some other creative discipline that isn't always widely known about them.

## IS ANALYTICS CERTIFICATION NEEDED, OR IS IT NOISE?

There has been a lot discussion recently about developing certification programs for analytic professionals. Such certifications would be similar in concept to how there are certified public accountants (CPAs) or certified financial planners (CFPs). Is there a need for analytic professionals to have a certification program that allows employers to identify who can meet minimum standards?

I've read about and had discussions about some terrific ideas in terms of the kind of programs various organizations are thinking of developing. The challenge is determining exactly what they are going to test. As we've gone through in detail, the things that would be easy to test, such as technical acumen, are just table stakes when it comes to finding a great analytic professional. It isn't too hard to validate if a person knows how to code or can identify the assumptions behind a linear regression. But how do you test creativity? How do you test intuition? How do you test business savvy? How do you test presentation skills? And how do you test those traits in the context of analytics? That is much more difficult.

It's not a bad thing to have analytic professionals demonstrate that they have the skills and motivation to pass a relevant exam. The issue is that any certification that is plausible to develop in terms of cost and validity will largely focus on technical skills. Such an exam may become a table stakes criterion, and at least it will prove that a person has been certified on the technical skills and had enough motivation to go out and get the certification. From there you can figure out if they have the other factors, like creativity, that you really need on top of those technical skills. Used that way, a certification program can be a good thing. Used as a benchmark or standard all by itself, a certification program will likely fall short.

Will a certification program be widely adopted in the analytics community? Certainly if all the various organizations trying to develop such certifications bring something to market, there will be some shakeout until one or two winners emerge. However, no matter how good the exams may come to be, organizations shouldn't hire purely based on a technical certification. Per the earlier conversation about job requirements, organizations may not even want to make it a firm requirement. Having such exams will be of value as long as they are put in context.

In the end, great analytic professionals simply get it. They "get" data. They know how to use it, they know how to organize it, and they can see the patterns in it. Great analytic professionals "get" the business problem. They understand why what a businessperson is asking is important and why it needs to be solved. They understand what constraints exist and how to provide answers that address the needs of those asking. Great analytic professionals "get" how to frame a problem correctly. Is revenue important, or is margin important? What's really the crux of the issue and why? How should the analysis be designed? Last, great analytic professionals "get" that they cannot view themselves simply as scientists. The best in the business are artists as well!

## WRAP-UP

The most important lessons to take away from this chapter are:

- When hiring analytic professionals, consider common technical and educational requirements a starting point, not an end point.
- Consider hiring analytic professionals who have differing industry backgrounds, as there is a lot to learn from what other industries are doing.
- Commitment, creativity, business savvy, presentation skills, and intuition are critically important, and often underrated, traits in great analytic professionals.
- Only a small portion of those with the required technical skills will cross the bar in the previously mentioned less-technical skills.
- Great analytic professionals focus on improving the business, not perfection. It is important to know when results are good enough to enable a decision and then move to the next problem.
- Great analytic professionals tie the level of concern about data's accuracy to the level of granularity of the decision required. Imperfect data can still have enough power to answer a lot of questions effectively.
- Today's offshore analytics offerings focus almost purely on technical skills. Use them only in conjunction with great analytic professionals on staff at home.

■ While getting solid results is important, as least 50 percent of the perceived success or failure of projects will be how analytic professionals present and position their results to non-technical project sponsors.

■ Analytics certifications are under development by a number of organizations. Time will tell if the exams will be widely adopted or not, but certainly they will only be a starting point in assessing a candidate.

■ One fact that surprises many people is that the greatest analytic professionals are data artists as much as they are data scientists. Do not underestimate the importance of artistic talents in a great analytic professional.

# CHAPTER 9

# What Makes a Great Analytics Team?

Many organizations struggle with how to structure analytics teams. Unlike human resources or finance departments, there isn't consistency in where analytic professionals fit in an organization or even the scope of their jobs. As a review, when we discuss analytics in this book, we are referring to things like predictive modeling, data mining, and other advanced analytics work as opposed to reporting and spreadsheet work. When we discuss analytic professionals, we're discussing the people who do such work. Many companies have different analytic professionals working for different parts of the company, where the problems they are addressing, the methods they are using, and even the kind of training they need are vastly different.

With other disciplines it's not always so complicated. Typically, human resources will be a centralized organization. Even if there are people assigned to help recruit for different business units, the definition of a recruiter and the job they're doing is fairly consistent, as are the skills that they need. This isn't as true in analytics. Imagine the difference between the analytics that an operations department needs opposed to what a merchandising department needs. Or how different the focus of a risk management team is opposed to a marketing team.

This raises some questions. How should an organization structure analytics teams? Where do the teams fit in the organization? What will set the organization up for the most success? How much of this must be figured out before getting started? This chapter is going to talk about some of the common challenges that analytics teams face, regardless of where they sit on an organizational chart. Those challenges must be overcome if it is desired to build a great analytics team that will be able to tame big data. Let's dig in!

## ALL INDUSTRIES ARE NOT CREATED EQUAL

Some industries have analytics highly embedded in their decision processes. Some of the best examples of this would be the banking, financial, and logistics industries. Companies in those industries have analytic professionals throughout their organizations. Risk management, for example, is driven by analytics. All the credit card solicitations you get in the mail are driven by analytics. Before a card application hits your mailbox, your data has been exhaustively analyzed, and it has been determined that you are a good risk for the offer in your hand. It's hard to find anything but a small regional bank that doesn't have a strong pool of analytics talent in the organization. Credit solicitations are one area where the power of analytics is so well established that nobody dares to act without analysis. Entire companies have risen to power by being better able to pick out customers who will not default on their credit card debt.

There are other industries where it's very much a mixed bag. In these industries there are some companies that are getting deep into analytics and other companies that have hardly started. Retail and manufacturing would be examples of this. There are some manufacturers that are very sophisticated in their use of analytics. At the same time there are some manufacturers that are household names doing hardly anything beyond spreadsheet-based analysis. How much better could those manufacturers be with even a little more analysis?

**KNOW WHERE YOUR INDUSTRY FALLS**

There's good news and bad news. If you are in an industry that is heavily into analytics, then there will be a lot of analytic professionals with the right experience to recruit. However, your organization will need to push to keep up with the leaders. If you are in an industry that doesn't value analytics, you'll have a chance to establish a lead on the competition. Unfortunately, you won't have as many winning formulas proven by others to follow.

There are nationally known retail chains that send the same mix of clothing sizes to all stores. Have you ever noticed how many stores never have your size, but they have a bunch of sizes you can't wear? Many retailers still haven't even tried to match a store's inventory to local demand. Even if their aggregate purchases are in the right size proportions, there is huge variation by store location based on who lives near and shops in the store. Size profiling is the process of determining the right mix of sizes for each store, typically for clothing, and stocking in that ratio. Some stores may require many more larges and some may require many more smalls. Many retailers have gotten wiser in this area, but many still have not.

Even within a company that is using analytics, it may not be consistent across the organization. A company may be highly sophisticated in certain areas of its business, but not at all in others. Perhaps a telecommunications company is very advanced in the analytics being done for marketing purposes to stop churn (the loss of a customer to a competitor), yet it is very unsophisticated in building models to predict the impact of product pricing.

There are a lot of challenges an organization will face in getting a great analytics team started. If a team already exists, there are challenges as it continues to grow. This is true regardless of where an industry falls along the spectrum. If you are reading this book, I assume that you want to help your organization do more with analytics in general and that you want to help it tame big data as well. If that's the case, then the need for a great analytics team is a given.

## JUST GET STARTED!

It is important not to get frozen in a state of indecision just because it isn't clear where to start. That would be the worst thing as it wastes time, prevents progress, and delays benefits from being realized. If the right people discussed in Chapter 8 are hired, they will help figure out how to best organize themselves to maximize effectiveness within an organization. Get the right people going after the right problems. Achieve that, and making a few tweaks to the organization chart over time is nothing.

A few years back, a company I worked with came to us and wanted to dip its toe into the world of analytics. We built the company its first marketing models. Over time, we also helped revamp the measurement techniques the company used for their promotions and campaigns, among other work. It was a very successful partnership. The company kept hiring us to do more and more over a period of several years.

The analytics we did together helped the company change a number of important things about its business. Staff at the company were able to identify segments of customers that they had been valuing incorrectly and marketing to with messages that weren't appropriate. They fixed that. They were able to agree upon a single view of promotional performance rather than the several views that were used in different parts of the organization. With a unified view, it was far easier to agree on where to invest and what was working. No longer was it finance's word against marketing's word. They were also able to implement a more customer-centric view of their business by adding customer measures to a wide range of operational reports and analyses.

After several years, the client started to ramp up their own team of full-time analytic professionals and made a commitment that over the long term the organization was going to invest in analytics. While we helped them derive their initial benefits and prove their case, they would have derived more benefits at a faster pace if they had committed fully sooner than they did. They were so concerned about where to start that they delayed the process for quite a while and didn't realize all of the benefits they could have.

## THERE'S A TALENT CRUNCH OUT THERE

As your organization builds and grows an analytics team, you're going to find that there are not enough good people. You'll need at least a few great, game-changing analytic professionals like we discussed in Chapter 8 in your organization as it grows, and such people are few and far between. While many fields lack enough good people, this is even more true in the analytics field than in most others. That's in part because of two things. First, the demand for analytic professionals is increasing rapidly. Books, articles, and blogs discussing the rapid increase in demand for analytical talent are everywhere. (Add this book to the list!) Second, the stream of analytical talent out of the educational system has always been fairly small. It is taking time for academic programs to adapt and scale to develop more talent.

Even though the economy is far from ideal as this book is written, it is necessary to compete and win out over other companies for the right talent. It isn't as simple as offering more pay or more benefits than an organization may be used to (although those will be important). It is also necessary to make sure that analytic professionals are given challenging problems and solid support for what they do. Once analytic professionals are on board, regardless of what they're being paid, if they realize that their employer is not serious about analytics and that they are not going to have an impact, then they will leave. Analytic professionals are going to want money just like anybody else, and also just like anyone else, they want to think that what they're doing is appreciated and is going to have an impact, and that they're going to have a chance to increase their skills.

 **BE HUMBLE**

It is easy in a bad economy to assume that everyone is desperate for a job. Analytical talent is in such demand that good analytic professionals are not desperate. If you take analytic professionals for granted and treat them as if they are dispensable, you'll lose them. It may be hard to get a raise approved for a new employee to get him or her in the door in a down economy. If that's what it takes to get the right person, it is a small price and a great investment.

Even in the horrible economic environment of 2009–2011, analytic professionals were able to find a position that has the preceding features. Recruiters routinely post positions and people in the community frequently discuss the jobs they've heard about. Great analytic professionals are in such demand that in one of the worst economies of the past century, they are still hearing about jobs and having recruiters contact them. Your company policy may be one of squeezing salaries and not negotiating in a bad economy. You need to accept the fact, and convince your human resources department as well, that to get the right analytics talent you may have to loosen up a bit. This will be even more true in the next few years until the very small subset of analytic professionals who have experience working with big data and the technologies utilized to analyze big data grows larger. Given how new many big data sources there are and how new some of the tools are that are used to tame them, those who can walk in with experience will be hard to find.

## TEAM STRUCTURES

How should analytical resources be aligned so that the various business units in need of analytical support get what they each need while maintaining some type of enterprise consistency? This question has been addressed by a variety of others, including Tom Davenport and Jeanne Harris.[1] Here, we will summarize the primary structural options, when each is appropriate, and how each works. Note that similar structures apply to other groups within a company as well, but we'll focus on how they apply in the context of analytics. The primary structures fall into the three broad categories of decentralized/functional, centralized, and hybrid. Deciding the best fit for a given organization can be difficult.

Recently, a company in the entertainment industry decided to pursue building a proficiency in analytics. The company had a number of different divisions that were independent operating entities. Since many of the divisions had been acquired, they were purposely kept separate because they each had their own type of work, style, and culture.

One of the divisions decided to delve into predictive analytics. When it came time to get started, a question arose inside the parent organization. The parent organization felt it was a great thing that this division wanted to start using predictive analytics, but there were other divisions that had no interest whatsoever. The question was: Should the parent organization let the division go off and do its thing, and then hope that other divisions would adopt the same approach? Would the method the first division chose to use be the right one for other divisions as well? Alternatively, did the corporate team need to come up with a cohesive plan and let this division be the first to apply it? The other divisions could then use the same "official" processes over time when they were ready.

There is not an easy answer to these questions. It is possible to argue to let the division go and build some successes. The company can then tweak the processes developed if needed for the other divisions. It is also possible to make the argument to get something more universal in place from a corporate perspective from the outset. The right answer is going to depend on an organization's culture and what an organization is comfortable with. The company in this example decided to meet in the middle: It allowed the division to take the lead, but the parent organization stayed involved in the process as well.

## Decentralized/Functional Structures

In a decentralized organization, analytics resources report through a specific functional business unit. An analytics team reports to the group that it supports. In this model, analytic professionals who are doing operational analytics report through the operations team and chief operations officer (COO). Marketing analysts report through the marketing team and the chief marketing officer (CMO). Risk analysts report through the risk management team, and so forth.

The advantage of this of configuration is that analytic professionals are embedded exactly where they need to be. They are immersed day to day with the businesspeople they support and the problems that they need to solve. This is usually the model where organizations start due to the fact that some part of the organization is going to be the first one to take the leap into analytics. As a result, the business unit that leaps first is going to be the first to hire an analytic professional. It is natural that the first hire will report to that unit. This is why it's almost a given that an organization will start with a decentralized, functionally focused model. At first, a decentralized model will be as simple as having one small analytics team reporting to a single business unit.

A downside of a decentralized model is that resources end up spread out across an organization. A lot of employees who have the same type of skills and background aren't part of the same structure. They will have no formal, and possibly no informal, connections at all. Each analytics team is only exposed to the functional unit it is a part of. This isn't an ideal situation over time. There may be no way for one team to borrow people from another in a time of need, for example, even if the other team has excess capacity.

Another potential issue with decentralized teams is a lack of career path. Consider an organization with five business units that each have three or four analytic professionals on staff. Within each of those business units there's not a whole lot of opportunity for those three or four analytic professionals to advance. At most, they can advance to running a team of three to four people. Even that is only possible when the current boss leaves. That is not a very compelling career path.

Across the organization in this example, there are up to 20 analytic professionals. None of them have a lot of career mobility, and most of them have no contact with analytic professionals outside their own group. As a result, decentralization in its pure form may be best as a short- to mid-term solution as an analytics organization gets started. Over the long term, organizations should consider evolving to either a centralized model or to a hybrid model.

This is not to say that there are not some cases where decentralized teams may make sense over even the long run. Within an airline, for example, there may be one analytics team focused on revenue management and another focused on marketing. The types of analysis, tools, and skills required for the two teams are different enough that it can be difficult to combine the teams effectively. If so, that is okay. Just be sure to consider the options periodically to ensure that making a change isn't a good idea.

## Centralized Structures

In a centralized structure of the purest form, there will be one core analytics team located in one spot on the organizational chart. That team supports all of the various business units and their analytic needs. One of the challenges of a centralized team is deciding where it should reside. There are centralized analytics teams reporting to a chief financial officer (CFO). There are centralized analytics teams reporting to a COO. There are centralized analytics teams reporting to a chief information officer (CIO). There just isn't a consistent model for where a centralized analytics team resides, and many organizations do it differently than others.

An advantage of having a centralized team is the ability to reallocate resources as needed. Consider an organization where the operations team has three analytic professionals and the marketing team also has three. Operations is having a slow period and doesn't have as much analysis to do or as much budget to spend as is typical. Marketing, however, is overworked due to some major new initiatives. In a purely decentralized setting, there's no way for members of the operations analytics team to move over and help the marketing department. With a centralized structure it is easy for the person who manages all the analytic professionals to shift them around. The centralized structure helps mitigate the risks of variation in demand over time.

Another big advantage of a centralized structure is that it provides the opportunity for analytic talent to get experience and exposure to multiple parts of the company and multiple types of analysis. Great analytic professionals are going to get bored doing the same stuff for 10 years. But if over those same 10 years a person can work with a variety of different business units, learn a range of new methods, and meet a lot of new people, then that's a terrific thing. Such a setting challenges and increases the skills of the analytic professionals on the team. It is a win for both the analytic professionals and the organization.

 ## CENTRALIZED, BUT DEDICATED

Even if your organization adopts a fully centralized analytics structure, consider assigning resources to focus primarily on specific business units. Having consistency in the analytic professionals that business teams work with will help them grow more comfortable with analytics. The relationships developed with their regular analytic professionals can't be underestimated in value.

A disadvantage of centralized teams is that it is possible to end up with a lot of generalists who can do analysis across the organization, yet there are no individuals who can go deep in any specific area. It can also be disruptive to a business unit if different analytic professionals are popping in and out of the picture over time. For this reason, even a fully centralized team may still allocate specific people to help specific business units on a dedicated basis. Analytic professionals can report officially into a centralized group, but in practice they're embedded with the business unit they are assigned to. From a day-to-day perspective the analytic professional is more or less considered a part of that team.

A centralized analytics team will often charge back for their services to the business units. Sometimes, however, the team is considered corporate overhead. It's probably easier from a perspective of making sure people are doing what's really important if the team charges back. This makes the business units prioritize efforts. At the same time it is much more difficult to get innovative and exploratory analytics underway when a specific unit will have to pay for the efforts. Ideally, there will be some level of corporate budget set aside for the analytics team to work on new and innovative projects outside of what the business units individually fund. The taming of big data is a terrific target for such a budget. Fund early work at a corporate level and then let the business units fund later work once the value of big data has been proven.

Don't underestimate the importance of structuring an organization so that there is an ability for innovative analytics to occur. Expecting specific business units with tight budgets to fully fund innovative work is a stretch. New analytics need to be sponsored and supported at a high level and considered a strategic corporate investment.

## Hybrid Structures

Hybrid structures are just what the name implies. In a hybrid structure there is a centralized team as well as dedicated teams within specific business units. This type of structure can arise for a variety of reasons. A common path leading to a hybrid structure is when one business unit led the charge with analytics. That unit may have a built up a solid analytics team and isn't willing to give up control of that team. At the same time, other units have started ramping up their analytics efforts. To support the other units, a centralized team is formed. The original team, however, stays within the unit where it started.

Another common hybrid model is where there's a centralized core team, often called a center of excellence (COE) or center of expertise (COE as well), with analytic professionals who are tasked with keeping an enterprise view. While most analytic talent is embedded within the business units, there are a few resources who float and are tasked to make sure there's consistency in the approaches and the tools being used across units. The COE team also focuses on capturing the knowledge gained from what the analytics teams in the business units have been successful in doing. The central analytics team can have either direct/formal or dotted line/informal reporting relationships with the business units' analytic teams depending on the company.

 ## DON'T STRESS OVER STRUCTURE; STRESS OVER PEOPLE

It is worth reinforcing that the most important thing isn't how you structure your analytics teams. The most important thing is that you have the right people doing the right analytics for the right reasons. It is also important to focus on creating an environment and culture that allows your organization to hire, grow, and retain the right analytics talent.

## KEEPING A GREAT TEAM'S SKILLS UP

Within an organization's analytics teams there will be differences in the skills and responsibilities of people of different levels, just as there are on any other team. There will be a seasoned executive or two along with fresh new hires straight out of school. As a team is initially built, it is necessary to focus on the specific skills critically needed at that point in time for the problems at hand. The team won't be large enough to round it out better.

However, as the team expands, it is important to consider specifically bringing in people with different analytic skill sets. Perhaps your organization's initial hires had a very heavy background in data mining. As the team grows, it may be wise to consider someone with a strong optimization background or a strong forecasting background. Having analytic professionals with experience in different areas of analytics only provides more opportunities to identify new ways to add value to the business. In addition, as the team grows, it is possible to focus on creating career paths for the team. Initial hires are usually fairly experienced since they'll have to successfully work on their own with little guidance from other experts. As the team grows, it is safe to start hiring less experienced analytic professionals and grow them.

## The Matrixed Approach

One approach that helps keep analytic professionals' skills sharp is what can be termed a "matrixed" approach. This is a non-hierarchical approach to running the team. The way it works is that for a given project, what is often called an analytics lead is assigned. The analytics lead takes care of several key functions. First, the lead will handle project management activities. Luckily, the amount of project management isn't too daunting for most analytics projects, but the lead is responsible for whatever amount there is. Second, the lead has responsibility for setting the direction of the project, laying out the analysis plan, and making sure the team is meeting deadlines. Third and most important, the lead has ownership of compiling the results, interpreting and building recommendations from the results, and getting any required deliverables compiled. Underneath the analytics lead on a project will be one or more analytic professionals. They are responsible for executing the project work on a day-to-day basis under direction of the lead.

An organization won't necessarily have anyone with the title of analytics lead on the team. This is because being a lead on a project isn't about a title or grade level; it's about what's needed for a given project. For example, a team may have two analytic professionals, Bob and Sue. On project A, Sue may be the lead, with Bob working under her. At the same time, on project B, Bob may be the lead, with Sue working under him. The lead for each project is based on who is the best fit. If a project is heavily forecasting oriented, then a person who's highly familiar with forecasting problems will be the lead, for example.

**ENTER THE MATRIX!**

A matrixed approach to managing an analytics team can be a terrific way to boost productivity, build team cohesiveness, and keep analytic professionals challenged. By keeping the focus on what people have to offer rather than their title or tenure, you create a culture where people are more likely to succeed and where everyone is focused on getting the right answers, not on who comes up with them.

Over time, of course, the strongest and most senior analytic professionals are going to be leads more often than not. Similarly, newer and weaker analytic professionals will fill the team member role more often than not. By not assigning projects purely based on level or seniority, however, it mixes things up. This is why using a matrixed approach to running an analytics team can be a good idea. By requiring the team to work together in different capacities, it's amazing how tight-knit and cohesive the team can become. Egos are better kept in check since all team members know they will have to work under each of their peers from time to time. The team will really get to know each other and each member's respective strengths. They will also learn a lot from each other, which brings us to cross training.

## Cross-Training

One of the most important things to do with an analytics team, regardless of how it is structured, is to ensure that analytic professionals are cross-training each other. If one person is just an absolutely amazing programmer, make sure that he or she is from time to time doing a lunch and learn for the team, or writing a document with tips and tricks, or mentoring others one-on-one, or even putting together a short class. The team is going to want to keep growing and be challenged. One of the best ways to do that is to let them delve into analytical areas they don't know as well by working on projects with their peers. The person doing the teaching will find it rewarding along with the person being taught.

## Managers Can't Lose Touch

Analytics managers and executives need to stay engaged and to keep their skills from eroding. People in any line of work hate the "empty suit" who may be high up on the organization chart, but is perceived as not really knowing how to do anything. In some cases, the empty suit used to know how to do a lot of things and just lost it over time. Regardless, an empty suit is perceived as someone who currently just can't do very much. He or she might talk the talk, but can't walk the walk.

Analytic professionals are often even more sensitive to such things than the average person. Many technical fields have the same issue. Technical people don't tend to respect leaders who are telling them what to do, looking over their shoulder, and critiquing their work if the leader can't walk the walk. If an analytic professional perceives that his or her management team is going to talk the talk of analytics, but can't walk the walk of analytics, it's going to be virtually impossible to keep his or her respect. This isn't to say that it isn't possible to manage analytic professionals if a manager isn't as deep in every aspect of knowledge as the analytics team is. The key is for the manager to acknowledge the limits of his or her background and to trust the team on details that go deeper than his or her experience.

### KEEP MANAGER'S SKILLS FRESH . . . LIKE A JEDI KNIGHT!

In the *Star Wars* series, Yoda was often behind the scenes guiding the action. However, he was able to jump in and do battle with the best of them when required. Similarly, a great analytics manager might not be in the field every day, but when the time comes, he or she should be able to do analysis with the best of them. A team will stay on its toes when it knows its leader can still personally take care of business if required.

To keep skills up, consider requiring that every analytics manager change duties at least once a year, go into the field, and actually do some analysis. This is a great way to keep their skills current, although it is a difficult plan to stick to. There are companies that use such an approach in general. I know of one restaurant chain that requires every employee to work in a restaurant a few days every year so that everyone will understand what's happening on the front lines. It keeps everyone in touch with the real world, and those I know who work there find it a very valuable exercise each year.

## WHO SHOULD BE DOING ADVANCED ANALYTICS?

There's a topic that comes up again and again on analytic community discussion boards and in conversations. I've even discussed this topic in my blog.[2] The question is this: Given that there are now software tools with user-friendly interfaces for performing advanced analytics, is it a good idea to let people who aren't trained in analytics do their own analysis using these tools?

The issue underlying this question is that many people assume that having a tool that's easy to navigate via a nice point-and-click interface implies that it is easy to use the tool correctly and appropriately. As we discussed in Chapter 6, this is not true. Just because a tool is easy to use does not mean it's easy to use it correctly. In fact, the ease of use makes it incredibly easy to do exactly the wrong thing fast and unwittingly. For example, tools that generate SQL through a point-and-click interface will let users join data together in any way they please. It will put the syntax requested in place, but there is no guarantee that the syntax created makes any business sense at all.

An organization needs to make sure that anyone who is going to use a tool of any type has the right skills, experience, and perspective to use it. An analytics tool may save a user some programming, but he or she still needs to understand the analytics that are being generated. If you were confident that a novice was asking the right question, that all of the data to answer it was ready and waiting in exactly the right format, and that the precise algorithm to apply was known, then virtually anybody could succeed. Under those terms, everything is laid out perfectly and the user is truly just going through the motions of hitting the buttons. In the real world, this perfect setup is never actually the case.

A lot goes into building an appropriate analysis or model. The process goes beyond pointing and clicking in a tool. Is the right behavior being predicted? Is the best set of independent variables to support that prediction available? Does the analytic professional have the experience to know when things don't look right? Does the analytic professional know how to address problems that arise? As we discussed in Chapter 7, there is no magic "easy" button for generating advanced analytics!

This is not to say that novices without much training or skill can't add value to an organization. It is simply a matter of ensuring that they don't overreach their bounds and get into areas they shouldn't. Most people within an organization should be sticking to predefined templates or reports, perhaps with a bit of basic ad hoc analysis on top. The heavier lifting should be left to the experts. The formal analytics team should be made up primarily of these experts.

## Illustrating Inconsistency

The comments in the prior section sometimes lead people to the thought that analytic professionals are just being defensive. In fact, the points made are well accepted in many other lines of work. Somehow, people who don't understand analytics don't apply the same logic they would apply elsewhere. Let's take a look at some illustrative examples that demonstrate why care needs to be taken to ensure the correct people and teams are performing advanced analytics work.

Jane has decided she doesn't want to be an analytic professional anymore, but wants to develop copy and artwork for her marketing department. She has installed on her computer the same modern, powerful graphics and content generation tools that the marketing team uses. She has taken hours of training on using those tools. She can create brochures, graphics, or whatever else she wants easily, because the software makes it simple to point and click and arrange pictures, images, and text. She walks down to the marketing department and says, "I've installed all your software tools on my computer. I've taken all of the available training. I'd like to join your team and create direct mail pieces, magazine ads, and product brochures. Do I have a job?" Jane would be laughed out of the room. Creating good marketing content is about more than simply pointing and clicking in a tool.

John has decided he'd like to work on the CFO's team and close the books each month. He found out what accounting software his company uses. Similar to Jane, he gets a lot of training on the software. He then goes down to the accounting department and says, "I'd like to help you close the books each month. I don't have any finance or accounting background. However, I took all the courses offered for the software package that you use. I know which menu items to choose at each step of the monthly book close process. When can I start?" Do you think John will get that job?

One last example: Joe's neighbor has a big tree he needs taken down because it's very sick. He asks Joe what tree service Joe would recommend. Joe responds, "You don't need a tree service. I just bought a top-of-the-line chainsaw. I've read the manual cover to cover, the blade's all sharpened, and it's ready to go. I can be your tree service. Let's go cut down that tree!" What neighbor would even consider such a silly proposition?

 **DON'T TAKE THE EASY WAY OUT**

Most people laugh at the idea of a novice generating copy and art for a major marketing initiative, or a novice closing the corporate books, or a neighbor with a high-end chainsaw cutting down a tree. Why is it, then, that so many are willing to assume that a person with absolutely no relevant experience and a little bit of analytics tool training can build accurate, high-quality advanced analytic processes? Don't fall into that trap.

If an organization is to have a great analytics team, it will need to remember the art and science that make up effective analytics. Just as great artists likely didn't paint a masterpiece the first time they painted, neither will great analytic teams be great from day one. It is something that evolves with practice and experience. Just as in other disciplines, there are complexities and nuances that are not obvious to those who aren't familiar with the field. If someone wouldn't allow a novice without the proper skills, training, and experience to do his or her own job, then he or she shouldn't allow a novice without the proper skills, training, and experience to build advanced analytics processes. It is critical to build an analytics team from a base of qualified analytic professionals as discussed in Chapter 8, and not simply shift people from other parts of the organization and give them a new role and title.

## Enabling Analytic Novices to Succeed

Let's now turn to a much more positive viewpoint. There are many people in an organization who want to leverage advanced analytics. Let's assume Barb from marketing is one of them and she's prepared to champion analytics for her business unit. She's prepared to push to move things ahead. That is a terrific thing, and an analytics team certainly wants to support Barb and help her make that happen. The answer isn't putting software on her computer so she can start cranking out her own analysis, however.

We need to circle back for a moment to the idea that friendly analytic tools are productivity enhancers. Objecting to tools being given to people who don't know what they're doing is not about someone protecting analytic professionals' jobs and rejecting new technology. If the concern was protecting analytic professionals' jobs, people would be against user-friendly analytic tools across the board, not simply such tools in the wrong hands.

A person with limited vision could argue that if he or she is part of a team of 10 analytic professionals and a productivity tool cuts the time it takes to do analytics work in half, that means half the team is going to get laid off. Anyone who would view the situation that way should be removed from the analytics team as they can't possibly be a great analytic professional. The right way to look at is that there are 10 people who have justified their existence based on what they're doing today. If suddenly they can get the current workload done in half the time, they now have half their time to address new problems and add even more value. Modern, friendly tools will only further justify analytic professionals' existence, help them grow in skill, and provide them additional challenges. It's a win all the way around.

 **FOCUS EVERYONE ON WHAT THEY DO BEST**

Businesspeople with no analytical expertise may want to leverage analytics, but they don't need to do the actual heavy lifting. The job of the analytics team is to enable businesspeople to drive analytics through the organization. Let businesspeople spend their time selling the power of analytics upstream and changing the business processes they manage to make use of analytics. If analytics teams do what they do best and business teams do what they do best, it will be a winning combination.

Hopefully you're convinced that user-friendly analytic technologies themselves are a good thing. So how should an organization use them? The key is to enable Barb to reach her goals. That is not the same as having Barb actually do the dirty work. The analytics team should partner with Barb, help Barb get the analytics she needs, and allow her to run reports that summarize the performance of the models the team has built for her. Customer focused results should be mapped into Barb's customer relationship management (CRM) suite. The results should also be made available to any other corporate applications that would benefit from them. Barb should be given the tools to leverage the analytics that the analytics team develops for her. She probably doesn't *want* to do the dirty work herself any more than she *should* be doing it herself.

## WHY CAN'T IT AND ANALYTIC PROFESSIONALS GET ALONG?

A big issue organizations face as they build a great analytics team is the struggle between analytic professionals and IT. There is long-term animosity between IT and analytic professionals in many organizations. Believe it or not, there are actually logical, valid reasons why this tension arose in the past. It no longer needs to be this way, however. To understand why, let's start by looking at the roles that IT and analytic professionals are given by an organization.

As can be seen in Table 9.1, an analytic professional is hired and tasked with pressing boundaries and making new things happen with corporate data. An analytic professional needs to do new and innovative things and think out of the box. IT, however, is being paid by the same company to make sure systems are running smoothly and that everyone can get the work done that they need done. IT needs to ensure that resources are appropriately allocated and keep things under control.

IT professionals and analytic professionals clash in part because the charters they are each given by their organization are inherently in conflict. They are paid by the same company to pursue conflicting priorities! One team is specifically tasked with locking down the data, controlling the data, and controlling resource usage. The other team is specifically tasked with crunching through the data, using lot of

**Table 9.1** The Roles of Analytic Professionals and IT

| Analytics teams are asked to: | IT teams are asked to: |
| --- | --- |
| Heavily utilize system resources. | Tightly manage resource usage. |
| Create tables and use a lot of space. | Limit table creation and space usage. |
| Run complex ad hoc queries. | Minimize use of complex ad hoc queries. |
| Go outside the box. | Keep users within the box. |
| Experiment with new approaches. | Stick to approved approaches. |
| Work with limited rules and restrictions. | Enforce rules and restrictions. |

resources in the process, and doing things differently. It's almost impossible not to have conflict in such a situation.

What makes things even worse is that analytic professionals are typically reporting to the business while IT reports through the CIO. The very first person in an organization that has direct authority over both teams to make them work more nicely together is the CEO. It's going to be very rare that two C-level executives want to go to the CEO and ask him to resolve disagreements between their teams.

## IT AND ANALYTICS TEAMS MUST SIGN A PEACE TREATY!

It is crucial that your organization gets its IT and analytics teams to sit down and come to agreement on how they're going to work together. It is entirely possible with the technology available today for both teams to co-exist peacefully and even help each other prosper. The hardest part is getting people past the historical biases and the pent-up ill will that may exist. Make the effort, or it will be difficult to build a great analytics team.

As a result of all this, analytic professionals are often viewed by IT as cowboys developing a "shadow" IT environment without any respect for rules and policies. At the same time, IT is often viewed by analytic professionals as a bunch of uptight control freaks who do nothing but stifle progress and put in place roadblocks.

The good news is that a lot of the things that drove this animosity are no longer a factor. We've talked about the advent of sandboxing, in-database processing, and the convergence of the data analytic environments in Chapters 4 and 5. With these developments, it is possible to get past the gap between IT and analytic professionals. It is important that your organization bridges the gap if it is to build a great analytics team.

One fact that can be hard to get analytic professionals to admit is that they would love to reach an agreement with IT. They don't want to manage a separate system unless they view it as a necessary evil to get their work done. Why? Because great analytic professionals often work themselves out of the job they enjoy! Let's explore how.

If an analytics team has their own analytics environment that they have to maintain, it effectively makes the analytics team system administrators, production schedulers, and so forth. An analytic professional builds a great new analytic process that needs to run on a weekly basis. Guess what happens? He is the one who gets stuck babysitting that process every week. He is the one who has to monitor it. He is the one who has to figure out how to account for changes to the data feeds, or other system changes that impact the process.

Analytic professionals don't really want to do those things. Worse yet, as an analytic professional builds four, five, or six new analytic processes, pretty soon his or her job is almost entirely consumed with babysitting the production processes he or she has created. There is no longer time to do any new analytics! That's a miserable outcome. The fact is that great analytics teams would love to hand over system administration, scheduling, backups, and such to IT. IT has people who do those things for a living, enjoy it, and are good at it. It's much more efficient and everyone will be happier. It will free up time for the analytics team to focus on being great rather than just getting processes to run.

## WRAP-UP

The most important lessons to take away from this chapter are:

- Instead of evaluating how to structure a team indefinitely, make the first hire and get some great analytic professionals starting to address the right problems.

- Be choosy in whom you hire. Success is far more dependent on the individuals who make up an analytics team than it is on the organizational structure in which that team is working.

- There isn't enough great analytics talent out there. Be prepared to be more aggressive than usual to bring the right team members on board.

- Most organizations start with a decentralized, functional analytics team structure. Over time, a company often moves to a centralized or hybrid structure.

- The organization should encourage, if not mandate, that analytics team members cross-train each other and push each other to expand their skills.

- Consider a matrixed approach to analytic project work. Have a strong lead oversee the work of others on each project.

- Analytic managers need to keep up with their skills and be able to still do work just like Yoda in the Jedi Knight example.

- Easy to use tools are not a magic "easy" button that enable the unqualified to generate good analytics. They make it easy for unqualified people to do the wrong things.

- Analytics teams need to enable their business partners to succeed with analytics. Analytic professionals should do the heavy lifting, but then make the results accessible to the business community.

- Broker a peace agreement between the analytics team and IT. Nobody, especially the business partners both teams support, benefits from a dysfunctional relationship.

## NOTES

1. Tom Davenport, and Jeanne Harris. "Organizing Analysts," International Institute for Analytics, webinar executive summary, June 23, 2009.

2. You can find my blog at http://iianalytics.com/category/faculty-blogs/bill-franks/.

# PART
# FOUR

---

# Bringing It Together: The Analytics Culture

CHAPTER **10**

# Enabling Analytic Innovation

**W**hat is innovation? According to Merriam-Webster, innovation is

1. "The introduction of something new," or
2. "A new idea, method, or device."[1]

The formal definition of innovation is disappointing to me because it misses the power of what innovation can do in business and in the world in general. Without innovation we'd still be living in the Stone Age because innovation is what drives change and progress. Unfortunately, innovation is not something that's always given the focus it needs in today's business environment.

Very few businesses succeed by simply following the competition. Innovation is one key to success. If an organization sits back and watches the competition begin to work with big data, it will have a problem. This is particularly true if there is gloating about how the competition is spending money in their efforts while the organization in question is not. Perhaps once the organization hears what the competition has been able to do with big data, it will get the motivation to go and do the same thing. That is simply playing catch-up. The effort of those who lead is spent to get a competitive advantage while the effort of those who follow is spent to catch up with the leaders. That is not a winning formula.

In this chapter, we'll review some of the basic principles behind innovation. Then, we'll apply them to the world of big data and analytics through the concept of an analytic innovation center. The goal is to provide readers with tangible ideas of how to better enable analytic innovation and the taming of big data within their organizations.

## BUSINESSES NEED MORE INNOVATION

From 2008 to 2011, the economy has been so bad that many companies have been in survival mode. Anything that isn't directly tied to surviving this month, this quarter, or this year is getting pushed to the backburner. The fact is, however, that even when times are good very few companies put enough emphasis on innovation. Ironically, one of the best times to surpass the competition is during bad times. While the competition is hunkering down, a company can invest in innovation and surpass them. In bad times, the status quo won't suffice anymore. This is sometimes the driver for organizations finally trying new ideas. It isn't possible to sit back and watch the same old strategies continue to succeed. Something new must be done, so why not get creative?

Without a steady stream of new ideas, products, and services, a company is not going to be able to compete in the long term. This has always been true, but in today's global, interconnected, fast-moving world it's more true than ever. Innovation is a key to survival, and innovation in the area of analytics and how data is used is an area that deserves focus. How will an organization use analytics to identify patterns that can be leveraged, and how will those analytics be acted upon? Analytics is an ever more important tool that organizations use to drive competitive advantage. Those who first and best tame big data and drive new, high-impact analytics with it will have a big lead on the competition.

Companies that develop consumer products have product labs that focus on bringing new and innovative products to market. Having labs focused on innovation with analytics and data is also important. In the analysis of big data, few companies have much of an edge yet since it is relatively new. But from an analytics perspective, as we talked about in Chapter 1, big data is not that drastically different from the other intimidating data sources that have evolved over time. There is no reason organizations can't get started with big data today.

**ENABLING INNOVATIVE ANALYTICS REQUIRES EFFORT**

How do you enable innovative analytics in your organization? It will take a concerted, focused effort to do so. Putting effort toward innovation in analytics needs to get similar attention to developing product and service innovations. Analytics should be considered a pillar of a business, and not an optional add-on.

There are so many new, large data sources becoming available that nobody is up to speed on all of them. There may be only a few people in a given industry who have actually worked in any depth with some of these new sources. In fact, there are some new data sources that are planned, but that aren't even being collected yet. The point is that much of big data is too new to have been totally figured out and tamed. However, someone is going to figure it out soon. The question is: Which organizations are going to be leaders and which are going to be followers? More important, what choice will your organization make?

## TRADITIONAL APPROACHES HAMPER INNOVATION

In organizations today, especially large ones, there's often an embedded culture of bureaucracy. Large parts of that bureaucracy are the long-established guidelines and policies on how an organization does things and how it doesn't. The typical process for trying to get something new underway is time-consuming and painful. This can be particularly true with an innovative use of data and analytics because many people aren't comfortable with analytics in general. All of this hampers innovation.

A typical corporate process leads to long delays in starting to investigate a new idea. It will take even more time to get a project fully approved and an even longer time to get the idea implemented. It's a long, risk-averse, highly formal process. Such a process involves a lot of documentation. For the person who wants to first attack a big data source, many of the following will be required: a business case, a project plan, financial projections, a staffing plan, an analysis plan, a contingency plan, a risk assessment. There's probably more that has been missed as well!

But here's the catch: If you're looking to do something innovative and new, then by definition you don't know enough to confidently produce all of the documents and figures that are typically requested. If using data in a different way to drive new analytics was fully understood, the idea wouldn't be innovative. It can be very difficult to get an innovative analytics project approved without setting up a mechanism separate from the standard processes.

The main roadblock will be that it won't be possible to convince everyone that the idea is risk-free. But, of course, the idea *isn't* risk-free. That is the whole point! An innovative analytics project isn't going to be risk-free. Following the standard process, an idea may be rejected. Over time, individuals who bring forth ideas and continually get rejected are going to either leave their company or quit trying. Without an alternative to the standard risk-averse process, an organization will find it difficult to innovate in the area of analytics.

 **INNOVATION REQUIRES RISK**

An innovative idea for new analytics using big data won't be risk-free. It is a challenge to get people to accept the idea of pursuing an initiative when they honestly aren't sure how it is going to work. A big data source won't be understood, and how to use it won't be totally clear at the outset. That doesn't mean it isn't worth taking on the challenge to figure it out.

Imagine the concern in a typical corporate environment when an analytics team shows up to a meeting with executives to put forth an idea. They discuss a new source of big data that has never been collected before and say that they want to go collect it. The analytics team is not entirely sure what's in it. They're not even exactly sure how the company will use it, but they have a lot of ideas to try. They are sure, however, that by the time they get this data, analyze it, and figure out what's in it, they'll be able to drive a lot of value. Exactly where the value will come from will become clear as the effort unfolds. It will take some effort and planning to get the executives to buy into such an effort. Are there ways to make it easier? Yes. We'll investigate some as we proceed.

## DEFINING ANALYTIC INNOVATION

Let's define analytic innovation as any type of analytical approach that is new and unique. It is something a given organization has not done before, and perhaps something nobody anywhere has done before. To qualify as an innovation, an idea has to be out of the ordinary. It can't be a rehash of an old idea. Tuning the settings of an existing algorithm or adjusting how some metrics are computed isn't innovation. Trying a completely different modeling technique while leveraging some new data sources at the same time is.

An innovation can't be something that's already readily available off the shelf from an existing software package or services offering. Those software or service offerings may be new to a given organization, but they don't count as an innovation. In other words, something can be a highly innovative approach for a given organization, but if it's a well-documented product or process that many others have already implemented, pursuit of it isn't really innovation. It is catching up with the market.

 **BE INNOVATIVE, NOT INCREMENTAL**

Innovative analytics are about trying something new and different. It isn't a matter of adding a small extension to an existing process or approach. An analytic innovation should be focused on analyzing a new data source, solving a new problem, or a combination of both. Of course, the analytics should be focused on an area where a company has a lot of opportunity.

Innovation specifically is not doing common ad hoc analytics. It's not that ad hoc questions and analytics aren't highly valuable. A request to dig into why a sudden drop in sales suddenly occurred can lead to a lot of value. But standard ad hoc requests should be in the regular flow of what an analytics team does. Most ad hoc requests don't require innovative analytics even if they are focused on a new problem.

## ITERATIVE APPROACHES TO ANALYTIC INNOVATION

In order to pursue analytic innovation and explore big data, it will be necessary to employ some different, iterative approaches that better enable such activities to occur. These approaches have an emphasis on collaboration and flexibility. The idea is to have a small team working together daily to figure out how to make an idea work. The team will address the problems that pop up and have the flexibility to change direction as needed to move things forward. For an approach to enable innovation, it needs to value response to change versus sticking to a predefined plan. If something needs to be changed and it makes sense to deviate from the initial plan, then so be it.

For example, a team begins an effort to analyze a new big data source. Unexpected issues in the content and structure of the data will certainly be found. The team will need to adjust plans as required once those problems are identified. The focus is on the goal of getting the data in a state that it can be analyzed as opposed to sticking to an exact plan as laid out at the start. Perhaps some of the intended metrics don't work well, but others are identified that do. Make the changes. If, at the end of the first phase, the data is in the state it needs to be for the upcoming analysis, then it is a win regardless of the specific steps taken to get there.

To continue the success after the data is prepared, it is necessary to focus on getting working prototypes built quickly. The goal is to get to something that proves that an idea can work. The prototype needs enough detail so that people can understand the bigger picture of what's possible if the organization goes after the idea in earnest. Back to our example, it isn't necessary to do a perfect analysis the first time using the data. The initial analytics don't need to be bulletproof. Rather, the intial work needs to be solid enough to show the merit of the approach. There is plenty of time to bulletproof the process later. Without buy-in that the approach has merit, time won't be given to make it bulletproof. A rapid prototype will lead to that buy-in.

The keys to all this are shorter iteration cycles and tackling small chunks that are digestible. This is partly so that progress can continue to be shown and is also due to the fact that there is some uncertainly in the process. Tackling small steps one at a time makes it much easier to deal with the unexpected and account for anything new learned in each step.

 **BE FLEXIBLE**

When exploring an innovative idea for analytics, the scope is never going to be 100 percent understood up front. The plan isn't going to be fully baked. The project team won't have it all figured out when they start. That is why it is critical to embrace an iterative, flexible approach to exploring ideas. Adjusting plans as more information is learned is part of the fun.

As the analytic professionals in our example dig into their big data they're going to need to be very flexible. The data may not be as clean as hoped. It may not be as complete as expected. The data may not have the predictive value anticipated for some of the specific uses planned for it. That's okay. Once the analytic professionals get in there and start working with the data, they may realize that the next couple steps they had planned aren't quite right. They can adjust plans and move forward if they are working under a flexible, iterative approach and not bound firmly to the initial project plan. As long as the team knows the goal of the analysis effort and what they are trying to prove, then they can ensure the adjustments made keep things on track.

## CONSIDER A CHANGE IN PERSPECTIVE

Retirement planning is all about managing the risk you're exposed to. At some date in the future you plan to retire and retirement planning is about making sure that on that date you have the assets needed to do so. As Table 10.1 shows, venture capital follows a completely different model. When investing in a venture capital environment you're investing with a goal of scoring big in a relatively short time frame. At the same time, in a venture capital model there's a reasonable risk that you'll lose all or most of your investment.

There's a risk/reward trade-off. Both of these approaches are completely legitimate if investors understand what they're getting into and they use the options appropriately. Many well-known companies

**Table 10.1** Retirement Planning versus Venture Capital

| Retirement Planning | Venture Capital |
| --- | --- |
| Selects established, proven companies | Selects new, unproven companies |
| Balances chances of loss and gain | Focus on gains, not losses |
| Targets a mix of moderate outcomes | "Goes big" or "goes home" |
| Volatility managed tightly | Volatility is high |
| Used for retirement and everyday assets | Not for assets critical to survival |

today, especially in the technology, ecommerce, and social media arenas, were funded by venture capital. Venture capital spawns amazing things. But for every Google or Amazon, there are many more companies that fail.

Just like it isn't smart to risk all retirement assets in venture capital style investments, it isn't smart to invest all corporate resources into risky or innovative initiatives. It is necessary to ensure a company will survive and grow at a pace that enables it to hit its goals just like people have to hit their retirement goals. As a result, the amount of capital put toward riskier activities must be managed. But even retirement accounts will have some portion of funds placed in riskier assets.

 **DIVERSIFY!**

Organizations need diversification. Just as it is prudent to put a small amount of retirement savings into riskier investments, it is prudent to put a small percentage of corporate people, systems, and assets toward innovative analytics efforts. Not having investment in innovation included in the mix can be as risky as having too much.

There's a flip side that people often don't think about, however. One of the biggest risks that people end up facing in their retirement account is caused by playing it too safe. If a retirement account holds 100 percent government bonds, for example, it is a risk because those bonds might barely keep up with inflation. The account may not grow enough to meet its goals even while it is virtually certain not to lose money. It is completely possible to be guaranteed not to lose money, yet also be guaranteed not to have enough money to retire on time!

This is the exact same thing companies faces when using nothing but a "play it safe" process when it comes to big data and analytics. It is necessary to mix in some riskier initiatives if a company is going to get where it needs to be years down the road. An analytic innovation center is a terrific mechanism to do this.

## ARE YOU READY FOR AN ANALYTIC INNOVATION CENTER?

One concept that can help with both the world of big data and the world of advanced analytics in general is the concept of an analytic innovation center. An analytic innovation center is intended to facilitate the rapid exploration of an idea, and reduce the latency between idea formulation and the formal execution and implementation of that idea. An analytic innovation center does have an oversight mechanism and a process for filtering ideas. It's not about a state of anarchy where anything and everything goes. However, decision and approval processes are greatly expedited compared to a typical corporate bureaucracy. Let's walk through how it all works.

 **BRINGING THE CONCEPTS TOGETHER**

An analytic innovation center brings together the concepts outlined in the first nine chapters. It makes use of the big data sources discussed in Part One, the tools, processes, and technologies outlined in Part Two, and the people and approaches outlined in Part Three. An analytic innovation center is one way to approach taming big data and driving new analytics from it.

### Component 1: The Technology Platform

An analytic innovation center will need a technology platform to house and analyze the data required for the projects it pursues. The infrastructure of the innovation center needs to be logically separate and distinct. The center's team will need dedicated database resources, analytic tools, network bandwidth, and so forth. An enterprise data warehouse (ideally), analytic appliance, or data mart is a starting point. To handle big data sources, the center will also need a system that helps process large streams of semi-structured and unstructured data. As we discussed in Chapter 4, a MapReduce framework is an appropriate option for this need.

The environment will require access to the data already on existing platforms, because any of that data may need to enter into an analysis. On top of that, the center will need an ability to load and analyze data from new sources. A lot of the projects an analytic innovation center will pursue are going to involve experimenting with a new data source and seeing if it can be combined with other data to drive value.

The technology of the analytic innovation center is actually very straightforward, given the topics we've already covered. From an implementation perspective the analytic innovation center infrastructure can be as simple as the analytical sandboxes we discussed in Chapter 5. Just as sandboxes are set up in an enterprise data warehouse or data mart for day-to-day analytics, a dedicated sandbox environment can be set up for an analytic innovation center. However, the resources allocated to the center's sandbox should be separate from those allocated to the day-to-day sandbox. When it comes to the center's MapReduce environment, it is possible to set aside a portion of an existing environment for the innovation center or a separate, dedicated MapReduce environment for the center can be implemented.

Setting up the infrastructure for an analytic innovation center shouldn't be that difficult. All of the pieces are already in place in some form for the other analytics an organization is doing. It is just a matter of partitioning off some of those resources for the center. By following the principles of in-database analytics and sandboxing, it isn't necessary to buy an entirely separate set of licenses or equipment.

## Component 2: Third-Party Products and Services

An analytic innovation center will need to leverage third-party products at times since there may be additional functionality required to effectively pursue an innovative idea. The tools already present may not have the algorithms or other capabilities that are needed. For example, perhaps there's a boutique modeling tool that contains a new algorithm that the team wants to utilize as part of an exploratory analysis. Buying the software or having a trial license for the project would make sense.

An organization may also need some help from outside consultants with experience in a subject area being explored. No organization will have analytic professionals on staff with all the skills that will be required over time. This is especially true as an organization looks to break new ground. Internal resources may not have the time, either. The chances of an innovative analytic endeavor working out well can be greatly enhanced with appropriate support from outside experts who already know what to do.

## Component 3: Commitment and Sponsorship

An analytic innovation center is going to need a commitment to pursue new ideas using the iterative processes we discussed earlier in the chapter. To help with that, it will need executive sponsorship, guidance, and involvement. An analytic innovation center is something that has to be sponsored from an executive level. After all, it's going to be a sizeable investment that will be considered risky by some people. Only an executive can drive the support required to get it approved and to push against established bureaucracy.

It is equally important that there are sponsors for each of the center's individual projects. The project sponsors must be active in the execution process and have the authority, ability, and intention to act on ideas that are proven. This is critical since it won't do any good to prove that an idea has huge potential if no one is going to champion it and make sure it gets deployed. Without executive support and vision, a project can be a technical success, but still lead to no positive changes.

## Component 4: A Strong Team

An analytic innovation center needs a team with a range of skill sets across business, IT, and analytics. The most important part of the center is the team assigned to it. Business resources will help define the problems and ensure practical considerations are accounted for. Analytic resources will dig through the data and perform the required analysis. IT resources will help manage the data volumes, equipment, and processes that the center uses.

It is absolutely critical that the people assigned to an analytic innovation center are some of an organization's best people. It should be an honor to be assigned to the center, and people can rotate on and off over time. Ideally, some people can be assigned to the center full-time. If it is not possible to assign people full-time based on budget constraints, then the center has to be a formal part of the team members' jobs. If people are supposed to spend 20 percent of their time on the analytic innovation center, they need 20 percent of their time formally allocated. If the plan is that the team first gets all of their other duties done, and when they have time they will work on innovation center projects, that's not going to work. Nothing will ever move forward because they'll never find the time to put toward it.

## Component 5: The Innovation Council

The final component of an analytic innovation center is an innovation council. This council is made up of members of the center's team, its executive sponsors, and representatives from the relevant business units. What the council is going to do is review ideas and choose which ones will be pursued. Similar to a pitch a startup might make to a venture capital firm, someone will do a quick presentation of what an idea is, why it would be valuable, and what the plan is to explore it and build a prototype. The council listens, asks questions, and then discusses the ideas presented. It then decides if each idea is something that is worthy of pursuing or not. If an idea makes the cut, it gets added to the list of projects.

The council will also monitor projects once they are underway. Interim results, as well as problems, can be brought to the council for discussion. The council may also have ideas about how to proceed as the project unfolds and more facts are learned. If a project hits a major issue, the council can decide to abandon it. We'll discuss how to handle failures in more detail later. The point is that the council keeps tabs on everything that is happening in the center and directs activities to the best ideas that are most likely to drive value.

## The Guiding Principles of an Analytic Innovation Center

As discussed, an analytic innovation center needs to be autonomous with the flexibility and resources it needs to succeed. The dedicated environment outlined previously has to be unconstrained by production demands or processes whether it's physically distinct or simply logically partitioned. This doesn't mean that the center can take up all the capacity of the available system resources. All it means is if it is decided to dedicate 10 percent of the available resources, then 10 percent of it needs to be available for the processes that the center is running. Of course, the people assigned need to have time dedicated to developing and pursuing the center's ideas. Working on projects for an analytic innovation center can't be on top of someone's day job. It needs to be part of that person's day job.

When laying the ground rules for the center, including how the innovation council will work, rapid response should be the focus along with a minimum of bureaucracy and red tape. If the center is assigned the high-end people it needs, it isn't necessary to "red tape" them to death. A lot of red tape is oriented toward stopping dishonest people from being dishonest and stopping incompetent people from doing things wrong. Honest, highly competent people don't need a lot of that red tape because they're naturally going to tend to do the right thing in the right way. This is certainly true of the great analytic professionals that we discussed in Chapter 8.

Another important guiding principle is that the analytic innovation center should follow a venture capital model, not a retirement model. The projects it chooses to pursue should have the potential to provide a large positive return and advance one or more strategic initiatives of the company. Some of the ideas are going to fail, and that's okay. The goal is to have them fail quickly. The aim is to find a few big winners among the losers and avoid the mindset of considering a failed idea as an entirely bad thing.

## Analytic Innovation Center Scope

We've talked about the fact that an analytic innovation center is supposed to address problems that are not common or simplistic. If you ever find your center doing routine data analysis or ad hoc reports, stop! If you find your center doing minor product enhancements, stop! If your center is testing out a new application just to see how it works, stop! If your center is working on a formal production implementation of an analysis process, stop! Even a highly successful project in the analytic innovation center will go far enough to prove that the concept explored can and will work. The center is not meant to be part of the long-term plan.

 **DON'T BE INAPPROPRIATE!**

An analytic innovation center should be used only for the purposes for which it is intended. Initial exploration, focused research, and initial prototypes are fair game. Once planning starts for a larger, more formal implementation of a prototype, it is no longer in the domain of the center. At that point, the center's resources need to move on to the next problem and pass the project off to an implementation team.

Within the process of pursuing innovative analytics there are multiple stages. As Figure 10.1 shows, it's clear where the role of an analytic innovation center stops. The process gets started with an idea. First, there is some initial exploration to get the team's minds around the problem. From there it moves on to deeper, focused research to really dig in and get to the meat of the problem. That will lead to development of a prototype to show how the idea might work. Up to this point, the analytic innovation center is appropriate. As soon as it is time to start building a formal version of this prototype targeted for deployment, the project needs to move out of the center. Once an idea is proven, it is time to move it to a more traditional path but with an expedited priority.

A concern with what is being suggested here is that after a successful prototype, the project is kicked back into some of the very bureaucracy the center aims to avoid. However, when it is time to put

An analytic innovation center focuses on only the initial
stages of the work process for an idea. Fewer projects
make it past each step.

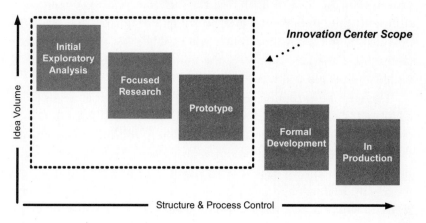

**Figure 10.1** Analytic Innovation Center Scope

something in place that a company is going to use to make multimillion-dollar decisions, it is a good idea to play it a little safer and make sure it is implemented consistently with other corporate deployments. The analytic innovation center enabled a shortcut to be taken to get to the point that an idea is ready to be implemented. The key to success is to continue an expedited treatment of the idea, just with the necessary testing and process change planning to make sure the implementation succeeds.

For example, consider an organization that decides to explore the analysis of customer service emails to identify sentiment and developing product issues. Initially, a sample of e-mails is collected and provided to the analytic innovation center team. The team uses trial licenses of a text analysis tool to develop an initial set of analysis. In this initial work, the team is able to identify a handful of compelling results, which leads to support for the idea being implemented on a broad scale.

The implementation should move out of the center, and it should become a formal project. Licenses for the text analysis software will need to be procured and installed, an ongoing feed of e-mail records will need to be established, and the analysis techniques used in the prototype will need to be refined. These steps shouldn't be part of the innovation center. The innovation center's job was complete once it proved that the idea of analyzing the customer service e-mails had sufficient value to make it worth pursuing. Presumably, the evidence provided by the innovation center will enable a fast track implementation. Since the idea is proven, the money being left on the table is visible and people will want to start picking it up.

There is one exception to these clean scope lines that needs to be addressed. Consider a case where an analytic innovation center has created a new analysis process that is quite powerful. It has proven that a new big data source has an amazing capacity to help the business. It is even known exactly what needs to be done to put that new process in production, and a plan is in place to do so. This is the one scenario where it can make sense to bend a bit on the analytic innovation center's scope.

It is silly to tell the business community that there is a terrific new analytics process that's going to help them and that there is even a prototype working in the analytic innovation center. However, the process will be turned off while it is put into production. In three to six months the process will be turned on again in the production environment and the business users will be able to start driving results. That doesn't make much sense. It makes sense to let the process run out of the analytic innovation center for the period that it's being formally implemented so that it can start driving results right away.

Making the prior exception takes a lot of discipline. If an organization is not serious about getting the process put into production and getting it done quickly, it has entered a dangerous, slippery slope of having the center running pseudo-production processes. That isn't good. In particular, people can't slack off on the implementation because the process is running out of the analytic innovation center. They may think that they can safely put their time into other projects first because at least the center's sponsors can get their results for now. The analytic innovation center needs to break free of the ideas it proves as soon as possible and get on to the next idea. At the same time, don't starve the business sponsors of the information they've been waiting for just to follow the rule of not going past the initial prototype to the letter.

## Dealing with Failures

A fact of life with an analytic innovation center is that failures will occur. Not every idea will work out. Failures can occur at a couple of different levels. We will discuss a few.

The first type of failure is a total failure. In this case everyone may feel the team was totally off base in thinking that the idea would work in the first place. Or maybe it was a great idea, but pragmatically speaking, given the realities of the data and business processes involved, it just doesn't work out. Failures of this type lead to abandoning the idea. Note that even in this case, there can be many important things learned about the data and learned from the problems experienced. All of those new lessons can be leveraged in the future. Just because the idea as put forth in the analytic innovation center isn't going to work, that doesn't mean that important knowledge isn't gained.

Another type of failure is where an idea is failing at present, but the team feels that the idea will succeed at some point in the future. Perhaps some new data will be available, or a more powerful system is being put in place that will be able to handle the processing, or some upcoming tweak to the company's business model will make the process changes required feasible. Failures of this type are put on hold until a later date when the barriers to success are lowered. Once again, there may be lessons learned that can immediately be applied to other efforts.

A final type of failure involves an idea that actually does work. There is merit in the idea and the company can make money from it. However, the return isn't high enough for the level of effort it would require, or there are other potential projects that have an even higher return. In this case the idea is either tabled or abandoned as appropriate.

As failures occur, there are three principles to remember to help to manage them. First, on any given project the goal is to risk the minimum amount of resources necessary to show if the idea has potential or not. The purpose of an analytic innovation center is defeated if multiyear, multimillion-dollar projects are being assigned to it. Projects in the center should be on the order of weeks to a few months. If a fairly large effort is required to fully tackle a problem, then scope an initial, shorter phase that will provide insights into whether additional phases are warranted.

Second, don't tackle projects that are so big that a string of losses can't be absorbed if the center has a streak of bad luck. This principle can be illustrated by considering professional poker players. One of the golden rules in professional poker is to only play in games when the stakes are set at levels where you can afford to lose everything you bring to the table. No poker player takes all of his or her money into one game. The reason is that it is possible to have a very improbable run of cards that cause a player to lose a big hand or two and lose most or all of the money in play.

I once sat in on a poker hand where four aces lost to a straight flush. The odds of seeing that occur are very low to say the least. Most people will lose all the money they have when holding four aces since they would be happy to bet it all. After all, the expectation is that somebody is giving you free money when you hold four aces and they call your bet. Statistically, it is the right thing to do by far, since the odds of losing are infinitesimal. However, it is possible to lose.

The point is that when professional poker players play, they risk amounts where they are going to be able to outlast any reasonable run of bad luck. Once the unlucky run ends, they will have survived, and the statistical probabilities ensure that they will eventually have a run of unusually good luck to balance it out. The worst thing to do is to go bust before the streak of bad luck ends.

 ## IF YOU NEVER FAIL, YOU AREN'T SUCCEEDING!

If there are not some failures experienced in an analytic innovation center, and if a couple of those failures aren't spectacular and complete, then the center is playing it much too safe. Innovation is about pushing the envelope and taking risks. It is possible to learn as much through understanding why a new analytic process failed as by understanding what made a successful one work.

The third and perhaps most important principle is to remember how much there is to be learned through a failure. When a failure occurs, it's not fair to look at it as nothing but a failure. It's a learning experience. It is now known both why it was originally presumed a failed idea would work and why it didn't work. The reasons why the idea didn't work can be incredibly important in assisting the design of processes in the future. If, through a failed project, a new limitation is found in the data or a new problem is uncovered with some of the assumptions that an organization makes, it can be validated that those same problems aren't affecting other processes. The new knowledge can impact both existing and future efforts.

Over time, as an organization embraces the concept of an analytic innovation center and proves its value, it can be expanded by adding more people and more technology to the mix. The principles that drive the need for an analytic innovation center, as well as the way it is implemented, can also apply to other areas of a business. It's not just analytics that needs its own innovation center. There are surely other areas of a business that do, too. Once an organization is comfortable pushing for innovation in one area, it will be easier to expand to others.

## WRAP-UP

The most important lessons to take away from this chapter are:

- Innovation in analytics and in how data is used and acted upon is an ever more important area for organizations to pursue.
- An analytic innovation should be focused on analyzing a new data source, solving a new problem, or a combination of both. It isn't a simple extension of current practices.
- By definition, an innovative idea has risk and isn't fully understood. It requires an iterative, flexible approach to drive innovative analytics. Plans will have to be adjusted on the fly.
- Some portion of corporate resources should be allocated more like a venture capital model than a retirement model. An analytic innovation center is a great way to do so.
- An analytic innovation center will have people, processes, and technology dedicated to innovation along with a cross-functional oversight council that helps guide it down the right path.

■ It is critical that the people assigned to work on projects within the analytic innovation center have a formal set of hours allocated toward it. It can't be an extra credit assignment.

■ Do not use an analytic innovation center for production processes or to complete a full build-out of a proven prototype. The scope of an analytic innovation center stops at a prototype.

■ Only risk enough resources to prove the potential of an idea, and don't tackle projects so big that a run of misses would be devastating.

■ Failures in the analytic innovation center need to be identified quickly so the team can move on to different problems.

■ A lot can be learned from failures. They aren't all bad. Failures can be quite valuable if what is learned in the process of failing is applied broadly to improve other past and future processes.

## NOTE

1. *Merriam-Webster,* "Innovation," www.merriam-webster.com/dictionary/innovation.

# CHAPTER 11

# Creating a Culture of Innovation and Discovery

If you are a parent, can you say what the next big toy will be that your kids will just have to have when their birthday comes around? If you aren't a parent, can you say what the next trendy electronic gizmo will be that people will stand in line for as they did for the iPhone™ or Wii™? Can you say what the next totally ridiculous trend like Pet Rocks will be?

Most people will claim to have no idea. And that's okay, because innovative approaches are never obvious until you see them. If the ideas were obvious, they wouldn't be innovative. If someone had the ability to foresee such innovations on a regular basis, he or she would be retired on a nice, pretty island somewhere enjoying well-earned riches!

In this chapter, we will wrap the book up with some perspectives on how to create a culture of innovation and discovery. This chapter is meant to be fun and lighthearted and provide some food for thought. Most of the concepts are commonly discussed, but it is worth reviewing them and considering how an organization can apply these well-established principles to the area of big data and advanced analytics. By the way, if you like Pet Rocks, check out the modern USB Pet Rock at ThinkGeek.com![1]

## SETTING THE STAGE

Silly Bandz® and Jibbitz™ are just two recent examples of innovative products that came out of nowhere and took off. In case you don't know, Silly Bandz are basically colored rubber bands shaped like animals, toys, or other everyday items. Kids love to wear them, trade them, and collect them. They are so popular that they have been banned at my children's school due to the distraction they cause. Jibbitz are little figures that attach to the holes in Crocs™ shoes. Look down at children's feet when they have on Crocs and most will have some Jibbitz in place. Crocs and Jibbitz are both examples of someone having a new and innovative idea and following through on it with great success.

Such innovation isn't new. Millennia ago, Pythagoras first pushed the theory that the earth was round instead of flat. Centuries ago, Copernicus broke the mold by declaring that the sun, not the earth, was the center of the solar system. Decades ago, Einstein came up with the theory of general relativity.

Some innovations are stand-alone. Other innovations are only possible by building upon previous innovations. For example, Jibbitz would not have made any sense if Crocs did not already exist. In every case, someone had to have the nerve to conceive of a crazy new idea and then pursue it fully. To successfully innovate, an organization will have to develop a culture of innovation and discovery that encourages experimentation, pushes people to challenge assumptions, and tries to change how business is done. It isn't easy, and it takes effort and focus. However, without such a culture, an organization will slowly fade away as the competition relentlessly takes away its business.

Has your company already embraced big data and made efforts to tame it? Has your company developed some new analytic processes that take advantage of big data? Does your company have a vision of combining big data with other data to drive additional value? Has your company tried a few "crazy" analytics ideas recently? Without a culture of innovation and discovery, the chance of a yes answer is greatly decreased.

## The Unlikely Story of Crocs and Jibbitz

Just imagine the conversation related to the invention of Crocs. One day, someone says, "I have a great idea! Let's make some solid rubber shoes. They won't look particularly nice, and won't be cheap. Nevertheless, people will like to wear them to the pool, to do their yard work, and so forth. In addition, kids will like them because they can get them dirty and not get in trouble. Parents can simply hose them off." Many companies would not have gone for that idea and wouldn't have had the nerve to pursue it. Most people would not have believed the success that Crocs achieved.

Now consider Jibbitz. The inventor of Jibbitz has a pair of Crocs and realizes, "There are little holes on top of these Crocs. Maybe I should invent something to fill those holes! I'll make some little clips that fit in the holes that will have cartoon figures, flags, or other everyday items on them. I'll bet kids will love to put them on their shoes to customize them. It will help them identify which pair is theirs out of the four pairs of red Crocs on the playground. The best part is that they will cost very little to manufacture but we can charge $3, $4, maybe as much as $5 for every single one. We'll make a killing!"

Would you have quit your day job and risked your savings to go after that idea? In the end, however, Jibbitz became a runaway success. In fact, a couple named Rich and Sheri Schmelzer started a company to sell Jibbitz in 2005. One year later, they sold it to the company that makes Crocs for $20 million. Now that is a successful innovation!

In the analytics world, consider the idea of a software suite oriented toward statistics and analysis. Such a thing didn't exist 40 years ago. In 1976, after SAS software had some success as a project sponsored out of North Carolina State University, several professors left their jobs to create a startup called SAS Institute Inc. The company was "devoted to the maintenance and further development of SAS."[2] Who could have guessed it would become a multibillion-dollar organization that would play a role in countless analytic innovations over the years?

## Making Innovation Work

Think for a minute about what had to come together for Jibbitz to succeed. The Schmelzers had to have the totally novel idea of filling the holes in a pair of Crocs. Then, they had to have faith that they could make it work and fully commit to it. It's a big effort to go from the concept of Jibbitz to actually getting them manufactured and into a store. With their $20 million in hand, the Schmelzers surely have absolutely no regrets about the path that they chose.

Will every idea pay off like Jibbitz? Of course not. That's the whole point about innovation. You won't win every time. That's okay. The problem is, you'll never get a payout like Jibbitz provided without trying some new ideas. You won't be guaranteed to win if you play, but you absolutely have to play in order to win. The Schmelzers played. The Schmelzers won. Would you and your organization have done the same?

 ## YOU HAVE TO PLAY TO WIN

Not all innovations will succeed. You aren't guaranteed to win just by playing the innovation game. However, you are guaranteed *not* to win if you don't play. You have to play to win! Without making an effort to tame big data, your organization will not tame it. Nor will it realize any of the benefits the analysis of big data can provide.

What have you and your company done recently to create a chance to win with advanced analytics and big data? How much energy are people putting in daily, weekly, and monthly thinking up new analytics that your organization could be doing? Who in your company is tasked with creating a culture of innovation and discovery? If it is unclear who is driving analytic innovation in an organization, it probably isn't happening at a substantive level. If nobody has explicit responsibility for it, chances are that nobody will step up and get it done. Do you want to be the person associated with making the "next big thing" happen with analytics in your organization? Let's talk about how.

## OVERVIEW OF THE KEY PRINCIPLES

There are three key principles that must be followed in order to create a culture of innovation and discovery capable of producing innovative analytics and taming big data:

- **Principle 1: Break out of your box.** This means that a groundbreaking innovation does not simply add a new twist to an old concept. It breaks the mold. It does things in a new way.

- **Principle 2: Ride the ripple effects.** This means that the best innovations enable other innovations to build upon them even though the later innovations aren't anticipated or planned. One innovation begets another, which begets another, and the cumulative ripple effects can dwarf the impact of the original innovation.

- **Principle 3: Align all eyes on the target.** An organization's leaders have to set a common vision. They have to set clear priorities. They have to tie compensation to that vision and those priorities. Unless everyone's eyes are aligned on the same target, they will not develop a culture of innovation and discovery.

While these principles aren't new, they are important. It is good to review and focus upon the basics from time to time. Let's dive deeper into each of these well-established principles and how they apply to the world of big data and advanced analytics!

## Principle 1: Break Out of Your Box

The first key principle is to break out of your box. Every one of us is stuck in a box. That is true as individuals, as teams, and as companies. You may not think about it all the time, but your box is around you right now. The box is made up of all the things you know you can and cannot do, the things you know you should and should not do, the things you know will and will not work, the things you know would and would not be approved. Your box is based on budgets, experience, traditions, skills, systems, data availability, and any number of things.

To some degree, these boxes aren't bad. They help keep us focused. They help us get things done. They help us take into account impor-tant practical considerations as we do our jobs day to day. When you consider the boxes firm instead of pliable, however, you run into trouble. If you don't continually test your boxes, they become a huge hindrance. The key is to make sure you're not artificially limiting yourself and your organization.

Have things changed since you last defined the box of what can and can't be done, what should and shouldn't be done, or what is or isn't accepted within your organization? When was the last time you thought about why your organization uses the analytics it does? When was the last time you reviewed the principles of a great analysis discussed in Chapter 7 to make sure your analytics teams are on track? When was the last time you considered updating your processes and approaches as we discussed in Chapters 5 and 6? When was the last time you upgraded your systems to get the full benefit of current levels of scalability discussed in Chapter 4?

## WHEN IS THE LAST TIME YOU TESTED YOUR BOX?

Operating within a box isn't all bad. However, you must continually test your box to make sure that the limits that existed previously are still in place. Otherwise, you will be needlessly limiting yourself. Push to the real edges, not the presumed edges, of what is possible. The ability to scale analytic processes has improved so much in recent years that many organizations don't even realize the potential benefits they are missing.

A recent trend in analytics is the phenomenon of public analytics contests. In these contests, a dataset that is cleansed of any sensitive information is provided to anyone who wants it. Rules are posted as to what type of model or analysis is required and what the criteria for success are. The team who does the best by the end of the contest wins the prize money. By getting experts around the world to bring their techniques to the table, organizations are able to totally break free from their boxes. Outsiders don't bring any of the preconceived notions that the organization itself has. As a result, contestants often handily beat the baseline results of the sponsor organization.

To break your organization out of its box, you need to have your people challenging each other, testing assumptions again and again, and making sure that they're pushing to the real edges, and not the presumed edges, of what's possible.

### Follow the Lead of Copernicus

Copernicus is a terrific example of breaking out of the box. In the 1400s and 1500s, it was widely established that the earth was the center of the solar system. Copernicus looked at all the available data and decided that the sun was at the center of the solar system and not the earth. His innovation, the idea of putting the sun at the center, led to an entirely new era in astronomy. Copernicus is also credited with being a key factor in beginning the scientific revolution, which led to a rejection of doctrines that had prevailed since Ancient Greece.[3] The scientific revolution laid the foundation of modern science.

However, even when Copernicus came up with his findings, he was reluctant to go public. He understood the controversy that such innovative thinking would cause. The old model was that the earth was the center of the solar system and it was wrong. His new model would not be a popular model with people who were invested in the old model.

If you have the wrong model for how things work, nothing that follows from that model is going to fully make sense. Copernicus showed with his efforts that even successful innovations won't always be accepted right away. It took Copernicus years to publish his findings. It took nearly three centuries for full acceptance of his theories. In the end, the truth of his innovation prevailed. Keep in mind that Copernicus knew that, of course, the earth is still an important part of the solar system. It just isn't the center. Saying the earth isn't at the center doesn't mean earth doesn't have a very important role to play.

 **FOCUS ON PEOPLE, NOT TOOLS**

Copernicus showed that the sun was the center of the solar system, not the earth. Today, many organizations focus on technology and tools as being the central components of analytical success. In fact, it is not the tools and technologies, but the people who use those tools and technologies that are the central component of success. Until focus is on the right model, success will be greatly limited.

One common error in the business world is that organizations think tools like databases and software applications are the center of the advanced analytics ecosystem. Too many organizations talk about how they put the best tools in place, or have given their people the best software, or have implemented the best databases. All of that is certainly important. An organization absolutely benefits from the best tools, software, and systems. Tools and technology are critical parts of any organization's ability to innovate with analytics.

However, what makes these technologies drive business growth? The people who use them, the way in which they use them, and the decisions they drive. The people that we discussed in Chapters 8 and 9 who use the tools, software, and systems are the center of the analytics ecosystem. An organization needs to make sure that it is getting the right tools to the right people to get the right results. The most powerful system with the most sophisticated tools attached won't tame big data unless some great analytic professionals are driving the process.

## Applying the Principle

If an organization in today's world is committed to innovation, analytics are a key part of the foundation. There are recent innovations in the analytics space that an organization must be making use of if it is going to break out of its box and tame the big data tidal wave. One of those innovations is the use of in-database processing to enable scalable analytics, as discussed in Chapter 4. As with many innovations, those who espoused it originally back in the 1990s took a lot of heat. Many people, including those within the industry, initially greeted the concept with suspicion and scorn.

It is important to understand that in-database analytics has now gone mainstream. Companies around the globe and across industries have realized and documented orders of magnitude in speed improvements from leveraging in-database analytics. We're talking about running analytics processes 40, 50, even 100 times faster than is possible with traditional approaches. It's not an incremental improvement. Rather, it's a quantum leap. It is crazy not to take advantage of in-database analytics today. With a few minutes of effort, you can search the Internet and find examples ranging from conference talks, to articles, to formal case studies that outline how companies have completely taken analytic scalability to a new level with in-database analytics. A similarly compelling story is developing around MapReduce, which we also discussed in Chapter 4.

Imagine how much more time a great analytics team will have to focus on analytic innovation if they are using in-database analytics and MapReduce so that their processes run dozens of times faster. Many organizations don't even realize it is possible to get these results today. As a result, they are still doing things the same old way with the same old limitations and the competition is getting ahead of them. The box of what's possible in terms of analytic scalability has been expanded. Be sure your organization takes advantage of the extra space.

## Principle 2: Ride the Ripple Effects

If you're not thinking out of the box and pursuing innovation, it is not possible to ride the ripple effects. Many innovations, while highly impactful by themselves, are even more compelling when the later innovations they enabled are examined. The second principle is the ripple effect. The ripple effect is innovation to the power of two!

Truly innovative ideas often lead to other unforeseen breakthroughs that have an even larger impact than the original. The potential future impacts of an innovation can't be discounted. By not pursuing an innovation today, not only are immediate opportunities missed, but so are unknown opportunities of potentially game-changing magnitude down the road. Dismissing ideas too early and failing to pursue an innovation may cost far more in the long run than imagined. Let's explore a few examples.

 **LEVERAGE THE POWER OF TWO!**

Innovations can lead to other unforeseen innovations down the road. These innovations compound the impact of the initial one. Big data is so new that its future ripple effects are still far from clear. But, ripple effects will certainly evolve. Don't miss the chance to benefit from ripple effects by failing to start analyzing big data today.

### From Telephones to Internet to Social Media

The telephone totally changed the way people communicate, and it had a massive impact on society. Phone lines were placed all over the world for the sole purpose of enabling two people to pick up a phone and talk together. There was no grander vision in place at the time the lines were placed. If nothing else had ever arisen from the effort outside of facilitating conversations, the telephone still would have been one of the most impactful inventions in history.

However, someone eventually realized that the same lines could carry data. It started with simple things like faxes. Eventually modem usage became widespread. Those same old-fashioned phone lines enabled access in the early stages of the Internet. The Internet as it exists may not have happened at all, or certainly not nearly as quickly, if a critical mass of people didn't have access to it. That critical mass drove the demand that led to the explosion of the Internet. It all began with those simple, low-tech phone lines. The Internet is an example of the ripple effect of telephones. Nobody imagined when the first lines were put in place how the use of those lines would evolve, but their use evolved greatly. That's what the ripple effect is about.

## FROM TELEPHONE TO SOCIAL MEDIA TO ANALYTICS

The telephone revolutionized communications. Telephone lines later played a huge role in the rise of the Internet. The Internet in turn spawned social media, which has again revolutionized how we communicate. Imagine how different life would be today if those phone lines had not been put in place!

The telephone led to the ripple effect of the Internet and the Internet has led to ripple effects of its own. Even in the mid-1990s, few could have imagined all the innovations that would come from the Internet. One ripple effect is the explosion of e-commerce, including business model breaking companies like Amazon, eBay, and craigslist. Another recent ripple effect is the rise of social networking sites like LinkedIn and Facebook. These sites offer whole new ways to communicate and socialize. It is ironic that phones revolutionized how we communicate, then phone lines facilitated the rise of the Internet, and the Internet in turn revolutionized how we communicate through social media.

Other ripple effects of the Internet include massive multiplayer games with immersive worlds to explore in real-time with people from all over the globe. Another is a GPS-enabled cell phone that can tell you every Chinese restaurant within a mile of your current location and has the ability to make a reservation on the spot. What will be next? Someone out there is working on it right now.

The data generated by the Internet has drastically changed analytics already and will continue to do so. As Chapter 2 discussed, the analysis of web activity is a growing practice and there have been immense benefits from it. The analysis of social media commentary is another new analytics approach that has been enabled through the Internet. For as much benefit as the Internet has provided consumers, the benefits of the data it is generating is similarly having a huge impact on what analytics are done and how the processes are built. Nobody could have imagined text analysis against a social media site's commentary more than a century ago when phone lines were first put in place, but it has arrived.

### Social Network Analysis

A recent analytical innovation that is a ripple effect is the rise of social network analysis in telecommunication companies. It has changed how they manage their customers. We discussed this as well in Chapter 3. For years, telecom companies have captured the details of every call that every customer makes. What was the primary purpose of collecting it? For billing. Nothing more interesting than that. However, over the years, this data has also been used for a wide range of analysis outside of billing.

Recently, with increases in computing power and the rise of in-database processing, telecom companies started to seriously explore the network of contacts each customer has. Which customers are at the center of a huge circle of people that call among themselves? Which customers are isolated in just a very small circle, such as their immediate family? Such analysis is not only interesting from a social dynamics perspective, but it's also being used to increase the effectiveness of customer retention and recruitment.

How is that possible? It has been shown that once a key member of a circle defects to another carrier, the other members of that circle are at much higher risk of defecting, as they follow the initial leader. Knowing the total influence a customer has, and not just his or her personal value, can inform better decisions on how aggressive a company needs to be to recruit, retain, and reward a given customer. Reaching out to the members of an at-risk circle early can help to avoid what would have been a string of cascading losses over time. Customers who are part of a large circle may be given much higher retention incentives than they would warrant based upon their individual spending alone. This analysis wasn't feasible to any degree until the recent expansion of scalability available to analytic professionals, and it represents a ripple effect of the collection of call detail records for billing purposes.

### Applying the Principle

The question then becomes: How can your organization start to ride its own ripple effects? Once your organization has embraced in-database analytics, MapReduce, and big data to help you break out of your box, then you can look to ride the ripple effects that the initial in-database analytics enable.

 **RIDE YOUR OWN RIPPLE EFFECTS**

As an organization begins to successfully build a culture of innovation and discovery, the pace of innovation will increase. An additional benefit will be the growing ability to identify ripple effects to ride by building on past innovations. The data source captured today, or the process built tomorrow, may well enable something far bigger down the road.

The innovations of in-database analytics and MapReduce are leading to ripple effects of analytic innovation that has only just begun. With the extra capacity and scale that these approaches provide, what else can be done that couldn't be done before? With the ability to tame a new big data source, what new analytics are now possible? Organizations need to move beyond focusing on speed improvements, start to look for new analytics that can be done today that just weren't possible before, and push the new limits of the box.

Ripple effects have occurred across industries as data sources, analytic methods, and scalability have matured. Retailers began loyalty programs to reward customers, and the resulting data has shifted the retail business from a product-centric one to a customer-centric one. The data and analytics that underlie credit scores have totally changed the financial industry. The accuracy of credit models and the availability of helpful data have increased to a point where a robust range of financial products and services is now available for every type of consumer. The use of text analysis against customer service dialogues is only beginning to impact a wide range of industries. Neither the data, the tools to analyze it, nor the scalable systems required were widely available until recently.

An organization can't win by doing the same thing it sees its top competitors successfully do. It has to get there first. It needs to innovate not just for the immediate impacts, but also for the ripple effects that will come later. If big data can make a business more effective today, just imagine how effective it will be once ripple effects to pursue are identified down the road.

## Principle 3: Align All Eyes on the Target

To push an organization to break out of its box and ride the ripple effects effectively, management must align all eyes on a common target. That's the third principle. An organization cannot succeed unless it is aligned. This is a well-documented fact for business in general, and it also applies to the world of advanced analytics and big data. The alignment needs to be in place for the whole organization, each division, and each team. The following steps must be taken to align all eyes on the target:

Step 1: The organization must share a common vision of where it is heading.

Step 2: The organization must be very clear on what the priorities are for reaching that vision.

Step 3: The organization's people must understand how they will get paid for making it happen.

It isn't easy to define the right targets. It isn't easy to drive a vision through an organization. It isn't easy to have the organization embrace and work toward new priorities. Changing how teams and individuals think and act won't happen overnight, and the hurdles that must be overcome are not trivial. To have a culture of innovation and discovery will take effort. In the end, the dividends received when successful can be huge.

## Setting a Common Vision

Why is it so important that a team share a common vision and understand why that vision is in place? Consider two workers busy pouring a foundation for a new house. Each worker is asked, "What are you doing?" The first man says, "I'm filling these forms with cement to make a support wall." The second man says, "I'm building a house."

Why does the difference matter? At the end of the day, they're just putting in place a support wall, right? They'll both get that wall done by the end of the day, so why should we care how they view their job? It matters because, without the larger vision, it is not possible to successfully innovate. There will just be a lot of people building the "wall of the day."

In our example, the man who thinks he's just there to put in a wall in a specific spot that day does not have the larger view of why that wall is important and how it fits into the overall house. The second man with the fuller vision will do a much better job of dealing with the inevitable unexpected issues that arise. He will ensure that whatever adjustments he is forced to make to the plan will not only get a wall in place in that spot on that day, but will get a wall in place that will support the house that's going to be built on top of it. It is absolutely worth the time to ensure that people not only understand their specific tasks today, but also how those tasks fit into a larger vision.

The same principle illustrated in our foundation pouring example applies when doing analytics. It is too common that an analytic professional is asked to do an analysis without much guidance and perspective provided. He or she runs a bunch of numbers and comes back with a very detailed analysis and some very reasonable and valid results. Unfortunately, the person who initially requested the analysis thinks it isn't at all what is needed. The reason is often that the analytic professional was given a specific task, not a vision of the desired results. He or she was only able to do exactly what was asked because there was not an understanding what was really needed and why. Famous author and speaker Stephen Covey wrote the book 7 *Habits of Highly Effective People*. One of the habits is "Begin with the end in mind."[4]

## ANALYTIC PROFESSIONALS MUST BE PROVIDED A VISION

If an organization is to succeed in taming big data, its analytic professionals will need to have a vision of where they're trying to go. Otherwise, there will be a lot of interesting analysis that doesn't help the business move forward. Analytic professionals shouldn't be issued analysis tasks of the week, but rather provided a long-term vision to work toward over time.

The first step in taming big data can't be to simply tell analytic professionals to figure out what's there. Some unguided exploration can certainly be a component of the plan, but it can't be the only plan. It is important to discuss what the data is all about and how it might be able to help the business. What are some specific areas where the new data might be of assistance? What decisions might it be able to change? Understanding those points will help the analytic professionals go in the right direction.

For example, analytic professionals can't just be turned loose on the video game telemetry data discussed in Chapter 3. The types of micro-transactions that are important in the games should be discussed first. Analytic professionals should be informed of any research that is available on what players like most about the games. There should be a review of what the business would like to do better or differently. With that extra perspective and vision, the analytic professionals assigned to the effort will be able to find compelling results much more quickly.

Is the culture in your organization one where people think of themselves as building walls in a certain spot, or one where they see themselves building houses? Are people encouraged to ask questions and to understand the bigger picture, or are they encouraged to do what they're told? Who on your team is more of a wall builder than a house builder? Are there some changes required to get a team in place that can do what is needed?

## Establishing Clear Priorities

Another factor an organization cannot succeed without is a clear understanding of what its priorities are. As we discussed, it first has to define the vision of where it is trying to go. After that, it has to establish clear priorities in terms of how it will get there. The choice of priorities can drastically change the strategies and tactics the team will need to use to get there. For example, is the priority to be the biggest company in the industry? Or is it to have a solid base of the most satisfied customers? Or to have the highest profit margins? Or to have the lowest attrition rate?

Depending on which of those is chosen, different strategies will be needed and different outcomes will be pursued in terms of customer counts, customer value, total revenue, and profit. This, of course, will also completely change the focus and scope of any analytics required. Given the energy and time it takes to create a culture of innovation and discovery, an organization needs to make sure that everyone has their eyes on the same target and is driving to the same priorities from the beginning.

A colleague has a friend whose restaurant hosted a very successful happy hour. The happy hour got people to come and have cheap drinks, but it did not create any relationship with the restaurant other than being a place to come and get cheap drinks. What would happen if another bar opened up down the street with even cheaper drinks and a newer interior? The owner began to question if he had the right priorities.

The owner tried an experiment. He offered to sponsor a free birthday party for anyone, plus up to 10 guests, that would include food and drinks. However, there was a catch! The birthday boy or girl had to join the restaurant's fan club on Facebook and get a minimum number of friends to do so, too. In addition, the birthday boy or girl had to provide names and e-mail addresses of a minimum number of friends that the restaurant did not already have registered.

The idea was a terrific success. The people who attended a birthday party then wanted one of their own. Meanwhile, the restaurant's contact database was growing exponentially. Eventually, the owner ended happy hours and focused on the birthday parties. He decided he preferred to have loyal customers who wanted to come to his restaurant because of what he uniquely offered. He no longer simply wanted to pull in a large crowd of people seeking cheap drinks.

This is an example that wasn't feasible without e-mail and Facebook, but it was a ripple effect of those innovations. The owner broke out of his box, aligned his eyes on a new target, and went for it. Most of his competition still focuses on keeping up drink sales month after month. He focused on building a loyal foundation of customers that will grow year after year as people's birthdays came around again. The change in priorities led him to take a very different direction, but also led him to success.

 ## BE THE BEST . . . AT WHAT?

Many organizations want to be the best in their fields. But what defines the "best"? There are many ways to define *best*, and it is important to make clear how *best* is defined. Then, it must be clear what the priorities are to become the best under those terms. Otherwise, efforts will be disjointed and it will be very difficult to succeed. The analysis needed will change based on what the goals, metrics, and objectives are in becoming the best.

Similarly, every organization needs to check its priorities. Let's assume an organization has decided to pursue text analysis against customer service e-mails and social media commentary. What are the most critical problems to solve? Is understanding the general sentiment of the comments the priority? Is identifying specific individuals who need attention the priority? Is identifying trends in terms of how often products are discussed the priority? There are so many different directions to go with text analysis that, without clear priorities, it will be hard to succeed.

### Tying Compensation to the Vision and Priorities

Making sure a team knows how it will get paid is critically important. How people will get paid has, for better or worse, a huge influence on what they do. An organization needs to make sure that the team will get paid and promoted for driving analytic innovation or it's not going to happen. At the same time, be careful that the compensation plan really does drive the behaviors needed. It is easy to form a disconnect that can lead to totally unexpected and unintended consequences.

A while back, a large grocery chain collaborated with a large soft drink manufacturer to sponsor a huge sale. Store managers were told that they would be rewarded with a bonus based on how many soft drink sales their stores generated during the promotion. One store was selling an outrageously high amount of soft drinks, far more than any other store in the chain. Somebody decided to look into what was working so well.

What was learned? The manager in the top-selling store was friends with the managers of some of the local competition's stores. Ironically, the sale price was cheaper than the competing managers could buy the products for their stores, since the sale was a loss leader. It ends up that manager was actually selling pallets of soft drinks to the competition from the loading dock! Of course, these sales were all at a loss for his employer and a gain for the competition. Sounds crazy, doesn't it?

## PEOPLE WILL DO WHAT YOU INCENT THEM TO DO

If poorly structured incentives are put in place, an organization can't get upset when employees do unexpected things to get those incentives. Some of the best and most innovative employees may take unanticipated actions to get their rewards. Make sure your incentives drive the right kind of analytics for the right problems, not just any new analytics that somebody can dream up.

Was the store manager in the soft drink example dishonest? It is actually hard to say. He may be dishonest, but that's not necessarily the case. The manager was told that his priority was to sell as many soft drinks as possible. If he took that goal literally and he wasn't given a larger vision, then he wasn't necessarily dishonest but actually quite ingenious. He found an innovative way to sell more soft drinks than anyone else.

It can be argued that this store manager is actually the exact kind of employee organizations want. He focused on his goal, he was quite creative in how he went about meeting it, and he blew everyone else out of the water. What the chain's management accidentally did was set up a scenario where he had an incentive to do something that really didn't make sense. Once this employee's energy and creativity are redirected through better incentives, he can probably have a large, positive impact.

In the world of analytics, offering a bonus based on the number of models produced can lead to a lot of fairly useless models. Better to offer a bonus based upon the impact that models have. The better the models built, the better the bonus. Quality should take priority over quantity. If offering a bonus for finding opportunities in a new big data source, leave flexibility in what areas to explore. Perhaps many of the original ideas for analysis don't work well, but a few other opportunities are found that do work well. The bonus should be based on finding value, not on finding value for one specific problem. Otherwise, analytic professionals might focus too much time on a low-value problem just to get their bonus.

## Applying the Principle

Your organization needs to examine the vision, priorities, and incentives that have been set and to continually reexamine and validate them to make sure they are appropriate and synchronized with each other. It doesn't make sense to change direction on a whim. However, sticking to a bad vision, priority, or compensation plan can be just as bad as not having developed them in the first place. Driving off a cliff is not a good idea, even if the entire team is unified in its determination to do it together!

Let's go back to the example of in-database analytics and MapReduce and assume an organization has decided to pursue them as a way to improve its analytics and tame big data. What should be done to start? The analytics team should be tasked with moving analytics into the database and implementing a MapReduce environment by a defined date. A vision of how the organization's analytics processes need to evolve to handle big data should be established. Some clear priorities about what areas should be focused on first should be set. By then tying objectives and bonus payments to achieving that vision, the team will stick to the plan.

Your organization needs to demand that your analytics teams produce some different, innovative, never-before-tried analytics that are well out of the box of what is done today. Then you'll see some results. But if it's just a suggestion, a desire, or a wish, then it won't happen. The organization must align all eyes on the target to succeed.

## WRAP-UP

The most important lessons to take away from this chapter are:

- Without making an effort to tame big data, your organization will not tame it. You have to play to win! Commit to trying new analytic approaches with big data.

- There are three broadly applied principles that also apply to the area of advanced analytics and big data. They are: (1) break out of your box, (2) ride the ripple effects, and (3) align all eyes on the target.

- Operating within a box isn't all bad. But, you must continually test the box to make sure that the limits that existed in the past are still in place. Don't unnecessarily limit yourself.

- It is not the tools and technologies themselves that drive analytical success. The people who use the tools and technology are the central component of success.

- Big data is so new that its future ripple effects are still far from clear. Don't miss the chance to benefit from later, currently unknown ripple effects by not starting to analyze big data today.

- Move beyond focusing on speed improvements and look for new analytics that can be done now that just weren't possible before.

- Analytic professionals shouldn't be issued analysis tasks of the week, but rather provided a vision to work toward. This will enable them to keep their eyes on the target.

- The choice of priorities can drastically change the strategies and tactics used to achieve a vision. Make sure that there are clear priorities provided before an analysis begins.

- Develop incentives that drive the right results. It is better to offer a bonus based upon the impact that models have than on the number of models produced.

- Take action and push for a culture of innovation and discovery. Someone has to take the lead in pursuing innovative analytics and taming big data within your organization. Why shouldn't it be you?

## NOTES

1. Think Geek, www.thinkgeek.com/geektoys/cubegoodies/c208/.
2. SAS, www.sas.com/company/about/history.html.
3. *New World Encyclopedia*, "Copernicus, Nicolaus," www.newworldencyclopedia.org/entry/Nicolaus_Copernicus.
4. Stephen R. Covey, www.stephencovey.com/7habits/7habits-habit2.php.

# Conclusion:
# Think Bigger!

Well, you made it! You've read about what big data is. You've read about the tools, processes, and methods required to tame it. You've reviewed what makes a G.R.E.A.T. analysis. You've read about the people and teams required to perform great analysis. You've read about how to enable analytic innovation through an analytic innovation center and a culture of innovation and discovery.

In our discussion about taming the big data tidal wave, we've covered a number of concepts and how they can be applied to improve your organization's analytics and business today. Regardless of your background, you have hopefully learned a number of new insights that can be taken back to your organization as a result of reading this book.

A few key points that should be reinforced one last time, along with some actions you can take, include:

- Big data is real and it is here to stay. Don't ignore it or be afraid of it. Extend your enterprise data and analytics strategies to incorporate it. Put it to use to gain a competitive advantage.

- Scalability is more important than ever. Be sure your organization updates to the most current technologies, including in-database processing, MapReduce, and the cloud.

- New processes are required as well. Start using analytic sandboxes, enterprise analytic datasets, and embedded scoring to enable faster, more scalable advanced analytics processes.

- Implement new analysis methodologies such as text analysis, ensemble models, and commodity models. Don't just apply the same old traditional techniques to the new big data sources.

- Taming big data will require analytic professionals with the right talent. Great analytic professionals, whether they call themselves analysts or data scientists, have skills that include commitment, creativity, business savvy, presentation skills, and intuition. Go and hire some.

- Analytics teams can be organized in various ways. However, the focus should always be on enabling decision makers to get the information they need.

- Implement an analytic innovation center to assist with tackling big data. Create a culture of innovation and discovery. It will make taming big data much easier.

The push to data-driven decision making has been underway for quite some time. The number of data sources and the variety of advanced analytics used to drive those decisions is ever increasing. Big data is a new addition to the mix and it is nothing to be scared of. Organizations need to jump in and start leveraging it today. There is no reason to delay. While there will certainly be bumps in the road and some resistance to change, it is entirely possible to tame big data starting right now. Whether it is text data or web data or sensor data, there are already organizations actively capturing, analyzing, and making decisions based upon it.

The organizations that decide to be leaders will uncover new business opportunities and implement new business processes before the followers realize what has happened. It is rare to have a chance to be among the first to enter an entirely new realm of data and analysis. Don't let your organization miss the chance that is sitting in front of you today. Begin to uncover the ways that the analysis of big data can change how your organization does business. Reap the benefits. What are you waiting for?

# About the Author

Bill Franks is Chief Analytics Officer for Teradata's global alliance programs, providing insight on trends in the Advanced Analytics space and helping clients understand how Teradata and its analytic partners can support their efforts. Bill also oversees the Business Analytic Innovation Center, which is jointly sponsored by Teradata and SAS, and focuses on helping clients pursue innovative analytics. In addition, Bill works to help determine the right strategies and positioning for Teradata in the advanced analytics space.

Bill is a faculty member of the International Institute for Analytics, which was founded by leading analytics expert Tom Davenport. He is also an active speaker and blogger. His blog can be found at the following address: http://iianalytics.com/category/faculty-blogs/bill-franks/.

Bill's focus has always been to help translate complex analytics into terms that business users can understand and to then help an organization implement the results effectively within their processes. His work has spanned clients in a variety of industries for companies ranging in size from Fortune 100 companies to small non-profit organizations.

Bill earned a bachelor's degree in applied statistics from Virginia Tech and a master's degree in applied statistics from North Carolina State University.

# Index